Hvar, An Insi 2016 Edition

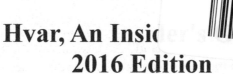

by Paul Bradbury

Table of Contents

INTRODUCTION

Why Hvar?

Among the top ten most beautiful islands (Conde Nast), one of the world's sexiest islands (Forbes Magazine), the sunniest island in the Adriatic and the new St. Tropez; it is not difficult to find superlatives about Croatia's premier island, enjoying a boom after the recent glitzy facelift to Hvar Town.

While the celebrity yachts of the likes of Bernie Ecclestone, Bill Gates and Roman Abramovich may grab the headlines, there is so much more to the island of Hvar than the exclusive party atmosphere of the main town. One of the island's strengths as a tourist destination is the sheer diversity on offer, with something to cater for every type of tourist.

Hvar Town – home of the oldest organised tourism in Europe – has plenty in terms of nightlife, beaches, cuisine, history and culture, as well as easy access to the stunning Pakleni islands a short water-taxi away, but the real diversity of Hvar can be found all over the island.

Archaeology buffs can delight in the ancient settlement of Stari Grad, dating back to 384 BC, and the immaculately preserved (and UNESCO-protected) Stari Grad Plain, or explore the delights of the Neolithic caves such as Grapceva. Lovers of tradition will find plenty to enthral, most notably the Easter Procession, a 500 year-old tradition of carrying the cross through the night on Maundy Thursday.

Hvar is a sailing paradise, with an endless stream of hidden bays and small islands to discover. With two ACI marinas and plenty of mooring space in the main towns, the island is a must-stop on an Adriatic sailing holidays. There are regattas, sailing schools and other water sports, such as sea-kayaking, on offer, while the range of pristine beaches – naturists, family and hidden – are an obvious attraction.

Hvar is a very popular year-round destination for cycling holidays, one of a range of activities adding to its diverse appeal. Rock climbing, hiking and off-road safaris for those looking to discover the more hidden parts of the island. The Hvar Half-Marathon takes place in August, as does the annual Faros Swimming Marathon.

Fine wine and fine dining are an important aspect to any holiday, and the winemakers of Hvar do not disappoint. Whether it be an organised wine tour, an impromptu drop-in or a bottle of the local red in a waterfront restaurant, the quality of the local wine, spearheaded by internationally recognised vinters such as Andro Tomic and Zlatan Plenkovic, is an added flavour to any trip to Dalmatia.

The range of Dalmatian fish and meat dishes, all served up with the freshest local produce, will ensure a gastronomic feast that will linger in the memory. Old stone waterfront restaurants serving up traditional local fare, washed down with the finest island wines against a backdrop of Dalmatian acapella music is an endearing memory in the minds of many visitors.

Away from the crowds, yoga and meditation, painting holidays, discovering the island's flora and fauna or taking part in the olive, lavender or wine harvests offers an opportunity to discover more of Hvar's nature. And for those looking to detox from stressful lives, very little can beat the sunny relaxation of people-watching on a pretty Dalmatian square over a coffee and strudel (or something stronger).

A backdrop to every visit is the wonderful climate, described as one of the healthiest in Europe. So convinced were the Austrians in the nineteenth century that they helped found the Hvar Health Society in 1868, the first organised health holidays in Europe. Whether or not the much-touted promise of a free night's accommodation in the even of snow still holds or not is unconfirmed, but one thing is sure – a holiday on Hvar is a magical experience in one of the world's most stunning settings.

When to Go

The best time to visit Hvar depends on what you are looking for in your holiday. Here are a few pointers:

Peak Season
If it is party action and blue skies and temperatures of 30 C plus that is your ideal holiday, book your flights for July and August. This is the peak season, a time when the yachts increase in size, the Italians come en masse, and the population of the island more than doubles. A time for partying, cocktails at the beach and late nights on the waterfront.

Easter
One of the highlights of the domestic calendar and a delightful time to visit, Easter tends to coincide with the official end of winter, the beginning of the season and returning family members celebrating this important religious festival over a long weekend. The overnight Easter Procession is an event unique in the world.

Olive and Wine Harvests
The main tourist season over, local focus turns to the fields, with agriculture a mainstay of the local economy and culture. All hands are turned to the fields for the grape harvest in September, and for the olive harvest in October/November (the merits of late and early picking are hotly debated in the island's cafes), while the lavender harvest in June/July is yet one more chance to engage with local people and nature.

Fields of Lavender

An arresting view round every corner, Hvar is famed for its colour and aroma. The picturesque basics – pristine turquoise sea and lush green hilly terrain – are interspersed with a colourful array of flora and fauna throughout the year, with perhaps the highlight being the fields of lavender, for which the island is famed, in June and July.

Shoulder Season: All the Benefits without the Crowds
While the occasional hardly soul swims all year, the generally-accepted swimming season runs from May to October. May, June, September and early October are excellent times to visit for people looking to beat the hordes, while being able to enjoy the benefits of everything open and a warm temperature. Locals have more time before the peak season madness, and these months are more relaxed in general.

Winter Regattas, Cycling and Tranquillity
While trying to sell Hvar as a beach resort in December might be stretching it, a visit to Hvar in winter gives an entirely different, but equally rewarding perspective. The lower temperatures make it popular with cycling groups, while the winter regatta in Hvar Town in December is a popular event. The biting *bura* wind and the frequent rain (yes, it does rain, how do you think it stays so green!) bring home the realities of the harsh realities of Dalmatian life. Not for the fainthearted, but a great web to blow away the cobwebs if looking for some isolation. With the arrival fo the seaplane service from European Coastal Airlines, year-round connections are now much better, and Jelsa is services by daily flights by the ever-increasing network.

Five Festivals Not to Miss

1. Za Krizen Easter Procession (March)
Inscribed as UNESCO intangible heritage, the 500 year-old Za Krizen (Behind the Cross) Easter Procession in the six towns and villages of Jelsa, Pitve, Vrisnik, Svirce, Vrbanj and Vrboska is like no other in the world, as 6 barefoot crossbearers lead

simultaneous processions, followed by their torch-bearing acolytes and pilgrims, leaving at 22:00 on Maundy Thursday, each from their respective community on a 22km procession via the churches of the other communities, before arriving back at their starting point, with the exhausted crossbearer running the final metres before kneeling and handing over the cross to the awaiting priest. Please note this is NOT a tourism spectactle, and applause is not welcome at the end of the procession, but visitors are more than welcome to tke part. It is one of the events on Hvar which makes Easter such a special time. This year's procession is on March 24.

And while the Za Krizen procession is the most famous, there are plenty of other processions over the Easter period, all unique and with fascinating traditions. Here is an overview:

Hvar Town
Hvar town procession „Po Božjim Grebima" (By God's Tombs) takes place on Good Friday at 3 pm, starting at St. Stephen's Cathedral.

The route of the Hvar Procession is: St. Stephen's Cathedral – Church of the Holy Spirit – Benedictine Convent – Franciscan Monastery - Church of Saint Mary Annunciation. There are different prayers and songs for each of the 5 churches and the whole processions take about an hour and a half.

The cross bearer is a member of one of the 2 brotherhoods in Hvar town. One year it is the Brotherhood of Saint Nicholas (Bratovstina Sv Nikolie) and the other the Brotherhood of the Saint Cross (Bratovstina Sv. Križa). The cross bearer is barefoot and masked, so until the end of the procession, nobody knows who he is.

The same day – Good Friday, there is another big procession in the evening. After the mass in the Cathedral, the procession starts

(8:30 pm – 9 pm depending on the service duration), going through the St. Stephen Square taking approximately 30 minutes.

Sveta Nedjelja
The procession takes place on Good Friday, starting at 4 am by a little pathway up the hill to the cave, then going down to Jagodna and coming back to Sv. Nedjelja at 7 am.

Stari Grad
The Stari Grad procession takes place on Good Friday starting at 8 pm going through the Stari Grad town and ends at 10 pm.

Dol
The 10 km procession takes place on Good Friday at 4 am, going to Stari Grad and comes back to Dol at 7 am. Until some year before the 2nd world war, there was a procession going from Stari Grad to Dol at the same time, and those 2 processions never met. The Dol procession carries 5 crosses, which unlike all the other crosses in the processions on the island are not covered with a black veil.

Zastražisće and Poljica
Zastražisće, little village with only few families living there through the whole year, but great many who left to find their happiness and earn their living somewhere in the world. The Procession starts on Maundy Thursday in the afternoon visiting all little churches and chapels in and around Zastražisće. After that, there is a break until the Good Friday's morning and at 6 am the procession continues from Zastražisće to Poljica and then to Vela Stiniva (wetting the cross in the sea as a symbolic connection for all those people living outside of Zastražisće) and then goes back to
Zastražisće.

Poljica procession takes place on Good Friday at 6 am going to Vela Stiniva, where the cross will be brough to the sea to touch it's surface (same as Zastražisće). After that, the procession continues through an old forest pathway leading to Zastražisće and it's churches and coming back to Poljica at 10:30-11:00 am.

Bogomolje and Gdinj
The procession takes place on Good Friday, starting at 8 am from Bogomolje to Gdinj through an old forest pathway and coming back to Bogomolje by road. The procession ends at 12 pm. Similar, there is a procession from Gdinj to Bogomolje, coming back to Gdinj throuth that old pathway.

Sucuraj
One of the most intriguing processions of all takes place on Good Friday at 20:00. taking about an hour and stopping at four places along the way. The crossbearer is masked and people are not supposed to know who he is, but in a small community, secrets are hard to keep. The crossbearer carries a hollow wooden cross, which can be filled with sand or stones to make it heavier.

2. Lavender Festival, Velo Grablje (June)

Being known as the Lavender Island is one thing, putting on one of the most unique festivals in Europe is quite another. One of my favourite places on Hvar with a current population of just five, Velo Grablje is undergoing a stunning renaissance, powered by the enthusiastic efforts of local association, Pjover. Workshops, stalls, a live concert, the live production of lavender oil, lavender ice cream for the kids, it is well worth the short trip from Hvar Town for a great insight into this wonderful tradition of Hvar.

3. Puhijada Dormouse Festival, Dol (August)

I have been to some strange places in my time in the deserts of Somalia and the wilds of Siberia, but the edible dormouse festival in Dol will certainly be in the top ten when my time is up. A really quite surreal evening that has to be experienced rather than described. I tried with words last year, but I will be here for sure this August. A great festival in yet another inland village with lots of energy and undergoing a revival. The highlight is the final night with the dormouse grilling and big live concert, but the Puhijada these days extends a whole week, with various Dol cultural manifestations on show.

4. Faros Marathon, Stari Grad (August)

When I first heard about the Stari Grad Faros Marathon, I wasn't sure what to think. A sixteen kilometre swim starting in Croatia's oldest town and heading out to the tip of the Kabal Peninsula and back sounded a little weird. It wasn't until much later that I realised the international reputation of the event, and the quality of the competition, which regularly features Olympic medal winners.

5. Jelsa Wine Festival (August)

The Jelsa Wine Festival is hard to put into words, but it is one of the street party events of the year - for all the family. Donkey rides, climbing the pole, street artists and food, drink, just a wonderful evening. It is Blackpool meets Oktoberfest with a family atmosphere for wont of a better description. The fact that it usually falls on the same day as the Faros Marathon makes the last weekend a great one to be on Hvar. The word is that this year's event will be a little different, with a more quality wine event also planned for the weekend before.

Five Tours Not to Miss

1. Secret Hvar Off-Road Safari
Not so secret any more, Sinisa's outstanding tour of the hidden places of the island has been discovered by Lonely Planet, for which hearty congratulations. The tour has been specifically designed by Sinisa, a native of the island, with as good an understanding and knowledge of Dalmatian culture and history as

anyone I know. The man is a legend, the tour fabulous - don't miss it. www.secrethvar.com

2. Blue Cave

Probably the most popular tour on Hvar, with different agencies offering a different version. This unique day on the sea starts with the majestic Green and Blue caves and includes Vis and the Pakleni islands! We'll begin by cruising between Hvar and the islets of Ravnik and Bisevo. First we will visit the Green Cave where we will get a chance to swim inside and enjoy the emerald light show!. Then we'll discover a picturesque hidden inlet called Stiniva, where you can enjoy a delicious swim or just relax and sun bathe. After Stiniva, it's off to experience the world-renowned Blue Cave, whose ethereal silveryblue color is created by the sun as it bathes the inside of the cave through an opening in the roof and is reflected back by the sandy surface below. Widely regarded as one of the world's most beautiful natural phenomena, this cave is a must see. Our trip continues to the legendary island of Vis and the authentic fishing village of Komiža. We will have an hour of free time to explore this charming seaside hamlet before we take off to enjoy the Paklinski Islands. We'll stop at one of the archipelago's most popular bays, Vinogradisce at Palmižana, where you can have a seaside lunch at some of the best restaurants in the Adriatic! After lunch, you can swim, relax or even go dancing at the Laganini lounge club beach bar, a famous island hangout!

3. Grapceva Cave

Travel back several thousand years to Neolithic times with a guided tour of Grapceva Cave near Humac on eastern Hvar. Guided tours are available from mid-June to mid-September, and by appointment at other times. Apart from the stunning cave, take in also the abandoned shepherd's village of Humac, from where the tour starts, ending with a great rustic dining experience at Konoba Humac. More information and tickets from the Jelsa Tourist Board

4. Get Active with a One-Day Adrenaline Tour

With so many great beaches to choose from, it is perhaps hard to find the motivation to pull yourself away from the sun and those lapping waves. But try, if only for a day. There are plenty of specially catered tours for those willing to explore Hvar a little further – from sailing and kayaking, to hiking, climbing and cycling tours. Don't limit your Hvar experience to just the beach and the nightlife. More information on what is on offer in our Activities section.

5. Hvar Tours Wine Tasting

Hvar's wines are attracting increasing attention around the world, as the secret of Plavac Mali is slowly coming out. Why not find out what all the fuss is about and take a wine tour with Hvar Tours, including a visit to the impressive Romanesque tasting rooms of Andro Tomicin Jelsa. Roman togas optional! www.hvartours.com

Events in 2016

Hvar has a very lively programme of events throughout the year. Unfortunately, most of them are announced much closer to the summer, and information should be available via the island's five tourist boards of Hvar Town, Stari Grad, Vrboska, Jelsa and Sucuraj (yes 5!). Their contact details can be found in the Useful Numbers section. Each tourist board hosts a cultural summer programme in addition to special events.

The big event of the year is the 2,400 year birthday of Stari Grad, one of the oldest towns in Croatia (some say the oldest). Not much information about the planned celebrations is available at time of going to press, but check with the Stari Grad Tourist Board.

Here are some confirmed events at the time of going to press.

Za Krizen Easter Procession - March 24
Gariful Kids Day - April 16
Feast of St Prosper - May 10
Carpe Diem Full Moon Parties - 20.06. / 20.07. / 18.08. / 16.09.
Lavender Festival – June 24/25
Hvar Etno Festival - July 8
Ultra Europe Beach Party - July 19
Tam Tam Festival in Sucuraj - July 29/30
Puhijada Dormouse Festival – August 8 - 13
Hvar Half Marathon - August 20
Faros Marathon - August 27
Jelsa Wine Festival - August 26/27
Days in the Bay – Stari Grad 2400 – September 8 - 11
Day of Hvar Town - October 1 - 6
Hvar Big Game Fishing Cup – October 6 – 9
Metropol Mora Traditional Sailboat Festival – October 11 – 13
European Laser Master Champioship – October 21 - 27
Peskafondo – October 25 - 27
Hvar New Year Regatta - December 28-31

Jelsa will also be holding Hvar Wine Association tastings with
live music every Thursday until October, starting at 19:00.

What's in a Name? How to Pronounce 'Hvar'?

So just how do you pronounce this beautiful island? And what are
the origins of its linguistically challenging name? For Westerners
used to a good coating of vowels in their words, Croatian can be a
handful to pronounce (For Trieste, read Trst for example), and
words in English beginning with H+V are in short supply.

There seem to be two approaches which seem to work. The first is
to ignore the 'H' completely and ask the ticket seller at the ferry
terminal for a ticket to Var. The other is it to insert an 'A' and
come up with Ha-var. You will sound like a tourist, but at least
you should get a ticket to the right island. The correct
pronunciation is somewhere between the two, a very shortened

16

'A.' If in doubt, just ask for Croatia's premier island.

The origins of the name seem to descend from the Ancient Greeks, who named the their settlement Pharos (lighthouse). The Romans derived the name Pharia, which then became Fara. This changed in the Middle Ages to Hvar, as the Slavonic consonant 'F' was superceded by 'HV'. This was sometimes spelt Quara or Quarra. To further confuse the issue, the Italians renamed the island Lesina in the 11th Century (or Liesena or Liesna in Venetian dialect), which was derived from an old Croatian word for 'forest'.

Exclusive Hvar: Which Celebrities Have REALLY Visited the Island?

2011 was the year of a British prince falling into a Hvar nightclub swimming pool, followed by a pregnant American popstar showing her baby bump to the world at a Hvar beach club (and then revealing she named her daughter Blue Ivy after a tree on Hvar), but Hvar has a long tradition of celebrities, and not only in Hvar Town – Jackie Kennedy was waterskiing in Stari Grad in 1964, the same town where Edward and Mrs. Simpson dined on their trip to Hvar.

For a Dalmatian island that has traditionally eked out a harsh existence based on olives, wine, lavender and fishing, Hvar has an exclusive image which has attracted many celebrities. Home to the oldest organised tourism in Europe, Hvar Town has been receiving distinguished guests since the arrival of Hapsburg Emperor Franz Josef I in 1875.

Many famous names have been cited as regular visitors to the island, but one organisation in possessions of the facts, the Hvar Town Tourist Board, has given some details about illustrious visitors in the past.

A Relaxed Atmosphere for Celebrities

17

It is worth noting that one of the attractions of Hvar for celebrities is the laid-back reception they receive from local people, and hounding by *paparazzi* is rare. The tourist board respects and protects the privacy of its more famous guests, keeping prying journalists away where possible, which is probably a major factor in Hvar's continued popularity on the celebrity circuit.

With its stunning scenery and historical towns, Hvar is an ideal film set (Indeed ex-Croatian President Mesic and Ashley Judd were both filming here in May 2011, the former in a new Croatian, the latter for her new ABC series, *Missing*), one which could command an all-star cast from its previous guests.

A-List Stars from the World of Film
Ever since Orson Welles filmed *The Deep* on Hvar in the 1960s, the island has attracted A-list stars from the world of movies. Visitors have included Clint Eastwood, Michael Douglas, Catherine Zeta Jones, John Malkovich, Brad Pitt, Jodie Foster, Eva Longoria, Gwyneth Paltrow, Stephen Spielberg, George Clooney and Jack Nicholson, while Kevin Spacey made world headlines during his visit in 2008 for grabbing a man's bare buttocks on a night out in Hvar Town. More recent A-lister visitors have included Demi Moore and Tom Cruise.

The James Bond Appreciation Society
Local observers could be forgiven for thinking a British espionage conspiracy was afoot on the island given the number of secret agents that have holidayed on Hvar. No less than three James Bonds - Sean Connery, Daniel Craig and Pierce Brosnan have soaked up the rays on Europe's sunniest island, as have at least two Bond girls, Gemma Arterton and Michelle Yeon.

Sporting Stars on Hvar
From sport, Hvar seems to provide a particular attraction to tennis players, with Croatian legends Goran Ivanisevic and Iva Majoli spotted on the waterfront, as have been Andre Agassi, Jennifer Capriati, Novak Djokovic and Gabriela Sabatini. Other sporting

stars who have spent time on Hvar are David Beckham and, from the world of motor racing, Bernie Ecclestone, Eddie Jordan and Michael Schumacher.

Continuing the Royal Tradition
The royal tradition has been continued by King Abdullah of Jordan, the King of Denmark, Prince Claus of Holland and Princess Caroline of Monaco, and some of the world's richest men - Bill Gates and Roman Abramovich - have sailed into the Hvar harbour.

From the world of music, Hvarites have glimpsed Simon Le Bon, MC Hammer, Beyonce and Jay-Z, as well as other celebrities Nicky Hilton, Ivana Trump (whose ex-husband owns a large hunting concession on Hvar) and Saif Al-Islam, son of the former Libyan leader.

The relaxed approach to celebrities is good news for holidaymakers to see someone famous. With Hvar making the Sunday Times list of Top 100 Affordable Places on the Med, there can be few other places where backpackers can mix so freely with the stars. Celebrities tend to be left alone on Hvar, something they tend to appreciate. Unless of course, they are a prince with a tendency to fall into nightclub swimming pools...

A History of Tourism on Hvar, the Oldest Organised Tourism in Europe

The First Visitors to Hvar
Interpretations by the Greek poet Apollonius place the island on the route taken by the Argonauts in search of the Golden Fleece, describing the island as idyllic Pityeia or covered in pine trees. What is known is that the Greek poet Xenphanes from Elea visited Hvar in the 6th Century BC, in search of fish fossils.

Rich Roman visitors came on individual visits during the Roman Empire (Diocletian's Palace in Split was built in the 4th Century for Emperor Diocletian), and there were many rustic villas built in the various bays of the island, which were known as *villae rusticae*.

On the Pilgrimage Route from Venice to Jaffa
There is more documented proof of religious tourism from the 15th Century, as Hvar featured as a stopping point for some on pilgrimages to the Holy Land on the popular route from Venice to Jaffa. Travellers were understandably from the wealthier classes and the writings of the period that have survived constitute the first real picture of life on Hvar.

Tourist impressions from the Middle Ages were in some ways not too dissimilar to the impressions today, with frequent mention of the stormy sea, the white stone, the palm trees, the playful dolphins (a regular sight even today), and the smell of rosemary below the fortress.

The period saw the emergence of what was called 'rural tourism', as the aristocracy and rich elite
spent holidays in villas in the towns and bays on Hvar. One of the best preserved of these is the summer palace of famous poet, Petar Hektorovic, in Stari Grad, called the Tvrdalj. It included a fishpond, walled garden, tower and dovecote. It is well-preserved and today houses the Ethnographic Museum.

A Royal Visit and the Emergence of Science Tourism
The 18th and 19th Centuries brought a new type of tourist, in search of scientific discovery. Dalmatia became a popular destination for scientists from Germany and Austria, and Hvar, with its rich flora and fauna, was an especially popular spot. Of particular interest to the scientists were the island's plants, insects, sponges and sea worms. There was even a royal expedition in 1838, when the King of Saxony, King Friedrich II paid a visit.

Founding of the Hvar Health Society in 1868

Hvar was formally established as a tourist destination in 1868, with the founding of the Hvar Health Society, following extensive scientific analysis of the island's climate. The climate was found to be an excellent environment for treating various illnesses, lung illnesses in particular. Thanks to the hard work and connections of Professor Oskar Schmidt and Dr Franz Unger, the Hvar Health Society, or Higijenicko drustvo u Hvaru, Societa Igienica di Lesina, Heil-verein von Lesina, was formed on May 15, 1868. The healthy climate and its recuperative powers remains one of Hvar's most attractive features for many visitors.

Royal Investment in Europe's Oldest Organised Tourism
With the founding of the Hvar Health Society on May 15, 1868, the first organised tourism in Europe came into being, tourism based on health and recuperation, rather than historical sites. While individual travel had a long tradition among the upper classes, the first organised tourist association in France only came into existence in Cannes in 1907 (Syndicat d'Initiative). The birth of organised tourism in Europe was announced as follows:

Having surrendered Venice, in all its vast dominions Austria does not have a single place on the coast suitable for people with chest illnesses to stay during the winter season, despite the fact that there are several such places in Istria and Dalmatia.

After due consideration, and with the approval of the most capable doctors and excellent naturalists, it has been established that nowhere is better than Hvar for those with chest illnesses. With its location, the particular nature of the town and the special features of its climate, it can not only rival Venice, Pisa, Nice and so on, but can often outshine them.

Guided by these reasons, and inspired by patriotism and humanity, in the belief that we can offer people from Austria and Northern Germany a superior and more accessible resort, we are establishing in Hvar, Dalmatia, a joint stock company called the

21

Health Society in Hvar.

The aim of the Health Society is to provide everything needed for
visitors to have a pleasant stay in this town, so that their
sufferings are eased and their diseased lungs can benefit from our
mild climate and health-giving air.

For this purpose, the Society will have at its disposal comfortable
accommodation for visitors, providing all services, and sparing no
effort to fulfil all their desires.
By October several houses will be ready and equipped for this
purpose.

Hvar, 15th May 1868.

The first hotel for the new society was a private house on the
main square in Hvar Town, owned by the Samohod-
Dubokovicfamily, which opened for business on October 15 1868
after a full renovation. The new hotel had 13 single rooms with
heating and a restaurant, and was staffed by a cook, two waiters
and a chambermaid from Trieste.

Funds for a more expansive hotel were sought but progress was
slow and the temporary hotel was moved to the former military
building on the Fabrika in 1872, with private accommodation
fulfilling any shortfall in beds.

The Hvar Health Society petitioned the Court in Vienna for
financial support to build a proper hotel, asking that the Empress
Elizabeth become patron of the new hotel, allowing it to bear her
name. She agreed and the first royal donation was made in 1869
with this reply:

To the honourable Management of the Health Society in Hvar,
Dalmatia
Her Majesty the Empress and Queen has very generously decided

to accept patronage of your Health Society, based in Hvar, and to allow the Clinic built by this Society to bear the name "Stabilimento igienico imperatrice Elisabetta" (The Empress Elizabeth Institution of Health). As a mark of her most gracious acknowledgement of the worthy aim of the aforementioned Institution, it is her pleasure to grant a gift for it of 200 florins from her Royal Highness' personal funds.

As it is my honour to inform the honourable Management of the Health Society in Hvar of the glad news of Her Majesty's decision relating to the request of the 20th of last month, and to pass on the above-mentioned generously approved sum, I ask you kindly to sign and return the enclosed confirmation of receipt of the same.

Gödöllö, 10th November 1869
B. Napcsa, on behalf of Her Majesty

Construction of the new hotel, where the ruins of the former Ducal Palace once stood, was slow, from plans drawn up in 1880 to completion of the first part of the building in 1898 and formally opened on April 1 1899.

The fully completed Kur Hotel Kaiserin Elizabeth opened in 1903, furnished from Trieste and boasting 35 beds, bathrooms, a reading room, restaurant and coffee-house in the old loggia. Some of the hotel's rules, included in the 1905 rule book (printed in Croatian, Italian and German), required guests to be clean and tidy, not to smoke at lunch, play dangerous games inside the hotel, bring in animals or hang washing outside.

Expansion of Tourism on Hvar
The Society's early efforts were both impressive and successful, with Hvar becoming known as the Austrian Madeira. The majority of guests were German, Austrian, Czech, Hungarian and Croatian, enticed to Dalmatia by some excellent tourism promotion by the Hvar Health Society.

In addition to the various leaflets, notices and reviews in Austrian journals, the first guide to Hvar, in German, was printed in Trieste in 1899, followed by a second with photographs in 1903. Things to do on Hvar included night fishing, bowling, the shooting range, concerts and music on the hotel's terrace, and the art collection at the Franciscan Monastery.

The tourism boom inspired others to jump on the bandwagon and the privately-owned Hotel Kovacic opened in 1914 on the waterfront, as did the Palmizana Manor House on the Pakleni Islands in 1906.

The financial dividends of successful tourism were somewhat reinvested in the town, and there were major improvements in this period, including fixing the promenades to the Franciscan Monastery and Majerovia Bay. Improvements were also made to the town's bathing beach, changing huts and tennis courts, trees were planted and ferry connections improved.

The most high profile visitor to Hvar in the early years was Emperor Franz Joseph I himself, who sailed in for a night in 1875, to be greeted with a spectacular reception, including fireworks, leading him to address the people of the town:

Thank you for the heartfelt welcome organized by this historic town. I have always believed in the sincere and patriotic feelings of these people, and I guarantee them my Imperial mercy and benevolence.

After a successful start, the Society's fortunes changed after 1910 and a combination of constant debts and the First World War led to the sale of the hotel to the owner of Hotel Royal in Zagreb in 1918.

Tourism on Hvar Between the Wars: 1921 – 1941
The Hvar Health Society was dissolved shortly afterwards, and

the period of 1921-1941 was one of great change, both politically and from a tourism perspective, as Hvar's rulers changed from Italian occupiers to the Kingdom of Serbs, Croats and Slovenes, then to former Yugoslavia and into the Second World War.

A new breed of tourism entrepreneur emerged, expanding the offer from traditional health tourism into more recreational and bathing holidays, and with the expansion, so tourism was opened up to different social classes. The Hvar Council Tourist Board came into being in the late 1930s.

A driving force in this expansion was the director of the Palace Hotel (as the Empress Elizabeth had been renamed) and leader of the town council, Dr. Josip Avelini, whose energy and enthusiasm led to the construction of new hotels and improved public services.

Work began on the large Madeira Hotel in 1929, the Palace was extended in 1935, and construction of the Dr. Jopip Avelini Health Centre finally opened at Hotel Dalamacija in 1948. Palm trees were planted along the promenade in 1924 and a new stone bathing station unveiled in 1927.

A small electric plant in 1925 lit up the town each night, while the water supply grid from the springs near the town was introduced in 1923. A road connecting Hvar with the northern coastal towns of Jelsa and Stari Grad was finished in 1939. Others followed suit, and Hotels Park, Overland and Slavija were built at this time

The boost in tourism was gratefully received by the local population, suffering as they were from poor wine yields, which had led to large-scale emigration. Records show that there were 3,065 visitors in 1930, for example, totaling 26,911 overnight stays.

As for Hvar's original hotel, the Empress Elizabeth was renamed the Grand Palace by the new owner, who himself fell into debt, and ownership transferred to a Serbian bank, who sold it to the Honorary Yugoslav Consul in Prague. He remained the owner until the break-up of the first Yugoslavia.

The most ambitious project was the spa Hotel Madeira, a 160-bed hotel where the present Hotel Adriana is located, with central heating and even a lift. Due to a scandal with one of the main investors, a government minister, the hotel was never built, and the site lay empty for forty years until the Hotel Adriatic was built.

Hvar under Communism: Mass Tourism and the Rise of Naturism
Emerging from the Second World War under Communist Yugoslav rule, Hvar's tourism suffered on two fronts: firstly, many of the traditional guests from Austria and West Germany could not easily visit; and secondly, the new authorities nationalised all the hotels and decided to focus tourism based on workers' trade unions, so that the majority of visitors were children, invalids and workers, with the only sizable foreign contingent being the Czechs.

In order to attract more quality tourism, the Hvar Hotel Company was established in 1959, an independent company managed by a young Hvar citizen, Tonko Domancic. A new leaflet produced in the same year, entitled "Come to Hvar this winter – the sunniest island on the Adriatic" marked a shift in emphasis in the Hvar tourism offer.

At the same time, several municipal projects, including the 364-bed Hotel Pharos and night-time restaurant on the island of Galesnik, opposite Hvar Town, increased the tourism offer, which also now projected Hvar as an ideal naturist resort, as well as a health resort.

It worked. Hvar became a very popular place to visit from Western Europe and Scandinavia, as tourists took advantage of the cheaper prices in Yugoslavia and the hospitable welcome and improved facilities, and the island once more regained its quality tourism image. Famous guests at the time included Orson Welles (who filmed The Deep on Hvar), actress Jeanne Moreau, actor George Hamilton, designer Pierre Cardin and underwater explorer Jacques Yves Cousteau.

Naturism was an especially effective tourism strategy and Western naturists, particularly from Germany flocked to the island from the 1960s. While the naturist tradition was at odds with Hvar's conservative society, the island of Jerolim on the Pakleni Islands was made available to naturists discreetly, the first such offer on the Adriatic coast. Hvar has been a haven for naturists ever since.

With the growth of mass tourism in the 1970s came the even stronger growth of the private accommodation offer, which is the backbone of much private income on the island, and has resulted in some lifelong friendships, as tourists return each year to the same families and apartments. In 1930, there were only 44 private rooms for rent in Hvar Town, a number that had increased to 700 by 1990.

War in Former Yugoslavia and the Arrival of ORCO Group
War, this time a more localised affair, decimated the tourist industry in the early 1990s, at a time when then Yugoslavia was the second most popular destination for British tourists after Spain. Not only were foreign guests not coming, but the hotels were filled with refugees and the displaced from mainland Croatia. The effects on the island's economy and the livelihoods of the many dependent on tourism was severe.

Recovery was initially slow in a newly independent Croatia, as many tourists stayed away, confused as to whether or not Croatia was still a war zone. A highly effective marketing campaign by the Croatian National Tourist Board, under the banner *The Mediterranean as it Once Was*, helped to dispel some of the myths and tourists are once more flocking to the island.

Hvar Town itself has undergone a major upgrade, both in terms of branding and renovation, with the arrival of Orco Group in 2005, who bought a majority share in Suncani Hvar, the Hvar Town hotel group. Since purchasing, millions have been invested into revamping the hotels and improving the town's image, so that it is now known as the new St. Tropez.

Now known as one of the premier spots on the Adriatic, the history of tourism on Hvar has been turbulent, but the fundamentals remain the same – it is the sunniest island with stunning scenery and pristine beaches, as well as an extremely healthy climate, leading Conde Nast readers to vote it among the top ten most beautiful islands in the world.

A Brief History of the Island

As one would expect for an island, the history of Hvar has been broadly shaped and influenced by outsiders, each invading force leaving their mark, which has resulted in a rich cultural, archaeological and architectural legacy. There is much to discover for visitors interested in the heritage of Hvar, as this brief overview of the island's history will demonstrate.

The earliest signs of civilisation on Hvar date back to Neolithic times and the so-called Hvar Culture of 3500 – 2500 BC. These estimates by archaeologists are based on artefacts and painted pottery in the caves of Grapceva and Markova Spilija, both of which can be visited today. Examples of the finds are displayed in the excellent Heritage Museum in Hvar Town.

Given its prominent position on a busy sea route, it is perhaps surprising that the island was not settled earlier that 384 BC, when the Ancient Greeks founded the settlement of Pharos (modern-day Stari Grad). The Ionian Greeks, the Parans, were in search of a base for military and trade expansion and the deep bay at Pharos offered the best protection.

The first recorded naval battle in the Adriatic took place just off Hvar, with the Greeks successfully taking on the native Illyrian tribe of the Liburni, an account of which was written by Diodorus of Sicily.

While there is some evidence of Greek heritage in present day Stari Grad, the most striking remnant is the UNESCO-protected Stari Grad Plain, a superbly preserved 80-hectare agricultural colony still in use today.

With the decline of the Syracuse Empire, Pharos enjoyed a brief period of local rule under Demetrius of Hvar, who kept the Romans at bay until they finally smashed the walls of Pharos in 229 BC. The Romans used the island as a strategic and logistical base, keeping their boats in the protected bays of the Scedro and the Pakleni Islands. Roman holiday houses sprang up in the bays close to fresh water, most notably in Hvar, Stari Grad and Jelsa. Archaeological finds confirm that the islanders were engaged in an existence of wine growing, fishing and trade.

There is little recorded about Hvar after Roman rule but the island was under a Croatian state of the Neretljani in the early Middle Ages, along with surrounding islands, before being briefly occupied by Venice in 1147. This was only temporary, however, as Croatian-Hungarian King Bela III managed to bring Dalmatia under his rule.

The Venetians were back in 1278, having been invited back by the islanders looking for protection from the pirates of Omis. One of the early changes the Venetians introduced was to move central administration from Stari Grad to Hvar, and the new centre became a regional centre of administration for Hvar, Vis and

Brac. A plan to build walls around the town and monastery was initiated in 1292.

Venice's rule was far from secure, and the island's noblemen rebelled in 1310, and the Hvar's rulers changed several times (Croatian-Hungarian kingdom, Bosnian kingdom and Dubrovnik) before, along with the rest of Dalmatia, a more protracted period of Venetian rule from 1420 to 1797.
Hvar became the main Venetian port in the eastern Adriatic, but was under constant threat of attack from the Turkish fleet which controlled the mainland near Makarska. A devastating Turkish naval attack in 1571 under Algerian commander Uluz Ali in 1571 laid waste Vrboska, Stari Grad and Hvar.

Matija Ivanicwas a prominent 16th century citizen of the Dalmatian city of Hvar that led the Hvar Rebellion (1510–1514) against the Venetian Republic. After the defeat of the Rebellion, Ivanicbecame a symbol of freedom in Venetian-controlled Dalmatia. Personifying defiance both against Venice and against the oppressive noble classes. He was mentioned in the well-known Dalmatian song which expresses these themes, the "Padaj silo i nepravdo" ("Fall, oh Force and Injustice!").
Hvar prospered under Venetian rule, and was known as a place for wine, lavender, olives, rosemary, fishing and boat building. More than three centuries of rule from Venice came to an end in 1797, when the Austrians briefly took over before themselves being usurped by the French. The Russians bombarded Hvar in 1807 in a period of general instability and warfare in Europe, until the Austrians retook control in 1813, a rule that lasted into the 20th Century.

Austrian rule was stable and brought prosperity, most notably in the development of health tourism on the island, with the founding of the Hvar Health Society in 1868. The oldest meteorological station in Croatia was also established in 1858. Austrian rule also brought infrastructure improvements to the island, with all the ports rebuilt, new lighthouses, malaria-infested marshland reclaimed, and a road connecting Jelsa to Pitve and Vrisnik in 1907. The old road from Jelsa to Hvar did not appear until the 1930s, and previous travel options were ship or 8-hour donkey ride.

The Italians were back in November, 1919, occupying Hvar once more after fierce fighting, an occupation which lasted until the 1921 Treaty of Rapello consigned the island to membership of the Kingdom of Serbs, Croats and Slovenes, later the first Yugoslavia and then the Socialist Federal Republic of Yugoslavia.

The region was subjected to more war less than 20 years later of course, and the British, Italians and Germans all left their mark on Dalmatia. One of the more remarkable stories of the period was the evacuation of about 25,000 (including several thousand from Hvar) civilians to a British refugee camp in the Sinai desert called El Shatt. The camp operated for two years, and even hosted the famous Za Krizen Easter Procession, before the refugees returned home after the war in 1946. Several people living on Hvar today were born in the Egyptian desert, and most families have someone who was born there.

Hvar's latest (and one would hope permanent) change of master occurred on January 15 1992, when Croatia was recognised as an independent state.

Hvar and the War (1991-5)
With the billionaire yachts moored up and the picturesque stone squares full of tourists in the numerous cafes, it is hard to imagine that the citizens of Hvar were caught up in war just sixteen years ago. A common request from incoming tourists is a simple explanation of the war in Yugoslavia, and while much has been written on the subject, rather less has been documented about the effects of the war on Hvar.

Naval Blockade

The former Yugoslav army (JNA) attacked Croatia in July 1991 and Hvar was blockaded the following month. The main effects of the blockade were shortages of foodstuffs normally brought from the mainland, such as flour, and no access to hospitals and main medical services.

After the sinking of some JNA ships from land fire on Brac and the Peljesac Peninsula, a ceasefire was signed and the navy left Sucuraj territorial waters on December 3 1991.

Arrival of Refugees and Internally Displaced Persons from the Mainland

The situation on the ground in the mainland was dire, with large tracts of Croatia occupied. A steady stream of refugees had to be housed, and a logical supplier of beds was Hvar, devoid of tourists due to the conflict. Refugees, particularly from the front-line town of Vukovar, began to arrive by boat.
The refugee situation deteriorated in 1992 as Croatia took in numerous refugees from the brutal war in Bosnia and Hercegovina. The effect of traumatised refugees replacing affluent tourist was two-fold: severe reduction in revenue and severe increase in wear and tear in the hotels.

Full Hotels but No Tourists

A UN fact-finding mission in August 1992 found that there were 624 displaced persons and 3,727 refugees on Hvar, of whom 1,323 were in private accommodation, the rest in hotels. Usually closed in winter, most of the hotels had no heating instillations, which caused problems for the new temporary residents.

Although never invaded, Hvar did experience enemy attack, and the tiny airstrip in Stari Grad was bombed at least twice. The main result of the bombing was denying local people emergency services on the mainland.

With the demographic balance upset both ways - increased population during the winter and decreased in the summer due to lack of tourists - the hotels were full all year, which had a negative impact on the condition of the buildings.

The absence of many paying visitors had a devastating effect on the island's economy which resulted in many cafes and restaurants closing. The cafes & restaurants closed because of the lack of electricity (because of the occupation of the Peruca dam, source of hydro-electric power) and the difficulties of obtaining necessary goods such as coffee, milk etc from the mainland. Many of Hvar's male population were drafted into the defence forces on the front line near Zadar, where one man from Stari Grad was killed and many more returned suffering from PTSD.

Ownership Issues

As former Yugoslavia's premier island, Hvar was popular with Serbs, many of whom had holiday homes there. Some of these were requisitioned for accommodation for the wounded and refugees from areas on mainland Croatia under occupation, while others were sold off cheaply by their owners who figured they would never come to the island again. Many others decided to bide their time and are once again regular visitors to Hvar.

A great hindrance to the post-war development of tourist infrastructure has been ownership issues of hotels and other such buildings, many of which were nationalised by the newly-independent Croatian government. One such example on Hvar was the Belgrade Resort, a 10,000m2 beach front complex with 400 hundred rooms and 25m indoor pool east of Jelsa.

It remains abandoned today despite much interest from large investment groups during the real estate boom of 2004-5, with ownership problems (the City of Belgrade was the pre-nationalisation owner) the main stumbling block. This ownership issue was repeated along the Adriatic coast and was one of the main reasons why hotels in prime locations remained derelict for so long.

Recovery of the Tourist Industry
The war had a devastating effect on the entire region, and recovery has been slow. In terms of tourism, the main challenge facing Croatia was to persuade potential visitors that the country was safe, not at war and open for business. A highly effective marketing campaign under the slogan *The Mediterranean as it Once Was* went some way to achieving this, but has still not fully recovered 16 years after hostilities ceased.

While the scars of the conflict, both physical and psychological, still exist, Hvar's tourism is once more booming, with Hvar Town in particular benefiting from a multi-million dollar investment in the town's hotels.

Is Hvar Really a Party Island?

One of the great charms of the island of Hvar is that it has something for everyone. While some go for the vibrant nightlife in Hvar Town, just a couple of kilometres away, a yoga retreat is taking place in an idyllic bay.

In recent years, Hvar has earned the label as a party island, one of the top ten party spots on the planet. The arrival of the Ultra Europe beach festival and the excesses of The Yacht Week have helped to enhance that image. So is it a party island, the new Ibiza?

If you are looking for a choice of places to party the night away, head to Zrce on the island of Pag. Hvar has just four nightclubs in total, the main one on an island just off Hvar Town (Carpe Diem Beach at Stipanska). There are plenty of bars and a lively atmosphere, but the new Ibiza? It should also be noted that the main nightlife of the main club at Carpe Diem Beach is only for the peak summer months of July and August.

Behaviour on Hvar: a Polite Request

In the summer of 2015, two Australian youths were arrested for climbing on the roof of the Hvar Cathedral. I interviewed one afterwards, and while he was sorry for what he had done in the sober light of day, his impression of Croatia was that it was a party place where everything goes, where walking around topless, sitting in the square drinking a beer on the floor were things that were acceptable. Things that he wouldn't do at home, but hey, this was Croatia!

A couple of years ago, in association with the local tourist board, leaflets with a code of conduct were printed, but never distributed for some reason. Here is the requested code of conduct:

CODE OF CONDUCT IN TOWN OF HVAR
Welcome to Hvar. We would like you to enjoy every moment of your stay in our town.
Hvar is one of the most famous tourist towns in Croatia, where organised tourism dates back 145 years. It has a rich cultural heritage, including the oldest public theatre in Europe, dated 1612.
In summer, Hvar buzzes with visitors and hums with activity. So that EVERYONE can enjoy being here there are certain public order rules which you are expected to respect and follow for our mutual benefit.

Please comply with the following:
- Respect the rule to walk through town dressed (you need to cover your beachwear) - our town centre is like a museum and a live stage at the same time.
- Look after the environment and do not discard any rubbish or cigarettes on the streets or in the sea - keeping our environment clean is our common goal.
- Not to shout, scream or argue loudly in public places
- Respect the rule of not drinking in open public places
For that purpose there are many bars and restaurants with varied

and quality offer
- Not to disturb public order by playing or reproducing music in late hours (on boats or otherwise)
Each person that is in town has a right to enjoy his or her stay. It is important to consider the needs of others as the freedom of one is allowed to the point if it does not disturb another.
- Not to use any inflammables or pyrotechnical goods by any means and do not light fires or barbecues in nature.
Care with the fires is necessary for the safety of us all.

Please respect our culture, customs and tradition - by doing this you will contribute to the efforts of local community to preserve our rich historic heritage.

We wish you feel free to behave in the same way as you would like others to behave in your house or your town. We thank you to chose our town for your holiday!

An Island with the Most UNESCO Heritage in the World

One of the more interesting facts about Hvar is that it has the most UNESCO heritage of any island in the world. In addition to one of Croatia's 7 World Heritage Sites, the Stari Grad Plain, Hvar also has various intangible UNESCO heritage – the Za Krizen Easter Procession in Jelsa and surrounding villages, the agave lace produced by the Benedictine Nuns in Hvar Town and – since 2014 – the Mediterranean diet, as Hvar, along with six other Mediterranean locations including neighbouring Brac, had a fourth UNESCO jewel to add to its crown. If you also count klapa singing for southern Dalmatia, the list rises to five. I think I am correct in saying that no other island has three. An island of heritage and tradition, and these treasures do not even include the oldest public theatre in Europe.

The Easter Procession: Za Krizen (Behind the Cross)
Za Krizen is actually six processions all leaving simultaneously

from the villages of Jelsa, Pitve, Vrisnik, Svirce, Vrisnik and Vrboksa at 22@00 on the evening of Maundy Thursday. Each group is headed by acolytes carrying lanterns to show the way for the cross bearer, who carries a wooden cross (weighing between 10 and 18 kg) barefoot the entire route. Each procession heads in a clockwise direction to the next parish church, praying and chanting along the way, before stopping in the church for prayers and the harmonies of the lament of Mother Mary.

After praying in each church, the procession continues along the circle of hilltop villages and along the coastal towns of Vrboska and Jelsa, before ending at the starting point, with the exhausted cross-bearer often running the last few steps before surrendering the cross to the parish priest. The deep male voices chanting through the night give the procession a special atmosphere, as does the practice of every household in the participating villages leaving a light on through the night.

The Easter procession is a popular event for pilgrims and tourists alike, the start of Easter festivities and a time when relatives return to the island for the celebrations. Each procession finishes about 7am and the paths to the churches are sometimes rugged, so it is not a pilgrimage for the fainthearted. Some cafes in Jelsa and Vrboksa remain open through the night, but refreshments are otherwise limited.

The Role of the Cross Bearer
It is seen as a high honour to be chosen as a cross bearer and there is a long waiting list for the privilege. It is a highly respected position and the krizonosa has a luminous cross displayed outside his home for the period before and after the procession. Competition is tough, and a 2007 applicant was told the first available opportunity to carry the Jelsa cross was in 2033. Although there is no age limit, a level of fitness is obviously required, especially as the heavy cross is covered in a veil for the journey, and can be severely unwieldy in the wind.

The krizonosa chooses a close circle of male companions to assist him through the night, and they are on hand in case he gets into difficulty. Dressed in black, they provide a stark contrast to the cream robes of the brotherhood worn by the krizonosa and the chanting acolytes. .

History of the Procession
The history of the procession dates back to the 16th Century and was placed under UNESCO protection in 2009. Its origins lie in a populist rebellion to the autocratic rule of the Venetians, and the procession has taken place every year, quite an achievement given the recent past with Communism and the war in Yugoslavia.

With the procession over, residents focus on the rest of the Easter celebrations, and the churches are strangely silent, the only time in the year when the church bells do not chime on the hour, although they more than make up for it with exuberant ringing on Easter Sunday, the highlight of the Easter celebration.

Agave Lace from the Benedictine Nuns
The Benedictine Nuns arrived on Hvar in 1664 and celebrated their 350 year anniversary in 2014. The house in which local hero Hanibal Lucic was born in 1485 was donated to the nuns by his descendants, and so started an important chapter in education in the town, as the nuns operated the first school in Hvar, from 1826 to 1866. They are still active today and, among other duties, produce some of the finest souvenirs from Hvar, in the form of intricate lace made from agave. Agave is the same plant which Mexicans use to make tequila. The Hvar agave lace is now under UNESCO heritage.

The Mediterranean Diet
For many, a key attraction to visiting Hvar is the gourmet scene. With some of the world's best olive oil, coupled with the fruits of the Adriatc and the freshest seasonal vegetables. In the words of

UNESCO:

"The Mediterranean diet involves a set of skills, knowledge, rituals, symbols and traditions... Eating together is the foundation of the cultural identity and continuity of communities throughout the Mediterranean basin. It is a moment of social exchange and communication, an affirmation and renewal of family, group or community identity. The Mediterranean diet emphasises values of hospitality, neighbourliness, intercultural dialogue and creativity, and a way of life guided by respect for diversity."

In 2014, along with the island of Brac, Hvar was one of seven locations throughout the Mediterranean which had its diet inscribed as intangible UNESCO heritage. Find out why on one of your visits to the local restaurants.

Village in Focus: Velo Grablje

If there is one place I would encourage you to visit away from the beach, it is the small village of Velo Grablje, home to a rather remarkable success story.

The village has enjoyed mixed fortunes. At its height it was the centre of lavender production for the whole of Dalmatia, but until recently, it was an almost abandoned village of just five people, despite its spectacular location with views toward the island of Vis. The association between Hvar Town and Velo Grablje is strong, and despite the lack of permanent residents, the Sunday morning mass is celebrated with 50-60 people, as Grablje men and women, now resident in Hvar Town, come back to their roots.

Several years ago, a group of young enthusiasts with ties to the village decided to do something about the decline. They formed an NGO called Pjover and set about reviving some of the heritage and traditions of the village, which included the first Lavender Festival. The local football team came alive again, and NK Levonda won the Hvar national league.

People got involved, more ideas flowed, and a few more initiatives were launched. Just a few years later, the full-time population of Velo Grablje is now 13, and the village now has the sound of child's laughter, as two kids are among the 13. A quality restaurant, Zbondini, has opened, serving excellent food and breathing a little more life, and if you are here on a Friday night out of peak season, head to Mali Zeleni, the only real pub on Hvar – and what a fabulous discovery it is too.

EU money is coming into the village, as part of a wider eco-ethno project, and it is heartening to see that with most people heading to the coast, small revivals in places like Velo Grablje are possible. It has a wonderful atmosphere and is well worth a visit, whatever time of year. Learn more about Pjover's activities on www.pjover.com

CHAPTER 1: GETTING THERE AND AROUND

Flights to Croatia

Split is connected to over 90 cities in 2016, a record number, giving travellers from around Europe a much better choice. But there are several other options to connect to get to Hvar. Dubrovnik, for example, is a popular entry point with much improved connections to Hvar for season 2016 (see below), while the Ryanair route to Zadar remains as popular as ever. Don't discount the capital Zagreb, a 5-hour bus or train ride to Zagreb, while Pula in northern Croatia is attracting more passengers each year, and you can now connect from downtown Pula to downtown Split by seaplane in just one hour – it is a spectacular flight. Many visitors take advantage of the one-way fares, and fly into one Croatian airport and out of another. For the most comprehensive (and current) list of flights to Croatian destinations, check out the best current online resource - www.visit-croatia.co.uk/index.php/travelling-around-croatia/flights-in-croatia

Seaplanes to Hvar

A revolution in travel to Hvar started shortly after 09:30 on August 27, 2014, when a European Coastal Airlines Twin Otter landed at the new seaport in Jelsa harbour, just 15 minutes after taking off from the seaport at Resnik, near Split Airport. After 14 years of fighting bureaucracy, the seaplane dream became a reality.

Since that time, the network has grown considerably, and internationally, and you can now fly from downtown Split to Pescara and Ancona for example. At time of writing, the following seaplane connections will be part of the network for

2016:

Dubrovnik Airport, Split downtown, Resnik (Split Airport), island of Lastovo, Vela Luka, Jelsa, Zadar Airport, Rijeka Airport, Rab, Losinj, downtown Pula, Novalja, Pescara and Ancona. Other key destinations are expected to be added. For the latest news and schedules, check www.ec-air.eu.

Some practical information. You are allowed 15kg luggage plus 5kg hand luggage, with each kilo 5 euro thereafter. Check-in is 30 minutes before the flight. If you are connecting from Split Airport to Resnik and on to Jelsa, there is a free shuttle to the seaport, where you can check-in, enjoy a welcome beer on the water, and travel to Jelsa in just 15 minutes. Nice! There are also transfers to Stari Grad and Hvar Town – just book those destinations and the transfer will be included in your ticket price. Prices can be surprisingly affordable, particularly out of season, and there are good discounts for advance payment.

As it is the first scheduled seaplane service in Europe, it is still something of a novelty, and many people have taken flights just for the experience, as well as a chance to fly low over the spectacular Adriatic coast. From Jelsa to Split, for example, you can see the famous Zlatni Rat beach at Bol, as well as the stunning bays of the Kabal Peninsula north of Stari Grad, while the flight to Pula takes in many fabulous sites and historic towns. An amazing experience. Don't forget your camera!

Ferries to Hvar

Most visitors arrive from to the main car ferry terminal at Stari Grad, a two-hour connection from Split, with additional services from Ancona, Dubrovnik, Korcula and Pescara. Three ferries run from Split to Stari Grad through the winter, with the service increasing in peak season. A full timetable can be found on the Jadrolinija website (www.jadrolinija.hr), while English-speaking phone enquiries are handled at the Split office (021-338333).

Smoking is not permitted inside.

There have been amazing advances in Jadrolinija service in recent years, and finally some of the basics are in place. Free WiFi is now available on board, although it does not always work, and you are advised to get online as soon as possible, as there have been reports that getting on later in the journey is problematic with too many people online. It is now possible to book tickets online, a major shift – this came into effect last year. All can be done through the website.

www.total-hvar.com/index.php/getting-here-2/ferries-to-hvar is the link which will give you all the information you need about procedures, prices and times of the ferries.

There are two ferry seasons with Jadrolinija, the summer one, which this year runs from June 3 to October 2, and the much longer winter one. Summer sees six ferries a day from Stari Grad, winter just three. The Stari Grad to Split journey is 2 hours.

Tourists heading up the coast from Dubrovnik have the option of the small car ferry from Drvenik to Sucuraj, on the eastern tip of the island. While Sucuraj would seem to be the logical choice from the map (the crossing is only 30 minutes, and journey time to Dubrovnik is about 2 hours, as opposed to almost 4 to Split), there are a couple of things to consider when planning the journey.

Firstly, the ferry only has capacity for 32 regular vehicles, which is not a problem in the winter or shoulder months, but it can be a major issue in peak season, resulting in long waits. The Sucuraj ferries run frequently (see timetable below), and the ferry runs continuously if there is a backlog, but the inevitable wait may mean that travel via Split is more appealing.

The second consideration is the poor road from Sucuraj to the more popular resorts on the western half of the island. The views are among the best on the island, but there is a fairly precarious one-hour drive for the uninitiated to the first major town – Jelsa – although it should be noted that the road infrastructure has improved in parts with new sections being built or widened in recent years.

While the Sucuraj route is undoubtedly quicker and more convenient, the uncertainty of ferry waiting times makes planning for onward travel somewhat difficult. One peak season tip is to make the effort to make the first departure of the day, at 0630, which would necessitate a 0445 departure from Hvar Town for example. The ferry is almost always empty, even in August; an early start, but worth it in terms of reduced waiting times.

Catamarans to Hvar Town and Jelsa

In addition to the car ferries, there are also options for foot passengers with various catamaran services, including the daily service from Jelsa to Split via Bol, and direct services from Split to Hvar Town.

The catamarans fill up quickly in peak season and tourists are often disappointed when trying to buy tickets to Hvar Town in particular. The ferry company keeps a reserve of tickets for the island of Korcula, the next stop, so one option is to buy a ticket for Korcula and get off at Hvar. It might be a little more expensive, but it has a better chance of getting you there.

Private company Krilo (www.krilo.hr) also runs catamaran services, and last year they initiated a very popular service from May to October, from Dubrovnik to Split via Mljet, Korcula Town, Hvar Town and Milna on Brac. The catamaran has a capacity of over 300 passengers, and was a welcome addition to transfer options to Hvar. This year, Krilo will be introducing another excellent service, Dubrovnik to Split by three-hour catamaran. A true revolution for those of us living here for years.

44

Check the Krilo website for more information and the latest prices and times. There are also international ferry and hydrofoil services from Italy to Hvar in peak season - a Jadrolinija ferry from Ancona to Stari Grad, and a hydrofoil from Pescara to Stari Grad (check www.snav.it for the latest schedule and pricing).

How to Buy Ferry Tickets in Split

The catamarans tend to sell out well before departure in peak season, especially to top destinations such as Hvar Town. This problem was compounded by the fact that tickets were not available on the day of travel to Hvar at times last August. The only other tip we can offer - apart from buy early! - is that some very popular destinations such as the catamarans to Bol on Brac and Hvar Town sell out, but it IS still possible to get on the boat. How? Bol continues to Jelsa and Hvar Town to Vela Luka and both boats have ticket allocations to these less popular destinations, which do not sell out as quickly, so if you hear that Bol and Hvar Town are full, ask for a ticket to Jelsa or Vela Luka instead. It may cost you more than you budgeted for, but it will get you to the beach quicker...

Tickets can be bought online via Jadrolinija's website, www.jadrolinija.hr, but thay must be more than 24hours before departure, and there are three Jadrolinija sales booths (which also sell Krilo tickets). The first booth is on the bend as the road passes the palace and hits the waterfornt; the second on the dock protruding at the centre of the harbour; and the third furhter down in the main terminal building (you will see a big sign for Imperium on the top floor). Blue Line, which also has ferries to Ancona, also has a ticket office in the main building. The catamarans usually go from the top of the harbour, as in this map - turn right at as the main road past the palace hits the waterfront - although they are sometimes switched, as at the Croatia Boat Show for example. Payment by credit card is acceptable. In times of bad weather, the catamarans sometimes do not go, and a judgement call is often taken at 13:00, so either check with the ticket office, or speak to the English-speaking staff on +385-21-338333 for the latest information and timetables.

From Split Airport to the Ferry Terminal

Travelling to Hvar from the UK should be seen as part of the travel experience and not just about the getting there. If you plan the journey and start adding up the time it will take you, you are missing the point. In all reality it is going to take the best part of a day of your life, so you need to see it as part of the adventure.

That adventure starts in the UK, usually at the mercy of one of the low cost airlines... We all know about this bit so see it as a necessary evil and try to not reflect on their definition of low cost by the time you have paid for your luggage, that limp sandwich, the pleasure of sitting next to your loved ones rather than fighting for space together and so on.

The crucial thing here is to book a flight that will enable you to get to Hvar same day. Flights and ferries need to be coordinated. So check the Jadrolinja website for ferry/catamaran times and allow for the flight to be late.The following assumes you are taking the easiest option and fly into Split.
On arrival at Split, 3 options present themselves – car hire, bus and taxi:

Car rental at Split Airport
Hiring a car is the preferred option simply because having a car does prove useful on Hvar and car rental opportunities are limited on the island. The downside is that you need to find your way to the ferry some 40 minutes away (depending on the traffic, your driving and your navigating...)
At this point you might want to know that you need to have said no to all offers of wine and beer on the plane - you need to be sober if you are driving here. The legal blood alcohol limit is lower than that in the UK (0.5%) and you don't want to start your holiday at the police station... Not sure the guide books have

enough handy phrases for that one!

Book your car in advance – demand in the summer months is high, and for Hvar you will be best with something smaller as some of the roads are narrow. You will need air con in Summer, but we have yet to see a hire car without air conditioning so it might not matter if you don't opt to pay for it... How lucky do you feel?

Don't be surprised if your car hire company leads you out of the airport and across the road to collect the car. Those cars seemingly abandoned by the side of the road really do belong to some of them!

Strangely the road signs out of Split airport direct you along the smaller road to Split, past housing, schools, shops etc. If you ignore these and turn out of the airport towards Trogir you will pick up the bigger faster road to Split only a couple of miles up the road. A much better bet and much easier to navigate.

When you get near Split you start to see the signs for Trajekt which means Ferry. The picture on the signs should give you a clue.. The signs work so follow them!

At the harbourside follow the signs for the Stari Grad ferry. You will be let under the barrier to wait on the harbourside if you are too early for your crossing. Useful to know as there is nothing like enough parking in Split. You can park in the queue and if time allows go off and look around Split, knowing that your car is safe and is parked for free.

Buy your ferry ticket from the Jadrolinija booths on the harbourside. They are usually manned by someone who speaks English. (Smiles not guaranteed though!) Be aware though that the booths may not open until an hour before the ferry is due to leave.

On the ferry most local people seem to go into the cabin inside. Far nicer is to go up on deck and enjoy the journey. The views are lovely, you sail close to other islands and can either enjoy the sunshine or enjoy the moonlight. Try to pick up something to eat in Split as the food on board is basic! You will need extra layers of clothing – it can be surprisingly breezy on top even if the sun is shining. And don't forget the sunglasses and sunscreen. You will be getting two hours of sunshine...

Bus to Split Harbour

You can take a bus from the airport to the harbourside in Split. The bus officially meets the Croatian Airline flights but there are many of those and it is likely that the bus will be there, or be due, when you leave the terminal building. It is a Croatian Airlines coach. Tickets (costing 30 kuna) should be purchased in the terminal building prior to departure.

Taking the bus is hassle free, and gives you extra options at the harbourside as you won't have to wait for the car ferry to Stari Grad. The catamaran takes foot passengers to Jelsa on Hvar via Bol on Brac. Another catamaran takes foot passengers to Hvar town. Again see the options on the Jadrolinija website as the timetables vary at different times of the year.

Tickets for the ferry and catamaran are purchased from the Jadrolinija booths on the harbourside. Make sure you find out where the ferry or catamaran departs from and be aware that the car ferry usually departs a good distance up the harbourside so if you are on foot from the bus stop and are taking the car ferry you will want a light bag or good wheels!

Finally, taking a **cab** from the airport is painless – there are usually plenty ranked up outside the terminal building. However the expensive cost of cabs is one thing that is likely to surprise you about Croatia! Why not look at prebooking a taxi with one of the companies offering transfers? Again forward planning usually pays off! See your onward travel options in the section on taking the bus.

Useful things to know:
- There is an ATM at the airport and places to exchange money. However they are not always open so perhaps pick up some cash at your departure point. Don't rely on being able to use your credit card – you will be surprised how many places do not take them.
- Car seats for children, sat navs etc are best booked in advance from your car hire provider.
- Some black cars are offered by the car hire companies and these get very very hot in the summer. If you are allocated one, perhaps consider asking for a different car!
- There is a Left Luggage booth at the harbourside in Split. This may be useful if you want to see Split before taking the ferry or catamaran.
- Getting a hotel room for one night in Split in the summer is very very difficult. Allow time for the flight to be late in your plans or accept that you may have to take a very late ferry if all doesn't go to plan. (There are some late ferries in high season.) If you want to spend a night in Split, book this in advance. The other option is to try the harbourside where local people will be trying to offer their rooms to those arriving off the ferries.
- Be aware that the Stari Grad ferry is usually met on Hvar by buses to other towns and villages. The Jelsa catamaran is not and you may find that there are no cabs either. Make your onward plans in advance and if in doubt ask your accommodation hosts!
- On the catamaran to Jelsa the destination is often not announced so it is easy for unwitting passengers to get off at Bol on Brac when they wanted to go to Hvar! I have seen this happen! (And yes I did stop them!)
- If travelling to Hvar via car ferry you might want to make the supermarket opposite the ferry terminal your first stop. It is the biggest supermarket on the island, and offers the widest range of

products. It is hard to find fruit juice without added sugar anywhere else...
- If you are returning by car ferry be sure to arrive at the ferry in plenty of time. In high summer the ferries are very busy and the queue of cars can be long. You may not get on the ferry if you don't and you may then miss your flight. Again make the journey part of your holiday and allow yourself time!
- Pack a picnic for your ferry home and enjoy the trip. There isn't much catering in the Departures lounge at Split (snack bar only) so make the most of dining opportunities elsewhere.
On arrival at your destination on Hvar, visit one of the recommended cafés or bars and reflect on your day. You have travelled, have arrived and are on holiday now! Look around. You made a good choice!

How to Get to Hvar from Dubrovnik

About 120km north of Dubrovnik is the small village resort of Drvenik, which operates a 30-minute ferry crossing to the earstern port of Sucuraj on Hvar.

While it would seem the most convenient option, there are two major factors to bear in mind: firstly, the ferry has a maximum capacity of 32 cars, so waiting times can be long in peak season; and secondly, there is no public transport to meet passengers for onward travel. Nervous drivers may want to avoid the winding road to the main tourist towns more than 50km away - a stunning drive, but not for the fainthearted. It should be noted that the first petrol station is 56km from Sucuraj, so it is advisable to fill up on the mainland (where prices are a little cheaper).

Ferry Travel: Split to Stari Grad, Jelsa and Hvar
Split is 86km further north from Drvenik, but the transport options increase considerably. There are regular car ferries to the main ferry terminal at Stari Grad, as well as daily catamaran services to Jelsa and Hvar Town. A bus service meets every Stari Grad ferry, with the exception of the high season 0130 crossing.

As with Drvenik, the car ferry may involve some queuing, although the ferry's capacity is far greater. Full information on ferry times can be found on the official Jadrolinija website.

Travel by Bus: Dubrovnik to Drvenik to Split
There is no train connection from Dubrovnik along the coast, buses are the main travel option. There are regular buses from Dubrovnik to Split and the journey lasts about four hours, depending on the coastal traffic. Although there are no scheduled services to Drvenik, buses pass just above the town, and the driver will stop to allow passengers to alight.

Crossing the Border through Neum, Bosnia
Many travellers do not realise that the coastal road from Dubrovnik to Split is not contiguous Croatian territory and that journeys involve transiting through Bosnia and Herzegovina through the so-called Neum Corridor. Questions over visa requirements and car insurance arise for the Bosnian leg. Transit passengers do not require a visa to pass though the Neum Corridor.

There have been some significant developments in the last couple of years, and if all goes well with negotiations, the seaplanes will be flying daily directly from Dubrovnik harbour to Jelsa, a journey of 45 minutes. Until then, the daily catamaran to Hvar Town from May to October, stopping at Mljet and Korcula Town, remains your best bet for the quickest and cheapest transfer. Private car transfers are also available, either one driver all the way to Dubrovnik, or much more practical, one driver to the Sucuraj ferry, then the passengers board the ferry on foot, to be met by a waiting car for the remainder of the journey. For more information about private transfer options, contact me on hvar@total-hvar.com

Buses and Trains to Split

There is no train service from Dubrovnik, but there is a regular service from Zagreb to Split, which terminates opposite the ferry terminal. The service has been upgraded in recent years and takes about five hours, although the slower, overnight service is popular with backpackers taking advantage of a free night's accommodation.

From Zagreb to Split
07:35 - 13:38
15:21 - 21:20
23:05 - 06:54 (season only)
From Split to Zagreb
08:27 - 14:30
14:35 - 20:50
19:12 - 02:52 (season only)
You are advised to double check the times, and the most reliable website (also in English) is www.bahn.de The over night train service is sadly now only available in the season.

Split bus station, next to the train station, is a hive of activity, with regular national and international departures. An online timetable exists in English while telephone enquiries (good luck!) should be directed to +385 (0)21 329-199. www.ak-split.hr

MUCH more reliable and information-friendly is the fabulous www.buscroatia.com website, which not only gives you the time and prices of every available option, but allows you to buy your ticket online. Another true revolution in Croatian travel.

Private Speedboat Transfer

Nothing quite beats arriving in style than by speedboat (although a seaplane is not bad...), and speedboat transfers from the airport to Hvar Town remain a popular way to arrive. Travel time is under an hour, a perfect way to kickstart your Hvar holiday in

style. Three recommended companies to check out:
www.rentaboathvar.com
www.hvarboatrent.com
www.mbrent.com

Car Rental: Mainland or Island?

One of the key considerations when renting a car in Croatia is where to start your rental. If you are visiting the islands, there are pros and cons of a mainland rental versus an island vehicle. On paper, the convenience (and lower price) of picking up a car at the airport would seem to be the sensible option, but there are several reasons why a more expensive island rental might be preferable.

Car Hire and Ferries in Croatia
The main issues surround the ferries, an integral part of any island-hopping trip. For such a sophisticated ferry network, there are surprisingly few connections between islands, with car transfers between Hvar, Vis or Brac, for example, all requiring a return trip to Split.

Another major consideration in high season with renting a car from the mainland is ferry waiting times. Even at the major ports such as Stari Grad on Hvar, the peak demand in late July can mean a wait of several hours for cars, while there is never any delay for foot passengers. Added to that is the price differential (a return trip from Split to Stari Grad is more than 100 euro per vehicle, as opposed to 11 euro per foot passenger), and island rental becomes a more interesting proposition.

Rent a Car or Rent a Scooter?
An additional benefit of renting on an island is the flexibility that it affords. Many tourists base themselves in the tourist towns, where all the amenities, including the beach, are easily accessible on foot. It is not uncommon for tourists to rent a car for one or two days of a week-long stay, when they can explore the island in more detail. While the daily rate is higher, it can work out to be a

53

more cost-effective alternative than having a mainland rental idly parked for most of the stay.

A very popular alternative to renting a car while on holiday in Croatia is to rent a scooter. This is a fun way for couples to explore, and they are widely available in the main towns. Helmets must be worn at all times when driving.

Car Rental on Croatian Islands and the August Shortage
For all the benefits of renting on the islands, the quality of the car rental offer can be variable, with various novelty cars available for hire. While undoubtedly cooler, they are not always as modern or reliable as their mainland cousins. Whatever choice you make, it is advised that you book in advance where possible, particularly in peak season. Apart the possibility of a better price for booking online, there tends to be a shortage of quality rental vehicles at times in the July 15 - August 15.

Ultimately, the decision of island versus mainland rental is a personal choice and comes down to individual circumstances. It would be a shame not to try out the scooter however - they are fun.

Sun City (www.suncity.hr) are a local rental car agency, with an excellent website, responsive team and reasonable prices. They have nice ideas such as one day rentals for day trippers, where they will meet you off the morning ferry and once more on the ferry home, thereby enabling day-trippers to get the most out of their day on Hvar.
Buses on the Island

The bus service, run by Cazmatrans, is the only means of public transport on the island, and is therefore a vital resource for locals and tourists alike. Schedules change several times during the year – check www.total-hvar.com/index.php/getting-here-2/getting-around-hvar/item/hvar-bus-timetable-2016 for the latest. A little unwieldy, so perhaps Google 'Total Hvar 2016 bus timetable' instead.

A key strategy in the bus schedule is coordination with the main ferry service to Hvar, the port of Stari Grad, which receives several ferries a day from Split, as well as occasional ferries from Dubrovnik and Italy. With the notable exception of the peak season 0130 crossing, all ferries from Split are met by buses.

There are two bus options on arrival: the first is to Hvar Town, the most popular destination on the island; and the second bus takes in the northern coastal towns of Stari Grad, Vrboska and Jelsa. Tourists arriving on the early morning ferry should either make prior arrangements or wait for the first bus leaving at 0710.

Travelling to Dubrovnik via Sucuraj
One of the common misconceptions tourists have about island travel is the availability of public transport from the ferry. Hvar has four entry ports, Sucuraj and Stari Grad by car ferry and Jelsa and Hvar Town by catamaran. Only Stari Grad has an inbuilt public transport connection. Travellers to Jelsa and Hvar Town face a taxi ride for onward travel, while tourists arriving in Sucuraj have a 56km journey to the nearest popular resort outside of Sucuraj.

Visitors wanting to travel south to Dubrovnik by public transport are better advised to travel via Split unless they can accommodate the sparse Stari Grad to Sucuraj timetable into their itinerary: 0430 from Stari Grad on Monday, Wednesday and Friday (to meet the 0630 ferry to Drvenik) and 1300 on Mondays and Fridays. Hitchhiking is an option, but there is little traffic after the ferry has unloaded.

Buses to the Southern Resorts of Zavala, Ivan Dolac and Sveta Nedjelja
The southern resorts of Zavala, Ivan Dolac and Sveta Nedjelja are

popular and full of tourist offers on the web, but hard to reach without private transport. There is a weekly bus to Sveta Nedjelja for example. If you plan to stay on the south side and are without car, rent a scooter.

Scooter and Boat Hire

A very popular way to explore Hvar is by scooter, and the island's roads are filled with the sight of young couples pootling around pointing to the latest stunning view. It is a fun way to travel and affords the greatest flexibility. Please bear in mind that helmets must be worn while travelling, as the local police will remind you - with a fine - if you fail to comply. Rental prices are in the range of 150 - 180 kuna a day.

There are various options for boat hire and these are discussed in depth elsewhere in the book, but as an intial guide, boat rental prices, including fuel, are in the region of 400 kuna for a 5 horsepower boat, 500 for an 8 horsepower.

Taxis

Taxis are expensive on Hvar, with a one-way fare from the Stari Grad ferry to Hvar Town in the region of 300 kuna, for example. Yet one more revolution will come to Hvar in 2016 with the arrival of the first online taxi booking service via www.hvartaxi.com. This is not Uber, but the service is cheaper than the established taxi drivers, who tend to operate without a meter. A nice aspect of this new online service is that you are able to get an online quote from the website, which is the fare you will pay. The Stari Grad ferry to Zavala for less than 200 kuna sticks in my mind as an example of pricing.

Hitchhiking

Hvar is a very safe environment, and the attitude to hitchhiking is very relaxed, especially out of season, and waiting times between Jelsa and Hvar Town are generally quite short. Many journeys are very local, however, as residents typically go to their fields. Traffic from Jelsa to Sucuraj is a lot sparser.

Driving on Hvar
Looking to avoid the driving stress of speed cameras, traffic lights and roundabouts? Step back in time and head to the island of Hvar, where such things have yet to be introduced. And while this may be a welcome respite from the daily commute to London, there are regional challenges to be encountered on Hvar that do not exist on the North Circular, such as roaming wild boar.

The Roads on Hvar
The island's road system was not built for heavy traffic and peak season can be a source of frustration for drivers keen to get to the beach. There is one single carriage road which runs from Hvar Town in the West to Sucuraj in the East, a road whose quality declines somewhat after Jelsa. For many travellers arriving at Sucuraj from Dubrovnik, the road to Jelsa is an endearing memory, although long-term visitors will be pleased to hear that the road has been upgraded in parts, and indeed a new stretch inland has cut out the winding approach to Jelsa along the coast.

While the roads are largely empty out of season with the most regular journey being to the family field, the roads are much busier in season, with a combination of tourists on scooters, holidaymakers with large caravans and impatient drivers providing a recipe for potential problems.

Nothing happens quickly in Dalmatia, and visitors who accept this also applies to the driving tend to endure less stress while on Hvar.

Alcohol and Driving in Croatia
After a period of zero tolerance in Croatia (during which one of the more interesting national debates in this predominantly Catholic country concerned the status of priests taking altar wine), the limit is now 0.5%. Police can - and do - stop cars for spot checks and a failed breathaliser can result in an instant fine or

something more serious. There is, however, zero tolerance for drivers under 24.

Seat belts, Headlights and Other Requirements
Seat belts must be worn at all times, and the fine for non-compliance is 500 kuna. It should be noted that tourists renting scooters are required to wear a helmet. Headlights must be on for the entire journey in winter (last Sunday in October to the last Sunday in March) at the risk of a 300 kuna fine, but the mainland requirement for winter tyres does not apply. This is an island where snowfall is national news.

How to Upset a Local: Parking Spots
If there is one issue likely to upset a Dalmatian in season, it is parking. Tourists looking to avoid car parking charges routinely park up on private property, leave the car and head to the beach. It is a source of more than mild annoyance, and easily avoided.

In Case of Accident
Whether it be swerving to avoid a strolling donkey, a nocturnal head-on with a wild boar (more common than one would imagine, especially on eastern Hvar) or a collision with another car, accidents do happen. Accidents must be reported to the police (dial 112), who must then fill out a police report. This can take a while and requires photographs and measurements - much better not to have the accident in the first place. Emergency road assistance is 987.

Speed limits are 90 km/h on the open road, 50 km/h in built-up areas and best adhered to, not only to avoid police attention, but also because cars are parked at the side of the main road near the family fields, and a speeding car coming round the corner has caught a slow-moving car leaving the field on more than one occasion.

Petrol Stations on Hvar

Motorists arriving via Sucuraj are advised to tank up before they arrive, as the nearest petrol station is more than 50km away in Jelsa. There are three stations on Hvar, one in Jelsa town, one on the main road to Stari Grad just outside Jelsa, and one in Hvar Town, while the marina filling station in Vrboska will sometimes provide fuel to motorists.

In general, driving on Hvar is problem-free, assuming one has adapted to the Dalmatian mentality.

A Brief Tour on the Main Roads

Hvar is long and thin, and one of the benefits of its layout is one is never far from the sea. The main road runs from East to West – Hvar Town to Sucuraj – with a journey time of about 90 minutes. The main highlights of the island can be introduced through four sections of road:

1. **The New Road from Hvar to Stari Grad**

Milna and Malo Grablje
With the opening of the new tunnel in 2000, the connection between Hvar Town and the car ferry terminal near Stari Grad became, quicker, more convenient – and safer. A trip on the old road from Hvar Town is an altogether more pleasant experience these days.

There is a steep ascent on the road out of Hvar, affording excellent views of the fortress and bay, before it winds along the southern coast. About 4km from the town, a right turn takes tourists into Milna, a delightful village popular for its excellent, child-friendly beaches and range of fine restaurants. The setting is idyllic and the various fish dishes do not disappoint.
Milna is a relatively new settlement, however, populated by previous inhabitants of the nearby abandoned stone village of Malo Grablje, where the most prominent surname is Tudor, giving rise to the local legend that there are descendents of Henry VIII

59

on the island.

Dubovica and Zarace

The road continues and straightens, passing the seemingly abandoned village of Zarace on the left. There are in fact signs of life, including the loving restoration of the first house in the village, which has been well renovated by its foreign owners, this after it had been on the market for years and was one of the most notorious properties on local agents' books. There are two restaurants in a quiet bay of the same name below the village.

Further on and just before the tunnel is one of the nicest bays on Hvar, the tiny hamlet of Dubovica, with its delightful beach. Access to the bay is on foot only, with parking on the main road by the telephone box, and is a fairly demanding walk down (read more on below).

The Road to Sveta Nedjelja

A long planned access road from Hvar Town to the south side of the island and the resorts of Sveta Nedjelja, Ivan Dolac and Zavala has recently opened, thereby reducing traffic and pressure on one of the great road experiences in Europe, the Pitve-Zavala tunnel, although the road is not paved and is not wide in parts. Proceed with caution, but try and enjoy the views.

Through the Tunnel: the Stari Grad Ferry Terminal

In stark contrast, the new tunnel is fast, modern and well lit. Emerging through the other side, the island of Brac and the Rudine Peninsula come into view, and it is a short descent to the ferry terminal at Star Grad, which handles most of the car and passenger traffic to Split. Opposite the terminal is a new shopping centre, whose main outlet is supermarket giant, Tommy - the biggest store on the island.

2. The Old Road from Hvar to Stari Grad

One of the best road trips in Europe, combining stunning nature and sea views, history and a challenging drive that is not for the fainthearted, the old road from Hvar to Stari Grad is an absorbing twenty-five kilometre drive, taking in near abandoned stone villages, which house, among other things, a lavender festival and the scars of the devastating European forest fires of 2003.

Throw into the mix a restaurant with a north and south-facing sea view, the path to the island's panoramic views from its highest point, an intricate stone terracing in the surrounding fields, and some of the scariest driving conditions in Europe, with unprotected sheer drops the norm, and all the ingredients are there for an unmissable adventure.

Brusje: Stunning Sea Views
Driving past the main Hvar Town car park, ignore the left turn to the town and take a right instead, along a road signposted for Brusje and Selca. The road is winding and climbs steadily, offering excellent sea views towards Split, before reaching the first village on the road, Brusje, a stunning example of a Dalmatian stone village, where even the ruins seem exotic.

A combination of the spectacular sea views, proximity to Hvar Town and authentic Dalmatian surroundings made Brusje one of the most sought-after villages during the Croatian property boom in 2004, as foreign buyers sought their piece of Adriatic tranquility in the sun. Mains water was added to the village in 2008.

Velo Grablje: Home of the Lavender Festival
The road straightens after Brusje, and drivers can relax a little and enjoy the scenery, in particular the spectacular stone walling that exists at every turn, resembling a chess board at times, as islanders throughout the ages have cleared the stony land to make it more fertile.

A right turn to Velo Grablje takes one to the village of the same name, a sparsely populated community, with excellent southern sea views. A rough road continues to the abandoned village of Malo Grablje. An interesting annual event hosted by Velo Grablje is the lavender festival, which takes place every year in June.

Konoba Vidikovac and Two Sea Views
The road is much quieter since the new Hvar - Stari Grad road was opened via a straight and well-lit tunnel several years ago. Prior to that German tourists, Italian caravans and Zagreb holidaymakers competed with local drivers to get to their destination on a hopeless inadequate road - overtaking on blind corners, never advisable, took on a new meaning with the sheer unprotected drops into the patchwork stone walls below.

The only place of refreshment along the way is the ideally located Konoba Vidikovac, a charming restaurant offering traditional Dalmatian fare, perhaps most memorable for its choice of excellent sea views - north-facing from some tables, south-facing from others.

Selca: Forest Fire Survivor
The road continues past a cemetery with excellent views again (a feature of cemeteries in Dalmatia, prime real estate in every location) and a sign for a bicycle route to the right leads to a rough road and access to the peak of the island, with outstanding panoramic views.

The main road continues to another semi-abandoned stone village, Selca, whose outer buildings still bear the scars of the savage forest fires of 2003, severe enough to feature by name in a report on European forest fires in this correspondent's edition of the International Herald Tribune on a flight back from Japan.

The views from Selca take in the Rudine Peninsula and the neighbouring island of Brac, as well as the incoming ferries to

Stari Grad, with which Selca is twinned. The winding road only takes a few minutes, but can seem a lifetime to motorists less than comfortable to the challenging conditions it offers. And then, as quickly as it started, one of the best road trips around is over, as a T-junction brings the car to the main Stari Grad ferry terminal.

3. Through the Pitve Tunnel

Surely one of the great undiscovered filmsets of Europe, the Pitve Tunnel is not for the claustrophobic, but there are few tunnels like it. Although no longer the only connection to the south of the island, it is still the busiest.

History of the Pitve - Zavala Tunnel
Work on the tunnel began in 1962 by local authorities, as a means of passing water pipes to the south of the island. Never intended to be a passenger tunnel, the drilling of the rock was crude and practical. The result, a 1.4km tunnel approximately 2.30m across, has been a lifeline connecting the southern settlements of Zavala, Ivan Dolac and Sveta Nedelja to Pitve, Jelsa and beyond, but the tunnel is definitely a case of practicality over comfort; there are no lights in the tunnel, water seeps the rock overhead, causing minor flooding problems, and passing options for two cars are extremely limited.

Tunnel Etiquette: The Occasional Traffic Lights
The tunnel has two distinct seasons, local and tourist. As the tunnel is not wide enough for two cars to pass, the tourist season has recently brought about the introduction of the first seasonal traffic lights on Hvar, an upgrade from a previous system operated by walkie-talkies.

Timing is everything. The lights remain green for sixty seconds only, followed by six minutes of red. In that time motorists are expected to navigate their way through the tunnel, although several tourists, unnerved by the sudden darkness and primitive conditions, have encountered numerous problems. While the sudden plunge into darkness and wading through surface water can be disorientating, it is nothing compared to the effects on the eyes when one emerges into the bright sunshine after 1.4km.

Tunnel Etiquette: Passing Places and Waiting Times
The lights come into operation in May and work until the end of the season, which is when the real fun begins in the tunnel. The local rules are simple: upon entering the tunnel, if there are no headlights coming the opposite way, one may progress; approaching headlights require drivers to wait.

That would be too easy. There are two roughly dug out passing points in the tunnel, and regular users who are confident in their abilities, feel able to judge the distance of the approaching car, making snap judgments as to their ability to make it to the first passing place on time. They do not always get it right. Throw a nervous tourist, unsure of the rules, into the mix, and the prospect of reversing back half a kilometre in claustrophobic darkness can cause chaos.

New Roads to Zavala and Sveta Nedelja
Fortunately for all, the opening of two new roads has helped to relieve the pressure on the tunnel, as well as alleviate some of the traffic congestion through the historic village of Pitve. A fire road over the top of the hill is passable for more vehicles, while the long awaited road from Dubovica to Sveta Nedelja has made the south side not only more accessible to and from Hvar Town, but also reduced the need to use the tunnel. Even if it is not on your route, it is worth a visit for the ultimate tunnel vision experience.

4. The Road of Hell – Jelsa to Sucuraj

Tourists arriving on Hvar by ferry at the eastern port of Sucuraj are often surprised at what they find. Far from 'the new St. Tropez', as Hvar Town has been labelled, they descend from a tiny ferry into a quaint sleepy Dalmatian village, with the next significant civilisation 60km away, and the only thing that separates the two is the Road of Hell. St. Tropez never seemed so far away. Here are some tips to survive the route.

Tourists sometimes make the mistake of thinking that, having arrived on the island, they have almost arrived at their destination. While there are distinct benefits using the Drvenik ferry for travellers from Dubrovnik, the main destinations are still some distance away – Hvar Town (80km), Stari Grad (65km) and Jelsa (56km).

The quality of the road is poor and the experience is not helped by the fact that it is hilly and winding, without protective barriers in many parts. While the road is wide enough for cars to pass with relative ease, an approaching truck on a bend with a sheer drop to the right can be intimidating.

Due to the lack of sensible overtaking points, frustrated drivers are more likely to take risks when overtaking, which can add to the stress. The good news is that a lot of money has been invested in a large stretch of the road in recent years. The stretched from Poljica to Prapatna was upgraded first, followed by a new inland road to Jelsa, which shaves some time of the journey and is infinitely better for the heart rate of nervous passengers.

Journey times to the nearest main town, Jelsa, are at least an hour, with another 20-25 minutes if Hvar Town is the destination. It should be noted that there are no petrol stations on the road before Jelsa, so it is advisable to fill up before catching the ferry. There is of course the option of the original last leg of the trip, as the road twists and turns at regular intervals, restricting speed. For confident drivers and relaxed passengers, the views are stunning.

Leaving the Ferry and Driving Styles
The small ferry carrying car passengers from the mainland to

Sucuraj can hold a maximum of 32 cars. If you are not in a hurry, it is perhaps best to have a coffee in Sucuraj and allow the rest of the ferry traffic to proceed. Impatient tourists and locals who know the road can make driving a less than pleasant experience, as they are in a hurry to get to their destination. While a few cars and caravans may turn off at Camp Mlaska, 2km out of Sucuraj, the majority continue to Jelsa and beyond.

Breaking the Journey: Humac
The Road of Hell passes through some pretty stone villages – Bogomolje, Gdinj, Zastrazisce and Poljica – all without running water and very depopulated, but steeped in their own histories and traditions. If you are not intending to spend time on this side of the island, one place which is worth seeing is the abandoned stone shepherd's village of Humac, about three quarters of the way to Jelsa.

It is abandoned and a magical place to walk around. Some restoration is now happening in this protected village, and there is an excellent restaurant at the entrance, which is well worth a visit.

Night Driving: Beware the Wild Boar
Driving the Road of Hell at night brings its own sense of fun. Apart from having to be careful that the road does not disappear due to the lack of street lights, there are some other factors to contend with, such as roaming wild boar, who tend not to look for the zebra crossings when moving around, as this correspondent's car can attest, having been subjected to a head on collision with a couple of hundred kilos of live pork.

If there is no rush, then the drive can be a pleasant one and the views of the Adriatic and neighbouring islands are breathtaking.

CHAPTER 2: WHERE TO STAY

The Hvar hotel scene is dominated by the Suncani Hvar group in Hvar Town, who own most of the hotels there, and whose fortunes are undergoing something of a revival since last year. After heavy investment from the ORCO Group in 2005, the company endured some financial troubles, troubles which have now thankfully been resolved, and Suncani recently reported their longest and best season ever in 2015, with their top hotel, Adriana, recording 180 days of full occupancy. The Hvar Town hotel scene will be welcoming its first hotel for millenials in June, with the old two-star Pharos being revamped into a four-star funky hotel for the new generation.

Suncani are not the only show in town or on the island. Here is an overview of the main hotels on Hvar.

Hvar Town

Hotel Adriana
Hvar's spa boutique hotel perfectly located and uniquely designed for the ultimate in relaxation and romantic experience. A luxury spa oasis for your most stylish and revitalising summer vacation. With clean lines accentuated by fine textured linens, intricately patterned fabrics, splashes of rich color, warm wood tones, and natural materials, the rooms at Adriana are designed to complement the sensory experience and health benefits gained from the hotel's spa facilities.

Adriana Spa Oasis
Inspired by the sensuous island environment the Spa oasis at Adriana is designed to bring holistic wellness to your life, offering experiences that will help you live healthier, look better and feel renewed.

The Top Bar

Featuring a wrap-around view of the ancient city, yacht harbour, bay, and Paklinski Islands, The Top is Hvar's premiere lounge bar. Perched on Adriana's rooftop, a sophisticated array of multilevel garden terraces and exquisite design create an outstanding atmosphere of luxury and relaxation.

Hotel Amfora
Hvar premier beach resort located in a private bay, features an exquisite cascading pool and offers a wide range of activities suitable for couples, families and business events.

Amfora's contemporary and stylish rooms are designed with clean lines, warm hues, fantastic patterns and textures that come together to highlight every nuance of the natural light.

Cascading pool
Amfora's spectacular new pool area is one of the features that make it the most exciting resort in the Adriatic, with an elegant array of cascading waterfalls and Mediterranean gardens.

Bonj beach club
Unsurpassed seafront ambiance, first-class amenities, and inspiring surroundings make Bonj 'les bains' a quintessential experience on Hvar. This white stone colonnade nestled under a pine grove on the eastern shore of Amfora's small bay is an architectural wonder from 1927.

Hotel Riva
Riva landmarked building with its unique and edgy design signed by Jestico + Whiles reflects a boutique nouvelle vague indulgence. Its prime location in the middle of Hvar's pulsating heart attracts a star - studded clientele since back in the day when the hotel was firstly opened in 1927.

Light, airy and intimate, Riva's rooms are sensual and glamourous.

BB Club terrace
On Riva's waterfront terrace the BB lounge is the coolest and
most chic place to chill out and socialise in style.

Hvar promenade
On the waterfront promenade in the heart of the medieval Hvar
town, Riva offers you the finest in Adriatic ambiance, full of
high-fashion Hollywood glamour.

Hotel Pharos
At Pharos, within the dynamic energy of Hvar Town, we've set
the stage to ignite island vibe and bring together those who push
boundaries creatively and crave a connection to other people,
cultures and ideas. We welcome wanderlusts of all ages and
backgrounds!

Surrounded by pines and olive trees, making the air magically
fragranced, from the moment you step into your accommodation
at Pharos bayhill hotel, you'll feel like you're a world away.
Lobby experience

It began with a passion to connect with our guests and experience
Hvar together! Our lobby is a giant living room, open 24/7, where
around every corner there is an opportunity to become part of
someone's story!

Pool & Bar
The Pharos essence is highlighted by its outdoor pool and bar- a
place where morning slowly drifts into day. It is a multi-level
playground for the senses where the local environment and
contemporary techniques come together to balance your mind,
body and spirit.

Hotel Palace
Perfectly located oldest hotel in Hvar's main square offering

amazing views, old-time charm full of history, comfortable rooms and friendly staff.

The rooms at The Palace have been equipped with simple fixtures and furnishings that provide comfort and convenience while allowing guests to thoroughly enjoy all the natural charm and beauty of this historical hotel. The Palace is ideally located in the heart of the old town overlooking Hvar Piazza, old town and marina.

San Marco Terrace
Being one of the most grandiose buildings in Hvar, this beautiful ornamented terrace floats above the city and gives great panoramic views of Hvar; ideal for a relaxed daytime coffee break or romantic dinners in a spectacular historical ambience.

Hotel Villa Dalmacija
Dalmacija Villa offers one of the best locations in Hvar, in the corner of the bay with stunning sea views and 5 minutes from the heart of the city. Beach lodge compliments the villa and sits right on the beach. Rooms in Dalmacija are simple, yet comfortable and affordable.

Peaceful bay, near the beach, 5 minutes walk from the city centre, vicinity of all local bars, clubs and restaurants.

Beach lodge
Affordable accommodation option in Hvar's premier location, simply designed, clean and comfortable, suited for younger travellers.

Hotel Delfin
Affordable city hotel perfectly located, offering simple and comfortable accommodation, sea views and harbour facing sports bar and grill. Available with sea or park views, Delfin's rooms provide tranquil Adriatic ambiance and practical comfort. They

are equipped with twin beds.

Hotel Delfin is perfectly located on Hvar's waterfront promenade overlooking the old town and marina at 3-5 minutes walking distance from the centre and local beaches.

Sports Bar & Grill
The view and vibe make Hvar's one and only Sports Bar & Grill at hotel Delfin a great place to enjoy exciting international sports TV programs. Sports Bar & Grill is home of great sport, great food and great times.

Hotel Croatia
Hotel Croatia is located in the city of Hvar at the so-called island, only about ten minutes walk from the old city centre and city port. It is situated by the sea in the beautiful park of pine trees at one of the most beautiful locations of the city of Hvar. It is built in 1936 and reconstructed in 1997 and again renovated in 2013. With its architecture, hotel is ideally set in the vegetation of Majerovica bay, reached by a beautiful walking area by the sea. Hotel Croatia is the smallest one in the city of Hvar, it is an intimate and very comfortable place for holiday throughout the year. Hotel Croatia is family-run hotel.

Hotel Park
Park Hotel is a boutique hotel situated in the heart of the town just off the main square, between the one time Rector's Palace and St. Mark church, which gives an indication of its long existence and the grand view of the south port and the Pakleni islands. There are 15 room in all, and the hotel is usually open all year.

Hotel Podstine
Our elegant hotel in a beautiful bay with its own private beach provides the opportunity for an unforgettable vacation... Just imagine, park your car on our parking lot free of charge, grab your swimming gear, choose a deck chair under a sunshade, and

let the sound of waves washing the shore take you to a happy place. Don't forget your sunscreen, and keep hydrated with fresh fruit & vegetable smoothies of your choice ...and an occassional cocktail or two! Although we suggest you log out completely, the wifi covers the whole resort, and is free of charge, of course.

Aparthotel Pharia
The only aparhotel in Hvar, located close to the beach on Hvar's northern side, and also offering four villas with pools.

Stari Grad

Stari Grad has a few hotels on the other side of the old town, and what they lack in luxury, they make up for in price and access to sporting and beach facilities. Four Seasons Hotels are in the process of applying to build a five-star resort with villas

Hotel Arkada
Hotel Arkada is close to the water with direct access to a pebbly beach. Situated in a pine forest, it is has a stunning location and excellent sea views. It is the biggest hotel in the town with 269 rooms, and is a natural base for a family holiday, with a range of facilities, including indoor and outdoor swimming pools, a sauna and a children's playground.

There are also plenty of sporting facilities within 100m, which is true for all the hotels, as they are all located in the same area. These include six tennis courts, a mini-golf course and handball, basketball and volleyball courts. Additional activities which can be arranged are windsurfing, water-skiing, boat hire and bicycle rental.

Hotel Helios
Another large hotel from the Communist Era is Hotel Helios, also positioned close to the water, with beach in front. Helios has 214 rooms, the majority of which have a balcony and sea view, and guests have access to the sporting facilities mentioned above.

Hotel Lavanda
Formerly the Hotel Adriatic, the 94 rooms at the Hotel Lavanda
are also ideal for a family vacation. The hotel has its own indoor
and outdoor pools, a volleyball court in the sand, its own
skateboard path and a playroom for children. Hotel Lavanda
offers all-inclusive packages.

Hotel St. Roko
The fourth hotel in Stari Grad is Hotel Roko, which, like the other
three, is owned by the same company, Helios dd. It is 50m from
the beach and close to Hotel Helios, which guests are required to
use for dining facilities.

And then, in 2014, some REAL quality came to the Stari Grad
accommodation scene:

Villa Apolon
Don sime Ljubić's villa was redesigned into a modern fully-
equipped villa with six suites/rooms, a restaurant and a wine bar.
Suites and rooms are designed for our guests' maximum pleasure
and satisfaction. Each suite is equipped with an air-conditioning,
cable TV, wireless Internet, mini-bar, electronic safe and other
additional contents. Your satisfaction is the top priority of the
educated, professional and friendly staff of the Villa & Restaurant
Apolon who also speak several foreign languages.

Reflecting Don Ljubić's fascination with science and art, each
room and suite in the Villa carries the name of one of the Apollo's
Muses – mythological patrons of arts and science.

Owing to the stunning sea and Riva views, modern design of the
Villa interior, the staff's attention to every detail and a pleasant
atmosphere, just one night in Villa Apolon will make it your
favourite place on the entire island of Hvar!

And then in early 2016, there was a press release from Four Seasons Hotels

Brizinica Bay Luxury Hotel and Resort

"Arqaam Capital ("Arqaam"), the specialist emerging markets investment bank, has entered into a partnership with Four Seasons Hotels and Resorts, the world's leading luxury hospitality company, to manage and operate Arqaam's luxury mixed use resort currently being developed on the island of Hvar in Croatia. Four Seasons Resort Hvar, Croatia is expected to open in 2019.

Located on a prime waterfront site at Brizenica Bay along the Dalmatian coast, Arqaam's luxury development will feature a 120-room Four Seasons hotel and a luxury residential community including 60 Four Seasons Private Residences ranging in size from one and two bedroom residences to three to five bedroom villas.

Riad Meliti, Chief Executive Officer of Arqaam Capital, commented, "We are creating a natural retreat within a stunning, secluded enclave in one of the Dalmatian Coast's most beautiful and private bays. Four Seasons was the natural choice for us as they share our commitment to elegance, unrivalled service and luxury. They have a long history, a strong and undiluted brand and an uncompromising dedication to the highest standards."

"In Arqaam Capital we have found the ideal partner for our entry into Croatia, one who believes in the culture of Four Seasons and shares our values," said J. Allen Smith, President and CEO, Four Seasons Hotels and Resorts. "Arqaam's long-term vision, combined with their extensive experience in emerging markets and project development are key to positioning this project for success."
Continued Smith, "Croatia is one of Europe's fastest growing tourism markets and a highly sought-after leisure destination for

discerning global travellers. We look forward to working together with Arqaam to create a world-class property in Hvar."

The resort will have its own private bay; multiple swimming pools and private infinity pools; a state-of-the-art spa and fitness centre; a selection of restaurants, cafes, bars and retail boutiques; and conference and banqueting facilities."

Vrboska

Possibly the most exciting development to happen in Hvar hotel accommodation for several years. Hotel Adriatic on Soline beach near Vrboska has long been a two-star hotel, and in recent years it has been rented out to the Czech government as a health resort for children, leaving Vrboska without a proper hotel. All that is about to change...

The Czech contract is finished, and some 4 million euro has been invested to give the hotel a complete makeover and an increase in stars. Renovated to 4-star standard, including spa and heated outdoor pool, but with 3-star categorsation, Hotel Adriatic has 184 full renovated quality rooms, and it will open for business in Summer 2016. Central Hvar has been in desperate need of a quality hotel, and Adriatic is sure to be busy.

Jelsa

Hotel Hvar (formerly Mina)
Splendidly located on a peninsula and overlooking a great (and partially sandy) family beach called Mina, Hotel Hvar is set in woodland on the outskirts of the town, a gentle ten-minute walk from the croissants and cappuccinos on the main square.

The hotel has 205 rooms, the majority of which have balconies and sea views. It is ideal for family vacations, with facilities including an indoor and outdoor swimming pool, fitness room and kids club, which offers a morning and afternoon programme, mini-golf, table tennis, a mini-disco and other games. The Cosmomedicus wellness centre offers classic and sports massage, pedicures, facials and waxing.

Active guests can take advantage of the indoor gym and eight tennis courts, while additional sporting activities available in Jelsa through the hotel include aerobics, scuba diving, cycling, volleyball, handball, basketball (indoor and outdoor). With the opening of the new sports hall in Jelsa, the hotel has benefited from several sports clubs undertaking their winter training in the town.

Hotel Fontana Resort
Run by the same Hungarian company who bought Hotel Hvar in 2003, the Hotel Fontana Resort is across the bay from Hotel Hvar in another stunning natural setting. It is a self-contained resort, about a ten-minute walk from the centre of town and a leisurely half-hour coastal stroll to the Vrboska, known as Little Venice and which houses the main marina on the island.

The hotel has 346 rooms, of which 234 are rooms and 112 apartments. Sporting activities and general facilities are very similar to Hotel Hvar, as they are owned by the same group. A great improvement in 2015 was the renovation and introduction of a selection of higher quality aparments, which have received 4-star categorisation.

There is no hotel in Sucuraj.

Hostels

The biggest shift in accommodation trends in Hvar Town in recent years has been in the explosion of hostels to meet the rise in popularity of Hvar Town as a backpacker and party destination. There are too many hostels to list, and they offer essentially a similar service, and you can check them out on www.hostelworld.com, but among the best are The Shaka,

Marinero, White Rabbit, Dink's Place, Hvar Out, Villa Marija, Luka's Place and Green Lizard. From no hostels in 2008, Hvar Town now has 16 licenced and 13 unlicenced hostels.

Private Accommodation: Booking on the Internet

As elsewhere, the power of the Internet has changed the dynamic of finding accommodation. Where previously it was the norm to go from apartment to apartment looking for availability, most tourists now book online. Many local renters are not comfortable with Internet marketing in English, and the descriptions and outdated photographs reflect that, but there are more professionally produced offers every year.

I debated whether or not to include a list of recommended private accommodation but decided against. Tourists booking online are very adept at finding accommodation, using recommendations from sites such as Trip Advisor, so I decided that it was an endeavour too far, although one can find a selection of recommended places on two great websites, www.villashvar.com and www.visit-hvar.com.

I will use this space, however, to do my one shameless plug in the book, for Apartman Milicic, private accommodation in Jelsa with balcony and sea views, run by the best mother-in-law in the world: mine. She has promised me I will be exempt from olive picking duties this winter if I generate enough bookings, so don't be shy! Contact us on hvar@total-hvar.com for more information.

Camping

There are numerous campsites on the island and most offer excellent facilities, also catering to the naturist market in Vrboska. Backpackers may prefer Jelsa as an entry point for camping, as it is the most accessible without transport, with the Mina campsite a short walk from the daily catamaran, which arrives at 17:50 from

Split.

Tourists of diverse backgrounds flock to Hvar every year, and there are accommodation options for all, be it luxury hotels in Hvar Town, private accommodation in Zavala or backpacking with a tent. Camping in Croatia is very popular, from the humble tent to the latest Italian motorhome, and the island of Hvar has plenty of choice for campers.

Camp Vira in Hvar Town
As with the various hotels in Hvar Town, the investment by Suncani Hvar in Camp Vira has resulted in a top-quality accommodation, arguably the best on the whole Croatian coast. Situated 4km north of the town in the tranquil setting of Vira, this four-star camp's amenities include plots connected to water and electricity, a supermarket, cocktail bar, playground, free Internet, restaurant, diving school and organized entertainment for children and adults alike.

The focal point of the camp is its excellent beach, one of the nicest on Hvar. Its 200m stretch of small pebbles is suitable for children and nonswimmers. Lifeguards are also on hand. The camp has won numerous awards from industry analysts, including the Croatian Camping Union, FederCampeggio and the prestigious ADAC *Campingplatz-Auszeichnung* award in 2008.

Camp Jurjevac in Stari Grad
Stari Grad's auto camp, called Camp Jurjevac, is located behind the Old Town on the road to the new ferry terminal. It is 300m from the waterfront and located in a forest in a quiet part of the town, with a capacity for 600 guests. Internet access is available, and the nearest shop is 200m away.

Camp Holiday in Jelsa
Located in the forest close to Hotel Hvar in Jelsa, Camp Holiday is a popular campsite for backpackers and caravan owners alike.

An additional attraction is the catamaran connection from Split, which means that it is the most accessible on the island by foot from the mainland. It is a pleasant five-minute walk from the catamaran. Jelsa's main beach, Mina, is next to the site. Internet access is available at reception.

Camp Grebisce in Jelsa
Those willing to walk a little farther or who are arriving by caravan from the challenging drive from Jelsa will find Camp Grebisce, approximately 1.5km from Jelsa. Facilities include a shop, fast food outlet, and a restaurant and bar. Accommodations come with or without electricity and running water, and there are some stone housing possibilities.

Camp Nudist in Vrboska (FKK)
Hvar has a long tradition of naturism, and still has several nudist beaches that dot the island. The picturesque village of Vrboska offers FKK Camp Nudist. The camp is about 1km away from the village, with a pleasant 200m-long beach. The beach is quite rocky but access to the sea is easy. Facilities include a restaurant, shop, gas station and various sporting activities.

Camp Mlaska in Sucuraj
At the other end of the island is the popular Camp Mlaska, 4km from the port of Sucuraj. For many arriving on the ferry from Drvenik, this is as far as they go on Hvar. The camp is in an idyllic spot on the northern coast. It offers facilities for caravans, and there are also bungalows available for hire. There is a restaurant at the camp, and one half of Mlaska is allocated for naturist campers.

Camp Paklina in Ivan Dolac
Those willing to brave the Pitve tunnel have the option of camping at Camp Paklina in Ivan Dolac on the south side of Hvar. The family-run camp is next to the beach, which is child-friendly.

Registering Your Stay and Rental Licences

Tourists are required to register their stay with the authorities and are liable for a daily tourist tax of one euro, and they must also de-register on departure. In practice this is done by hotels and apartment owners (hence the reason guests are required to briefly surrender their passports), although tourists should check this on arrival.

The tax is usually (but not always) included in the cost of the rental. A more serious issue to investigate is the owner's licence to rent out the property, as the authorities are starting to clamp down on the grey economy, and inspectors have been known to evict guests in unlicensed properties, although this is rare. It should be noted that peak season short-term rentals of less than three nights usually incur a 30% surcharge.

The 'Sobe' Ladies and Finding Accommodation

The Internet has changed one of the great institutions of Croatian tourism – the 'Sobe' lady (sobe means room). Prior to the Internet, this was the main way of finding accommodation. Signs with 'Sobe' outside vacant apartments, older ladies with 'Sobe' signs at the ferry. This practice has been all but surpassed in recent years, as tourists book their accommodation in advance, but if you are looking, then you will still find plenty of offers. Alternatively, check out what is on offer via the local tourist board in your part of town. They can ring through for you and find out what is available – useful in peak season.

One of my favourite stories about Hvar concerns the 'Sobe' ladies. An extract from Total Hvar.
I haven't laughed as loudly all year. So loudly in fact that almost every table at Sidro stopped talking to look around. Head barman Matko interrupted his babysitting duties to shoot me a smile. Or was it a scowl?At Total Hvar, we try and cover all aspects of the island. We have some way to go, and we are certainly enjoying

experiencing and reporting on the rich diversity of life on this wonderful island. One thing we have learned this year is that the island is perceived in many different ways by many different people, and listening to everyone's viewpoints leads to a more representative picture.

The reason for my laughter was a funny story I was being told at the end of yet another business meeting (a productive one this time...). We were discussing tourism and apartment rentals, when the couple I was meeting told me about their recent experience of a guest staying on Hvar. He was totally enthusiastic about the island, loving every aspect of it.

"The beaches were amazing. That water so clear. The women are stunning. The food, the wine, the architecture. Perfect in every way. There is just one thing I don't understand. In all this amazing setting and beautiful people, why are the prostitutes so old and unattractive? There are lots of them at the ferry and coming into town and at the bus station, and I didn't fancy any of them."

Couchsurfing

The cheapest price for accommodation is free, and the Couchsurfing concept has a number of members on Hvar. The basic concept - members host other members for free as part of a cultural exchange - has been a global phenomenon, and beds are available on Hvar, although it should be borne in mind that most islanders depend on tourism to some extent, and so beds may only be available out of the peak season.

CHAPTER 3: GUIDE TO THE PAKLENI ISLANDS

Standing and admiring the view from Hvar Town's Spanish Fortress, one is in heaven. A gorgeous historic town, whose harbour is glistening with boats and yachts of various sizes and price tags, and in the distance, a collection of emerald jewels, known as the Pakleni Islands. Perfect all, and different only in their size.

Or are they? There is nothing whatsoever uniform about these delightful islands, for as we shall see, they contain one of Croatia's hottest nightspots, CNN's top naturist beach in the world, an arboretum populated by peacocks, Roman mud baths, the lowest vineyards in Croatia, a resident donkey named Mercedes (sadly recently deceased), and an island which almost got renamed Facebook.

Sveti Klement, from Palmizana to Vlaka

We go back to 1906. The first organised tourism in Europe has started in Hvar Town some 38 years previously. The first hotel in Jelsa would be built five years later. Dr Eugen Meneghello has the idea to start tourism in a southern bay of the biggest of the Pakleni Islands, Sveti Klement, in a bay which is now commonly referred to as Palmizana. There is no water, there is no electricity, just wild terrain, and wild unspoilt beauty.

Progress is made, and while the water and electricity do not come for almost 100 years, tourism blossoms, as the rich and famous hear of an idyllic piece of Paradise off the beaten track, where the owner hunts the food in the Adriatic and the accommodation is basic at best. Meneghello's son takes over the business and marries a young Zagreb journalist called Dagmar Gebauer.

With their unique skills, determination and innovation, Palmizana is transformed into something unique in Europe, a paradise haven for celebrities, who arrive and depart with nobody aware of their presence, with an arboretum, an art gallery and a rich cultural programme with internationally famous artists to entertain them.

Last year Dagmar Meneghello marked 50 years living on the island she has come to love and which has become her home. The contribution she and her family have made to Hvar tourism is immense, and perhaps sadly not recognised locally. Palmizana regularly features in the international media as one of the top destinations in all Croatia, a testament to her work, and John Malkovich last year named it his most relaxing holiday destination after a 2-week stay. Learn more about the amazing Meneghello story and tourist offer – from restaurant, quality accommodation, arboretum, art gallery and cultural programme on www.palmizana.hr

Below her restaurant lies Toto's, a waterfront restaurant run by her son, surrounded by greenery and trees from all over the world, and easily the restaurant on Hvar with the most space per guest. Walk through a small gate, and the beach and divine Adriatic are yours. And yet, rather than being expensive for such a prized location, Toto's is one of the best value dining experiences on Hvar, especially when the location is taken into consideration. And if you like deep sea fishing, owner Djenko is your man – the main organiser for the annual Hvar Big Game Fishing Cup each November.

Others have come to put their stamp on Paradise, and there are now two more restaurants and a cocktail bar to share the view. Upscale Zori next door has the prime location in the middle of the bay and is a prime wedding destination. Next to that, offering shade under some truly impressive olive trees is Bacchus, traditional Dalmatian fare of exceptional quality. At the end of the row is Laganini, a cocktail bar which is becoming one of Hvar's hottest spots.

Palmizana is a popular stop for tour boats from the Blue Cave and elsewhere, but the cheapest way to reach it from Hvar Town is to take a water taxi from the Hvar waterfront near Arsenal. The 15-minute journey takes you to the ACI marina on the northern side of Sveti Klement. From there is is 200 metre walk though the trees until you come to a crossroads – advertising signs and different paths to the restaurant of your choice.

There is another settlement on Sveti Klement, much further from Hvar Town, on its northern shore, called Vlaka, another piece of Paradise, and home to the island's only permanent resident, as well as what many regard as the finest restaurant in the region, Dionis. I have heard wonderful tales about the temperamental owner, but the reports on the food have been superb, but sadly not a restaurant where I have yet had the pleasure. The same is true of Pansion Tonci, which also offers accommodation, and if you are looking to escape the pressures of modern life, there are few better options.

Here you can find an array of fascinating things, such as the vineyards of Bracanovic, just one metre above sea level, whose grapes are to be found in the wines of Luviji and legendary Hvar winemaker Andro Tomic. The Romans loved Vlaka, and came regulary (there are still Roman remains there) and enjoyed mud baths in the pretty bay. And if you are looking for quality, delicious rock salt, this is the place to come. Some kind local lady gave me half a kilo collected from the rocks in a scorching summer the year I picked grapes with Andro – it tasted more like childhood sweets than salt. You can reach Vlaka by water taxi from Hvar Town.

Marinkovac, from Carpe Diem Beach to Zdrilca and Mlini

For a Pakleni island of contrasts, look no further than Marinkovac, perhaps better known to many by its most famous bay, Stipanska. The party island! For here is the home of Carpe Diem Beach, home to the infamous Full Moon parties, as well as Hvar's most famous – and biggest – nightlife destination, with a capacity of some 2,700.

The peak season parties until dawn are legendary, with regular boats from in front of the main Carpe Diem bar on the Hvar waterfront, but Stipanska has much more to offer by day – an excellent beach club with great service by day, a popular wedding location, and a romantic evening dinner location, as long as you are finished by 1am when the party starts... www.hvar.com

And yet the hedonism of Stipanska is in direct contrast to the tranqulity of two bays on the other side of the island – Zdrilca and Mlini. Both have excellent beaches and cuisine, and both are accessible by water taxi from Hvar Town.

Jerolim

Are you a naturist? Then head to Jerolim, which was named by CNN as the world's top FKK beach in the world in 2011. Naturism has a long tradition on Hvar and on Jerolim, and there are only two places to check out.

The most well-known is Amo Beach, which faces Hvar Town, and is more of a beach club, as well as the location for the For Festival in recent years, and this is the arrival point, but the real gem is through the woods, perhaps 100m to the other side, to Mara's Place, my favourite bar in Croatia. For here is the most accepting and natural place I have found in Dalmatia, where guests are naturist, gay, families – it doesn't matter, and the attitude is mirrored by its divine setting. In the woods one can find random pieces of art, all created from wood washed up on the beach. The toilet is one of my favourite stories, but you will have to go and visit and ask Mara for that story. Vogue Australia shot here in 2013. It really is that kind of place – something for everyone. A treasure of Hvar with the perfect custodians.

Galesnik

The closest of the Pakleni islands is Galesnik, whose single-story building – a former ammuniation storage – faces the town. Today it is a fine restaurant on this eco-ethno island, but one which is only open by appointment. It is worth making the effort, both for the food and the view. As with all the finer things on the Pakleni Islands, arrangements are a little orthodox – go to the office of the harbourmaster close to where the catamaran arrives, and enquire.

Galesnik was more famous – and the inspiration for my last book, 'Lavender, Dormice and a Donkey Named Mercedes' – by its sole permanent resident, until she sadly passed away. Mercedes the donkey and I never met, even though she graced the cover of my book. A lovely lady who became a rakija addict over the years, her undoing was thanks to another Englishman, who was working in a hostel in Hvar Town.

Trying to impress his visiting girlfriend, he took her to Galesnik for a romantic girlfriend, where they encountered Mercedes on the rakija. The girlfriend informed his that donkeys were not meant to be alone, and that he should do something. At which point – and I am HUGELY impressed by this (and there IS a YouTube video to corroborate the story), the valiant boyfriend negotiated the purchase of a male donkey from the Hvar donkey capital – Brusje – and had to winch the poor male donkey (did I mention YouTube?) onto a boat in order to transport him to his future love.
Mercedes was at first a little reticent, but soon got the hang of male company, but the rumours sadly were that the couple's amorous endeavours proved too much for poor Mercedes, who has since moved to Donkey Heaven, where I trust there is rakija aplenty...

Vodnjak

Those then are the main Pakleni Islands, which gets its name from two sources depending on who you talk to. Some say Pakleni translates as 'hell' – if this is Hell, then show me Paradise... - while others say it is due to resin on the islands used in shipbuilding. I am of the second opinion, but one more Pakleni quirk is in the island of Vodnjak, complete with lighthouse. A few years ago, a former Mayor of Hvar invited Facebook supremo Mark Zuckerberg to visit Hvar, stating that if he did, the mayor would rename Vodnjak 'Facebook Island', with the lighthouse a symbol of connectivity. Needless to say, Mr. Facebook never arrived, the mayor got replaced, and the magic of the Pakleni Islands lives on.

Water Taxis

How to reach the Pakleni Islands? Some have their private yachts of course, and the main ACI marina for Hvar is housed in a nothern bay on Sveti Klement.

Speedboat transfers are also possible of course, and many excursion boats moor at Palmizana, but the vast majority of tourists arrive by water taxi. There is a very well-organised system of water taxis servicing the islands mentioned above. Each destination is clearly advertised, and return tickets only are sold, but they can be used on any returning boat. Boats leave in the morning until about midday, with returning boats starting about 16:00. The price for Palmizana, for example, is 60 kuna return.

CHAPTER 4: THE TOWNS OF HVAR

Top 5 Things to Do in Hvar Town

There are not many places on the planet like Hvar Town. History, heritage, beauty, charm, vibe and the perfect climate. It is no wonder that almost everyone falls in love when they arrive. But what to do? It is such a diverse place, attracting the mega-rich to the budget student traveller, but here are our top 5 things to do.

1. Take a boat to the Pakleni Islands

Yes, I realise I am sending you out of town immediately, but you will forgive me when you arrrive. The Pakleni Islands are an essential part of Hvar Town, and if you are looking for daytime beach action (or nighttime partying), they are an indipsenable part of your holiday. Watertaxis ply their trade daily from the main riva – choose from the various chill zones of Carpe Diem Beach and Palmizana, to lesser visited treasures such as Vlaka, Jerolim, Milni and Zdrilca. Boat tickets are return only, but they do allow you flexibility on the return, and you can choose from any returning boat. Prices start at 60 kuna return.

2. Take in the Spanish Fortress view

It does look mighty impressive, doesn't it? And it is. And while it might seem quite a hike, not only is the climb to the Spanish Fortress not too bad, but the views MORE than make up for it at the top. Spectacular vistas which take in the true magic of the Pakleni Islands, the yacht-sodden Hvar riva and the old town below maket the hike to the top a distant memory. Entry is 30 kuna and includes a visit to the fortress inside, complete with visit to the prison inside. And the good news is that the hike back to your celebratory beer below is a lot less challenging.

3. Do Nothing on the Largest Square in Dalmatia

What to say? Holidays are about activity for some, about relaxing for others. And if relaxing is your thing, then look no further. Simply grab a seat at one of the numerous bars and restaurants on the main Hvar square – all 4,500m2 of it, the largest square in all Dalmatia – and take in the vibe. This is people watching paradise, and one of the most relaxing things to do on Hvar is simply to take it all in. Do as the locals do – order an espresso and make it last an hour. And watch the beautiful people (for there are many) – a truly wonderful blend of all sections of society and budgets drawn to the magic of this incredible town.

4. A Walking Tour of Hvar Town

It was ten years before I did my first walking tour of Hvar Town, and I thought I knew it all. I was so wrong. There are plenty of tours available – I can thoroughly recommend both Karmen Barcot and Katija Vucetic from personal experience (ask at the tourist board), who both taught me an awful lot about the town and the island, with very personal input from their local experience. Not many people know, for example, that the father of fingerprinting, Ivan Vucetic, came from Hvar Town before emigrating to Argentina to make his discovery. Benedicting lace, fingerprinting, Franciscan monasteries and seemingly a story in every stone, a 90-minute walking tour will enhance your Hvar experience no end.

5. Breakfast at Hotel Adriana – Oh Yes

Am sure many locals will raise an eyebrow at this one, and I can understand. Hotel Adriana is the best hotel in Hvar Town, and all locals know that the best terrace is the fabulous Top Bar, with its unrivalled views of the main square, fortress riva and Pakleni Islands. Or is it? I stayed at Adriana a few years ago for the first time and had breakfast on the ground floor which is where I made this discovery. The Butchery and Wine restaurant is rather a find, and one that not many notice, despite its central position. A ground floor terrace which people walk past without noticing on their way to Hula Hula, which makes it perfect for people watching and relaxing. The price of breakfast (from 07:00 to 11:00) is I think 129 kuna, which may sound expensive, but trust me, you will not eat again before dinner, and with up to four hours on the best terrace on Hvar, overlooking the old town with its mega-yachts contrasting nicely with the fishing boats in front of the terrace, the perfect way to start the day. Open to non-residents.

A Tour of Hvar Town Restaurants

With more than 70 restaurants to choose from, it is safe to say you will not go hungry in Hvar Town... And while some say that the Dalmatian menu is the same in most restaurants, there are enough twists and turns in the top establishments in the town to satisfy even the most demanding of palates.

Where to begin? Perhaps with the undisputed market leader, king of the TripAdvisor rankings for more than 3 years apart from one week last year. **Dalmatino**, located in a small alley just off the main square by Hotel Palace, does not have the prime sea view location, which makes it all the more sure that the food is what people rave about. A fish and steak house, the zucchini carpaccio remains a Hvar culinary highlight three years after I first tried it.

But Hvar is about the water, and waterfront restaurants are where the attraction is for many. Top of the list for reputation and extensive wine list is luxury fish restaurant **Gariful**, a celebrity draw with the most exclusive wine and Champagne list on the Adriatic. Looking for a Chateau Palmer 82 or a jeroboam of Moet to celebrate the day? You have come to the right place. Signature dish – drunk lobster.

Round the corner is what many claim is Hvar's most romantic restaurant – **DiVino**. Stylish cuisine and an excellent wine list are only half the attraction, however. DiVino has the best setting in the town, with a spacious and aromatic garden overlooking those spectacular sunsets. Located back from the main throughfare, it is also one of the most private terraces on the island.

Keep going towards the 550 year-old Franciscan monastery, and just before it, you will come to a charming little beach and one of the best-priced and delicious restaurants – **Djordota Vartal**. Known locally as the meat maestro, Djordje Tudor is the embodiment of tradition and fine Hvar cuisine, and while meat may be the speciality, the fish options are excellent as well. Combined with the beach below and the location away from the main drag, it is perhaps one of the best dining options on the islands.

Continue your journey along the water and you will come to Krizna Luka, a much underrated bay well away from the main action in a residential zone. Here you will find one of Hvar's most decorated and eclectic chefs at **Lungo Mare** at his family home away from the water, or else try one of my favourite people on Hvar, Crazy Stipe at **C'Est La Vie**. Stipe ran the wildest restaurant at Lucullus for the last few years, but is now taking it easy away from the main action, with a quality slow fast food concept, with a terrace to die for. Highly recommended.

Hotel food is often overrated, and this is the case in Hvar Town also. One of the biggest surprises in the **Butchery and Wine** restaurant on the ground floor of Hotel Adriana, complete with – among other offerings – the first Kobe beef on the island. Add to that the first shrimp restaurant in all Croatia at stylish **Hotel Riva** on the main waterfront, and the romantic terrace at **San Marco** in Hotel Palace, and the Suncani Hvar restaurant contribution to Hvar cuisine is significant. Another hotel-related restaurant woth checking out, both for the food and the private terrace is

Restaurant Park below Hotel Park, just off the main square. Cafe Park below is an outstanding escape from the crowds, with its high ceiling, log fire in winter and live jazz and other music during the season.

Hvar Town has a repuation for being very expensive, expecially when it comes to restaurants, which it can be. This is the town where you can spend more than 100,000 euro on a 6 litre bottle of one of the world's most exclusive Champagnes, for example.

But it does not have to be. One of the strengths of Hvar as a destination is that there is something for everyone. It is a town where the backpacker can rub shoulders with the celebrities, and where everyone can find his own level of accommodation and level of dining experience. Here are four great value places to eat in Hvar Town, where you can fill up without emptying your wallet.

Villa Dinka Overlooking Hotel Amfora's pool and with a cool breeze and sea view, it is worth making the short climb to Villa Dinka (there is a path just before the hotel) for the ambience alone. But the pizzas are excellent, and start at under 50 kuna. Catch them on a day when they are roasting lamb on the spit for an extra treat.

Bistro Alviz Probably the most jovial of all Hvar's restauranteurs, Vjekoslav from Bistro Alviz(just opposite the bus station close to the car park) has built up a very dedicated following over the years, with a combination of warm welcome, excellent service and quality food delivered at reasonable prices. A full Dalmatian menu is on offer, or check out the range of pizzas, again in the sub-50 kuna bracket.

Marinero Fish plays a major role in the Hvar gastronomic scene, and prices can be high. There is no doubting the quality however, and one place to go for a fish extravaganza on a budget is

Marinero (tucked away in a pretty square near St. Mark's Church just off the main waterfront between Cafe Sidro and Hotel Adriana). The tuna steaks are probably the best value in town, delivered with frightening efficiency which produces everything itself, from the organic vegetables to the range of seafood via its fish business.

Mizarola Another of Hvar's smiliest welcomes, host Marino has built up a solid following of both locals and visitors in this excellent eatery on the main square in Hvar Town. Perfect location to watch the summer go by, and with a delicious menu and excellent prices. If you want to fill up for two days, invest 55 kuna in one of the lasagnes - 500g of heaven.

One of the most interesting gourmet parts of town is the area to the right of the main square as you enter from the bus station. Here you will find 'Gourmet Street', the finest dining per square metre on the island. And what an entrance with hsitoric **Giaxa**, arguably the most stunning restaurant heritage setting on Hvar, with a cuisine to match. 'Have You Ever Tasted Art?' You will have, after your first Giaxa dining experience.
Giaxa also run the welcoming restaurant on the other end of Gourmet Street – **Luna**. Famous for its romantic terrace carved out of the building's rooftop, I love the food but also the wonderful Hvar wine map in chalk on the ground floor. I will not spoil your surprise by elborating. Lucullus in the middle of the street is under new management this summer, so nothing to report as of yet, but opposite is **Zlatna Skoljka** (Golden Shell), a gourmet slo food extravaganza from one of Hvar's greatest chefs. Add to that the town's finest courtyard next door at **Paladini**, and the home of Hvar wine bar tourism opposite at **3Prsuta**, and why would you dine in any other street? And just around the corner going towards the cathedral is gogeous **Passarola**, which has become a firm favourite for fine diners despite being a relative newcomer to Hvar gourmet scene. A great addition this year will be the win bar basement directly under the restaurant, a great place for a pre or post dinner

drink in more exclusive surroundings.

Other restaurants deserving of a mention include **Macondo**, as traditional as you can get – no fancy hostesses or credit cards here, just excellent fish, simply and outstandingly prepared; **Menego**, up the steps and on the way to the fortress, and a regular source of column inches in international media; **Luviji**, to the right as you approach the cathedral, a bastion of Hvar tradition and home to the only Hvar Town member of the Hvar Wine Association.

There has been foreign influence too in recent years.. Hit the main square and you will find the biggest restauant on the square – **Asian Spice**, with a selection of Japanese, Chinese and Thai. Or the foreign-owned **Fig Cafe** and **50Hvar**, which have both become hits in their short existence.

The Legendary Hvar Town Nightlife

I am really not sure what to write about Hvar Town nightlife. According to the international media it is one of the top party places on the planet, despite having only two nightclubs, and the Carpe Diem Full Moon parties are the stuff of legend. What is true is that the nightlife is extremely good, but if you are expecting Ibiza, you are going to be very disappointed – go to Zrce instead. And if you are looking for a party outside June to the end of August, you really are in the wrong place.

That said, the nightlife IS good. **Carpe Diem** may not be as exclusive as it was when it opened in 1999, but it still has its appeal on the waterfront next to Gariful, and the summer programme at Carpe Diem Beach at Stipanksa is the stuff of legend. Veneranda, the nightclub where a certain British prince fell into the pool in 2012 is no more as a nightclub, but has been taken over by a local association with a rich cultural programme.

Pink Champagne is a basement club opposite the police station close to the bus station. Don't let its position put you off. After a slow start a few years ago, it is now firmly established on the Hvar nightlife scene. If you want to head a little further out of town, head up the hill on the road to Stari Grad to **Temple**, a club and strip joint that opened in 2015. A new club on the waterfront next to Sidro just off the main square is due to open for the 2016 season – **Seven**.

Most of the nightlife is centred around various bars. The arrival of the cancerous The Yacht Week has heightened Hvar's party reputation, and while I can understand what The Yacht Week gets out of Hvar as a destination, I struggle to see what benefit Hvar receives.

The main party action is set around a few bars in close proximity just off the main square heading towards Hotel Adriana, with licences until 02:00 – look out for Sidro, Nautica, Aloha and Kiva, the party centre of the town, while Jazz Bar just behind the main waterfront is also worth checking out. Many people start the party at Hula Hula, which has stunning sunsets, a 10 minute walk from the main square.

5 Cafes to Check Out

Coffee is at the centre of life on Hvar, and if you are trying to meet an official, forget trying to get to him via the office, find out where he takes his daily coffee and inform the waiter ahead of town that his coffee is on your bill – that is how business is done.

Everyone has their favourites, but here are five in Hvar Town worth checking out.

Caffe Pjaca. Location, Location, Location. It is had to go wrong on the corner of Dalmatia's largest square, looking over the oldest public theatre in Europe, the home of organised tourism in Europe and one of the most exclusive waterfronts in the world. Is it any wonder that Tom Cruise popped in for a coffee in 2014?

95

Caffe Sidro. A Hvar institution since the 1970s and one of the first bars in the town, Sidro has mastered the art of appealing to both locals and tourists alike. Reputed to be the best coffee in town by day and the best cocktails at night, why not find out for yourself? A superbly positioned people watching spot just off the main square.

Aloha. A Hvar legend until it shut down many years ago, Aloha recently rejoined the cafe scene, after it reinvented itself from an art gallery into a cafe/cocktail bar. Located a few metres north of Sidro, it retains its arty feel by day, and cocktail prowess by night.

Archie's. If you want to go local in a prime location, it has to be Archie's, a firm local favourite in the heart of the main square, right next to Caffe Pjaca. Waste an afternoon watching the world go by.

Rin Tin Tin. One of the most local bars of all, and one which offers a different perspective on Hvar, more of a working man's cafe. Located opposite the bus station and away from the main drag, it is a place of waiting, business and gossip, with reasonable prices for the town. Don't miss its star attraction, the wonderful pictoral map on the wall dispaying all the peculiarities of each Hvar town and village.

What to See

Tvrdava spanjola – Spanish Fortress
Towering above all the revelling and the mega-yachts is the Spanish Fortress, built in the early 16th century, and offering spectacular views of the town and islands below. The fortress is not the original, and the 13th century city walls, constructed soon after the islanders requested Venetian protection in 1278, predate it by almost 200 years.

Hvar was destroyed by the Turkish Fleet in 1571 and only the fortress saved the local population, but a freak lightning strike on the gunpowder stores caused further devastation, and many of the town's buildings can be traced to this period of reconstruction. The fortress can be accessed by car for visitors to Hvar Town and it is then a pleasant stroll down to the town.

St. Stephen's Cathedral and the Main Square
The central point of Hvar Town is the pjaca, or main square which, at 4,500m2, is the largest square in Dalmatia. Originally part of the bay, the land was filled in and fully paved in 1780; the fountain in the square dates back to 1520. In summer, the square is extremely busy, with all cafes and restaurants overflowing, but there is a much more tranquil feel after the season, as locals relax over a coffee.

At the far end of the pjaca is St. Stephen's Cathedral, which was finished in the 18th Century, with construction of the current building starting in the 16th century. The first church on the site was built in the 6th century and was granted cathedral status in the 13th century when Hvar Town assumed the Bishopric from Stari Grad. The intermittent construction period gave rise to different architectural styles, and there are elements of Gothic, Romanesque and Renaissance. Inside there are eleven Baroque altars made by artists from Venice.

The Arsenal and Clues to an Earlier Civilisation
Guarding the right-hand entrance to the *pjaca* is the impressive Arsenal building, with its 10m spanned archway. Built between 1579 and 1611 to house war galleys, the Arsenal is an imposing building on the waterfront and underwent renovation in 2009. It was also used as a storage facility for items such as cereal and salt. Coins were found in 1835 bearing the name Heraklea leading to speculation that the ancient Greek settlement of the same name may have been located in Hvar. Spectacular ruins were unearthened during renovation under the Arsenal floor in 2015, giving us one more layer to Hvar's rich heritage.

The Oldest Municipal Theatre in Europe
On the first floor of the arsenal is a delightful sight that tourists sometimes miss - the oldest municipal theatre in Europe. Built in 1612, the theatre celebrated its 400th anniversary in 2012, and the current interior was renovated in 1803. It owes its existence to the then Prince of Hvar Pietro Semitecolo, who was inspired by the Italian theatre at the time and arranged for the construction with money from the commune of Hvar. Events to celebrate the anniversary are planned for October.

Franciscan Monastery and Benedictine Convent
Walking along the riva past Carpe Diem, the Franciscan Monastery comes into view. Built in 1465, it was jointly financed by the nobles of Hvar and sea commanders as testament to their gratitude for many lives saved at sea near Hvar. The local contribution included 1000 gold coins from Antun Lucic, and his son, the famous poet Hanibal Lucic is buried under the main altar.

Hanibal Lucic also had a part to play in the Benedictine Convent on Hvar, which has played an important role in the town since nuns first arrived in 1664.

All the main sights in Hvar Town are within easy walking distance of the main square, and there is ample to take in a cultural tour before taking in another incredible sunset over an evening drink.

Museums in Hvar Town

The Archaeological Collection in Hvar
Started in 1966 and dedicated to the later Dr Grga Novak, a driving force in assembling the exhibition, the archaeological collection gives a comprehensive overview of Hvar's heritage.

Starting with artifacts dating back to 6,000 BC and the Neolithic era, and including finds from shipwrecks, and art and architectural fragments from Hvar's long history, the 2,500 exhibits, assembled by donation and private collection, offer a fascinating insight into the island's past. Opening hours 1000 - 1300 and 2000-2300 in summer, by appointment in winter. The collection is housed in the former Dominican church of St. Mark's.

Hanibal Lucic's Summer Residence

A famous poet and influential noble, the name of Hanibal Lucic is intricately bound with Hvar Town. There is a restaurant on the main square which bears his name and he is buried under the alter of the Franciscan monastery.

His summer house, the headquarters of the Hvar Museum, is a well-preserved example of the country houses of the Renaissance period, but with clear Gothic influences. Included in the museum is a reception room dedicated to the memory of Hanibal. The museum is also home to the local branch of the Croatian state archives. Opening hours 0900 -1300 and 1700 - 2300 in summer, 1000 - 1200 in winter (by appointment).

The Natural History Cabinet in Hvar

Located in the Hanibal Lucic Summer Residence, the Natural History Cabinet is a collection of 350 items which have preserved the natural history of Hvar. These include meteorological instruments, preserved plants and old history books.

Stari Grad

The former capital of the island, and orginally called Faros, is the oldest settlement on the island, after the Ancient Greeks arrived here in 384BC from the island of Paros, bringing among other things olives and grapes. In 2004, a boat set sail in the opposite direction, from Stari Grad to Paros, bringing olives trees and vines from Hvar which owe their existence to the original Greek colonisers. Stari Grad is considered by some as the oldest town in Croatia, and in 2016 it celebrates 2400 years, the highlight of which will be the Days in the Bay Festival from September 8-11 (details yet to be revealed).

UNESCO World Heritage Site – the Stari Grad Plain

Hvar has one of Croatia's seven UNESCO World Heritage Sites, located just outside Stari Grad, called the Stari Grad Plain, Hora or Ager, depending on who you are talking to. Rather than me blither on, the wonderful Go Hvar blog (gohvar.wordpress.com) run by Marion Podolski (with a little help from hubbie Zdravko) covers the essentials more than adequately in these three blogs. If you have not come across Go Hvar, I encourage you to check it out. It is rather eclectic, with a range of diverse topics about you Hvar you will not see elsewhere on the web, from earthquakes to birdwatching.

The only thing for me to add about the Stari Grad Plain is that the island's first lavender museum will open in the summer of 2016, at Agroturizam Pharos, one more great addition to the heritage of this fabulous island.

1. What did the Greeks do for us?

In the 4th century BCE, the ancient Greeks settled on Hvar at the head of a long inlet where the town of Stari Grad now stands. They called it Faros. It was a prime piece of real estate, not just for the protected harbour, but the adjoining land was the only flat fertile area in the Adriatic islands suitable for cultivation. They divvied it up, and gave each colonist a parcel. Fields were cleared of stone, which came in handy to construct dividing walls and pathways. Shelters were built, and irrigation systems installed. Watchtowers were constructed on the surrounding hills to keep marauders away. They grew grapes, olives and other crops for themselves and for export.

The amazing thing about this process is that it's pretty much all still there! Continuously maintained down the years, the Stari

Grad Plain is a living example of ancient Greek agriculture, complete with this year's vines and olives. It's still entirely recognizable 24 centuries later.

The fields are laid out according to the original measurements by the Greek surveyors. Starting from the only pond, they divided the land into standard-sized rectangular parcels (chora) which they then bounded with dry stone walls. The system included a rainwater recovery system of gutters and storage cisterns, and small stone shelters, known locally as trims (pronounced treems).

Walking along the ancient pathways, you can really get a sense for the continuity of a very successful system of agriculture, one that's in harmony with the surrounding nature. The original Greek walls are very easy to spot for the sheer expertise of the work. They have the smoothest, most regular blocks, and the wall tapers elegantly towards the top. Later constructions use rougher stone, and some very recent ones use, gasp, mortar to hold them together. Wild flowers grow everywhere – come May there are splashes of red poppies, rock roses, honeysuckle, lots of herbs and many other Mediterranean natives. No pesticides here.

In 2008, the Stari Grad Plain was designated a UNESCO World Heritage Site. For more information, maps, etc. check out their website here: http://whc.unesco.org/en/list/1240/

2. Maslinovik
Maslinovik is an old watchtower set on a hill on the north side of the Stari Grad Plain. Built in the 4th century BC by the ancient Greek settlers, it formed part of the line of defence for the fields, running from the town of Pharos (today's Stari Grad) to Tor, a second watchtower set high on the cliffs above Jelsa.

The existence of two massive watchtowers shows that the Greek colonists were not entirely secure on the island. In fact, the natives took great offense at the incomers and after the first year they called in help from fellow Illyrians on the mainland. The Greeks from the neighbouring island of Issa (today's Vis) also pitched in, and the resulting battle left many dead. The dramatic events were recorded in the first century B.C. by historian Diodorus Siculus. Following the battle, there seems to have been an uneasy peace, with the Greeks in Pharos surrounded by big defensive walls, emerging out during the day to farm the fields of the Stari Grad Plain. The Illyrians had the rest of the island, including the hillfort of Gracisce directly overlooking the plain.

The watchtower of Tor was built on a high cliff at the eastern end of the plain, providing a good view over the surrounding area, including the sea. But since it doesn't have a clear line of sight to Pharos, a second watchtower was needed on the hill at Maslinovik. If enemy activity was seen by the lookout on Tor, smoke signals would have been sent to Maslinovik, and on to Pharos.
Maslinovik is an easy walk up from the plain, starting from the one pond in the area. That's a distinct feature now as then, when the Greeks used it as the starting point to measure out the land parcels. Heading up the hill, take a right turn near the top, when you see a break in the wall. There's no sign, because everybody knows that's the way, right? Follow the path round to the right of the hill, and look for a left turn just as you reach the ruined houses. Again, it's pretty much just a break in the wall with some steps. Keep heading upwards to the top of the hill.

Finally, as you round some bushes, a large red signpost labelled Maslinovik appears! Very helpfully written in English (is no one else interested, I wonder?) it provides a description and an aerial map of the site. You're there!

Most of this tower has been recycled into nearby houses and walls, but the enormous square blocks of the foundation stones are still in place – the classic sign of a Greek building. Maslinovik is impressive for the sheer size of those blocks. Must have been murder to move, let alone cart them up a hill! Or perhaps they were cut from the ground up there? At any rate, those are good, solid foundations that haven't moved in 2,400 years.

And the views from that hill… beautiful in all directions! We had our picnic up there, sitting on the stone blocks of the tower, with nobody else around. Maybe Maslinovik gets more visitors in summer, but we had it to ourselves in May. Next to the tower is a pit, possibly a shelter related to the watchtower but it wasn't clear. A ruined house with a caved in roof stands to the south and is probably where a good few of the stones from the watchtower ended up!

We headed downhill a different way, circling round the hill to the east past what looked like a ruined hamlet. Interestingly, the garden plots were still neatly cultivated – it doesn't do to waste good growing soil! Lovely views over the island on the way down as we followed an old pathway, then turned right onto the road. You can't really get lost, not with the grid pattern of fields and roads!

3. Roman Holiday

Unlike the Greek settlers before them, the ancient Romans made themselves much more comfortable on the island. Of course it helps that they owned the mainland – Dalmatia was a Roman province, with a large city at Salona, on the sheltered northern harbour of today's Split. The modern city of Split started life as the retirement palace of the Emperor Diocletian, who was born in Dalmatia.

But back to the island. The Romans, then, having pushed out the Greeks in 219 BC had a relatively peaceful and prosperous existence on Hvar. They called the island Faria, and set about improving the agriculture, most notably the wine production. They dismantled the defensive walls at Faros, but presumably the merchants and traders continued business as usual. There was apparently a settlement in Vrboska, but the map isn't precise enough for me to tell exactly where it was. Would be interesting to know! It's a lovely harbour, and perfect place for a villa, if you're not worried about invading hordes from the sea. No, I'm not talking about today's yacht marina and excursion boat traffic, but attacking pirates and Illyrian resistance to the Pax Romana!

Whereas the Greek farmers had only small shelters in the fields, the Romans constructed more spacious villas with room for managers, slaves and livestock. The best known villa rustica on Hvar is Kupinovik on the Stari Grad Plain close to Stari Grad. Excavations show the extent of the buildings, the olive press and other signs of the ancient agriculture. You can imagine these ancient Roman landowners coming over for the summer season. Strolling around in their tunics and sandals, bathing in the sea, going for walks, admiring the Greek ruins, etc. The Stari Grad fields continued to be cultivated, property was expanded and the island was exporting wines and olive oil, just like today.

The Stari Grad Museum has a beautiful display of underwater archaeology- the cargo of a Roman shipwreck laid out like it was still on the seafloor. The galley sank in the Duboka cove on the north side of Hvar island near Basina, in the mid 4th century. You can see all the amphora strewn around – this was a serious export business!

But what of the Illyrians? As they didn't write things down, the end of their story is not entirely clear. I assume they got assimilated into the Roman Empire one way or another.

Top 5 Things to Do in Stari Grad

The Stari Grad Tourist Board recently published their top five things to see and do in Stari Grad, and who are we to disagree?

Petar HektorovicCastle
Petar Hektorović's Tvrdalj, with its fishpond and a dove-cot over

it, is the most famous building in Stari Grad. This renaissance poet built it throughout his entire life and it had the same importance for him as his literary work. There he realized his idea of a microcosms; a small, enclosed world where all divine creatures – fish, birds, herbs and people (himself, his friends, a holy woman, paupers and travellers) - had a space to live. The Tvrdalj is also a stone book – Hektoroviccarved more than twenty stone inscriptions in Latin, Italian and Croatian in its walls. One, which is in Italian, is his life motto: "Fede e realtà o quanto è bella!" ("Oh how lovely faith and reality are!").

Stari Grad Plain
This large plain occupies the island' s central area. Its name kept changing with the successive arrival of new masters. First known by the Greeks as Chora Pharu, it became Ager Pharensis in Roman times and was later replaced by the medieval name of Campus Sancti Stephani (the Plain of St.Stephen). It is now known as Stari Grad Plain, and has sustained the life on the island for thousands of years. The Plain is in fact a cultured landscape, formed by thousands of years of human labour. Its ancient man-made features originate from 24 centuries ago when Greek colonist divided the Plain into rectangular plots of 1x5 stadia, (ca. 180x900m), each enclosed by drywall.

The Plain was crisscrossed by major roads cutting through it in regular longitudinal and transversal directions. Today we can identify the point in the Plain from wich the Greek surveyor began his measuring located at a road intersection.

Kabal Peninsula
The Kabal peninsula, whose form resembles the fingers of a hand, is located in the north-western part of Stari Grad Bay. At the very entrance to the Bay is the Kabal cape - an eighty metre high rock - and on the end of the Bay is Stari Grad, one of the safest natural harbours in the Adriatic. During crystal clear days you will have the feeling of sailing into some kind of fjord. You will leave

behind high hills that drop steeply into the sea on the southern part, and far away, in the depth of the bay, is the town of Stari Grad.

Stari Grad Museum
The Biankini Palace – Stari Grad Museum –was the neo-renaissance family home of the Biankini brothers dating back to 1896. Interior decorations from the period in which the palace was built have been preserved, whilst in the garden there is a century-old Deodar Cedar, which is of the same period as the building itself. Museum collections on the ground floor and upstairs tell us the tales of Stari Grad's long history. The hydroarcheologic collection is in fact a tale about the sinking of a merchant ship full of amphorae which, in the 4th and 5th century, was sailing from North Africa to Pharia of the late antiquity period.The archaeological collection collection of artefacts tell us about the life of ancient Stari Grad – from the 5th century B.C. to the 7th or 8th centuries A.D. The Gelineo Bervaldi Salon invokes the times of the patrician salons from the end of 18th and the beginning of 19th century, whilst the Kapetanska soba (the Captain's room) from the second part of 19th century reminds us of the time when Stari Grad was a living port with large sailing ships. The works of art of two painters from Stari Grad - Juraj Plancicand Bartol Petric– together with other 20th century Croatian painters can be seen in the permanent exhibition of the Juraj PlancicGallery.

Skor Square
Of the numerous small squares in Stari Grad, the most picturesque one is theskor Square. Almost like a theatre coulisse (which it actually becomes during the summer cultural events), this square was formed , during the 17th and 18th centuries from a stretch of shallow water. It was once home to a shipyard which was covered and the square took its name from this (skor from skver, in Dalmatian dialect, means shipyard). This curved space where mythical Dalmatia lives is enclosed by typical dalmatian

working-class houses with picturesque luminari (roof windows) as well as sulari and skalinade (stone terraces with staircases).

Where to Eat

Stari Grad has the best selection of year-round dining on Hvar, with several restaurants open during the winter. The summer season widens the choice considerably, and there are plenty of places to indulge in some of the island's excellent Dalmatian cuisine in authentic surroundings. Here is a quick overview.

Opposite the Old Town: Ermitaz

For location, rustic environment and traditional local fare, it is hard to better Ermitaz, located on the water opposite the old town. Its waterfront location and natural setting in pine trees make it a desirable location to while away an afternoon in the company of good food, wine and service.

Atmospheric Old Town: Antika, Jurin Podrum,Kod Barba Luke and Pinetta. Kod Damira

The pedestrianised streets of the old town, which date back more than 2000 years, provide a wealth of choice of authentic stone Dalmatian dining. Among the best are Antika, whose tiny interior in winter expands to several tables in the nearby square in season (check out the cute leafy cocktail terrace on the first floor, Jurin Podrum, the old premises for Kod Damira (and location for a rather good royal lunch in 1936 when Edward and Mrs. Simpson popped in), and offering a warm welcome and hearty Dalmatian menu and Pinetta, a relative newcomer to the town's gastronomic offer, a combination of restaurant, cocktail bar and wine tasting venue, and with the oldest bottle of Prosek in Croatia on display. Or experience a wonderful fish extravaganza with the best desserts in town at Kod Barba Luke, which is the oldest restaurant in the oldest town in Croatia. And very good. At the entrance to the old town is Kod Damira, a heartbeat of the island all year round, with authentic food and authentic Hvar conversation.

Best Value on the Island: Marko's Pizzeria and a Little Indian and Chinese Action

For a combination of old town charm, excellent service and great value food, check out Marko's, the local expat favourite and arguably the best value on the island. Open all year, Marko's core offer is pizza and pasta, with a wider Dalmatian menu. Pet and child friendly, there is ample space inside and out. And perhaps the most unusual restaurant in Stari Grad, the new-look Galija next to Marko's run by a father and daughter team from the Midlands, and offering – in addition to the regular pizza and grill – a little Indian and Chinese fare. And rather nice it is too. I must admit I was surprised when I introduced myself to be met this reponse from the owner:

"My other daughter cuts your sister's hair in Stourbridge." And so she does.

Cafes, Bars and Nightlife

Tourists looking for raucous nightlife should head to Hvar Town or more local town of Jelsa, but there are numerous bars and cafes to have a quieter drink. The recently renovated Gradska Kavana (now called Espresso) is a grand cafe next to the court, a chance to combine wonderful sea views while overhearing hushed legal negotiations conducted over double espressos.

Round the corner is Stari Grad's largest square and home to the palace of Petar Hektorovic. There are several cafes to choose from, with Molo Misto, with its cosy upstairs, and Sokol, with its free wireless, the pick of the bunch. At the other side of the old town, next to the car park, Casper's offers the cheapest beer in town, at 12 kuna.

What to See

The old town is a great place to wander round and get lost in. There is seemingly a square and church on every corner, and among the things not to miss are:

Petar Hektorovic Trvdalj

The top attraction in Stari Grad is the Hektorovic Tvrdalj, the 'castle' built be one of Croaita's most famous poest, Petar Hektorovic (1487 – 1572). Situated at the back of the largest square in the town, close to the court, Hektorovic built an original legacy, and carved some of his writings in stone in Latin, Italian and Croatian.

With a long sea-facing wall preventing it from attack and intrusion, entering the courtyard is something of a surprise, and includes a large fishpool and herb garden. Above the entrance, carved in stone, he wrote "Petar Hectorović, son of Marino, at his own expense and by his own effort built this for the use of himself and his friends."

Biankini Palace

The impressive Biankini Palace, home of Stari Grad Museum, was the Neo-Renaissance family home of the Biankini Brothers and dates back to 1896. In the garden there is a Deodar Cedar which is as old as the building itself.

Dominican Monastery

Right at the back of the old town is the impressive Dominican monastery of St. Petar Mucenik which was founded in 1482, and then fortified with two rounded turrets in 1682 following the Turkish attack on the island. Here Hekorovic is buried, along with his mother, and his words are carved in stone above the church entrance.

There is an impressive array of art on display, of which the most valuable is The Mourning of Christ by Venetian artist Jacopo Tintoretto, and the oldest inscriptions in Croatia, written in Greek from the 4th to 2nd Centuries, are preseved in the small museum.

St Stephen's Church

St. Stephen's is a baroque church built after the old cathedral and bishop's court had been destroyed. Construction started in 1605, with the main façade thought to have been built by Ivan Pomenic from Korcula, who also constructed the current cathedral in Hvar Town. The interior is decorated with works by various Venetian artists.

St. Jerolim's Church
On the other side of the harbour, the pretty St. Jerolim juts out into the water. Hermit friars – the emerites – lived in what is now one of the island's best restaurants (Ermitaz) and the medieval church is now an art gallery.

Jelsa

These are exciting times for the home of the Total Hvar project. Home to the top destination of former Yugoslavia in 1983, home to the first disco in former Yugoslavia over 50 years ago, Jelsa has sadly experienced hard times in recent years, but the tide – it seems – is turning, and a new optimism has come to the town. New investments, a change of leadership, the arrival of seaplanes – they have all contributed to the town looking forward rather than back, and even though I may be a little biased as this is my home town, I predict great things for Jelsa in the coming years.

Top 5 Things to Do in Jelsa

1. Explore Hvar's Town of Wine
Jelsa is the centre of the Hvar wine story, and until the disasters which befell the island's successful wine industry in the 19th century (see wine section), it was a major exporter all over Europe and beyond. Today, just 280 hectares of vineyards are under cultivation (from 5,700 in the heyday), but what remains is of the highest quality. Jelsa itself has three exceptional tasting experiences – Andro Tomic, Ivo Dubokovic and Teo Huljic, while the village of Svirce close by has another two national names, the

Svirce Cooperative and Ivo Caric. If you are too tired to trek to the wineries, sample the range on the Jelsa waterfront at Artichoke, the first restaurant to sell Hvar wine by the glass.

2. Hike to Heritage and Nature
While most tourists understandably head to the beach – Jelsa has some of the best on the island – there is plenty else of interest closeby. Hiking from the centre of town can lead to some magnificent views, as well as an insight into Jelsa's rich historical path. Hikes to the Greek tower of Tor and Galesnik, for example, are both achievable in a half-day, and both take you through Hvar's pristine nature to get you there. More details at the Jelsa Tourist Board.

3. Get Active
Jelsa is in many ways the sporting capital of the island. It has a nationally renowned rowing club (and you may see them practicing in the harbour in the morning) and used to host professional football teams for winter training. These days, the rowing club is very active, there is a new sports hall with football pitch, tennis courts at the hotels, plenty of activities available from local agencies, as well as the fabulous Adventure Park Jelsa (see Activities).

4. Do Absolutely Nothing
Why come all this way and do nothing? Because it is Dalmatia... I have lost count of the number of guests who arrive with a plan to explore this and that, and they make the fatal mistake of starting their holiday on the lovely main square of Jelsa, the best chill zone on the entire island. And they cannot tear themselves away. And that, as they say, is that. The perfect chill holiday. Particularly recommended is late Sunday morning after Mass, when the locals come out from church in their Sunday best for coffee and gossip, with the little ones play freely in the middle.

5. Explore those Seaplanes

111

The arrival of the seaplanes has brought a different dimension to tourism in Jelsa. I am now able to go from Munich (the Total Project has now expanded to Total Munich – www.total-munich.com) to Jelsa in just 3.5 hours, unheard of before the seaplanes arrived. It also opens up a whole new dimension in day trips from Jelsa – UNESCO sites of Trogir and Diocletian's Palace less than 30 minutes away – as well as a fantastic panoramic experience along the way.

A Tour of Jelsa's Restaurants

The gourmet scene in Jelsa has changed in recent years, and for the better. Where once there was strictly traditional Dalmatian cuisine, now a few innovators have joined the scene, upping the quality and adding choice to an already high quality offering. In season, Jelsa has about 25 restaurants in all. In winter during the week, none...

Over the years, I have had the opportunity to dine in pretty much every restaurant in the town, and it is rare that you will get a bad meal. For the very best though, there are several options. The best in town in my opinion is **Me and mrs Jones**, an unusual sounding name for a rather unusual restaurant on the water opposite the old town. An innovative menu (love the baked goats cheese with cranberry sauce) and the friendliest service in town, perhaps the Jones experience is best summed up by a national TV journalist who was interviewing me there. "I have worked all over Croatia and eaten the best food, but never have I been to a restaurant where everything is done out of love."

A new kid on the block is the **Artichoke Wine Bar** directly opposite Jones on the Jelsa waterfront. With arguably the best interior design of any restaurant on the island in terms of quality, Artichoke, like Jones, has succeeded in getting people to come to Jelsa from Hvar Town. Traditional Mediterranean dining with a twist, Artichoke is also the only place on the island where you can try a selection of the best Hvar wines by the glass.

112

The main square is mostly cafes, but there is one great exception, **Pizzeria Jelsa** on the right hand corner as you enter. Connected to the ice cream Mecca Eis Caffe next door, the restaurant offers much more than pizza, with some of the best salads in town, as well as excellent pastas dishes, of which the Fiery Spaghetti is my favourite. Extremely well priced and located, probably the best value in Jelsa, and if you were looking for an ice cream close by after dinner...

Head into the old town for some additional treasures. Soon after I bought my house next to winemaker Andro Tomic, I went out in search of food and found myself at the atmospheric **Restaurant Faros**, whose garlic soup was an essential starter every night until they closed their doors for the season. Wonderful Dalmatian fare and a gorgeous outside space from a lovely hard-working family, who have been providing quality food for more than 30 years.

Head a little further up the main 'street' from the main church and you will find **Nono's** on the left, which has quickly become an institution since it opened a decade ago. One of the most gorgeous and traditional interiors on the island, the expanding outside space gives it additional charm to match the excellent menu.

Two more worth a mention in the old town. On the edge and just behind the petrol station as you enter Jelsa is **Murvica**, a wonderful German-Croatian combination of great hospitality, with apartments, restaurant and some of Croatia's best olive oil and home-made wine (they also have a rustic holiday home in the abandoned eco-ethno village of Humac). The fish pate is to die for, and the steaks among the best on the island. Deep in the heart of the old town, round the corner from Dalmacijaland gallery is **Pelago**, whose outstanding fish and meat offering highlights Dalmatian cuisine at its finest.

5 Great Cafes

1. Caffe Splendid

Where else to start but The Office? I first went for a beer at Caffe Splendid on the main square, liked the welcome, and have been there every since. During my real estate days, it was a place to meet clients, leave documents, and relax at the end of a working day. With the best pastries on the island, a quality place to hang out, and if you come around midday, you will almost always meet someone from the small but very friendly expat community.

2. Tarantela

Directly opposite Splendid is Tarantela, where the cool people hang out. Great for morning coffee, they also have a good range of cocktails, as well as a late licence, and if you are looking for somewhere on the square with an atmosphere in the evening, this is the place to be.

3. Eis Caffe

The best ice cream on Hvar? Many swear it is true, but whether or not the claim is right, there is no denying that the quality is excellent, the service fantastic, and the location outstanding. Guarding the entrance to the square on the left, the view from Eis Caffe takes in the whole harbour and sometimes snow-capped Mount Biokovo through the palm trees on the mainland.

4. Trick

Walk along the newly expanded Riva, past Artichoke, and you will come to Trick next door. Recently opened, it offers something a little different to the main square – an uninterrupted sea view for starters (and be careful how much you drink if you don't know about the seaplanes, as it is directly in the flight path, which can be a little unnerving as you watch a random plane on its descent). Trick is also a great year-round destination, with probably the biggest internal space in the town's cafes, a welcome addition in winter when the bura is blowing.

5. Skver

Continue on from Tirck to the end of the main waterfront, just before the boathouse which houses the Jelsa Rowing Club, and there is a small cafe called Skver. It may not look the most exotic,but the warm welcome from Ana is matched by the quality of the coffee and the energy she puts into events to liven things up, including live music and karaoke. A great place off the main drag to chill and take in the tranquil scene of the rowers in front.

The Jelsa Cockatil Scene

For some reason, Jelsa has always had a more lively cockail scene than its neighbours in Stari Grad and Vrboska. 2016 looks to be no different, and there will be a VERY interesting mojito event in July for the leading cocktail bar in the town of the same name. **Mojito** has a gorgeous location jutting out into the water in the picturesque harbour opposite the old town. Open all day, it has not only the biggest selection of Mojitos on the island, but also one of the most diverse and innovative programmes, with regular concerts and events, from jazz to magic.

There is another cocktail treasure in the heart of the old town is **Villa Verde**, a wonderful leafy and spacious garden just off the waterfront. Jelsa's oldest cocktail bar, it is still a firm favourite for many locals and returning guests, and there is a good programme of entertainment in peak season. The demise of Candela after just two seasons is offset with the opening of a new cocktail bar opposite the old town next to Me and mrs Jones, **Pulena**.

Although not a cocktail, another business opening in 2016 worthy of mention is **Flying Pig**, Hvar's first dedicated locale offering exclusively Croatian craft beers, as well as ribs, burgers and wings. Located in the old town, a great initiative and we wish the owners luck.

What to See

One of the relatively undiscovered gems on the Dalmatian coast for British holidaymakers is the delightful town of Jelsa, home of this guide.

The focal point of Jelsan life is the main square, or *pjaca*, a picturesque location on the waterfront, where seven cafes compete for the local and tourist business, but not too much, for this is Dalmatia where the emphasis is on taking life in its stride.

The Fortress and Church of the Assumption (of the Blessed Mary)

Daily life centres around the central square, the Pjaca, which is a hive of activity all year round. The Slatina stream runs under the square, offering a source of fresh water to the islanders, and the fountain was added in 1934.

Overlooking the square is the main church in this very Catholic town, the Church of the Assumption, which dates back as far as 1331. The original construction was strengthened and expanded in 1535 and today has four chapels, the two main ones dating back to the 17th century.
Inside are two paintings of interest: in the first chapel on the left, a relief by Antonio Poro and in the chapel on the right there is a work by Flemish-Venetian painter P. de Coster, entitled "Mother of God and the torture of Fabian and Sebastian."

St. Ivan's Square

To the left of the main square, there is a very pretty smaller square called St. Ivan's, whose centrepiece is a small octagonal church from the 17th century, which has elements of Gothic, Renaissance and Baroque. This is arguably the most preserved part of the old town, with its Renaissance lamps and balconies. Don't miss Wine Thursday, wine tastings with live music from the Hvar Wine Association each Thursday until October from 19:00.

116

Municipal Hall and Former Library
One of the most impressive buildings on the waterfront is the
Municipal Hall next to the entrance of the square. Built in 1895
from stone imported from neighbouring Korcula, the palace was
constructed in the Neo-Renaissance style and bears the 1871 Jelsa
Municipality coat of arms.

Disaster struck the building in 2003, when fire broke out in the
town's library on the top floor, leading to the loss of 10,000
books. Renovation has now been completed and the building now
houses municipal offices, while the library is once more thriving
in the town, having received numerous donations.

The Church of St. Roko
Behind the petrol station on the road out of Jelsa is the tiny
church of St. Roko, which was built in the late 16th Century.
Various additions have been made over the years to incorporate
Gothic and Romanesque features, and the church was last
renovated in 1999. Inside is a painting, allegedly by Palma il
Giovane the Younger (1544 - 1628), of the Virgin Mary below the
clouds, with Anthony of Padova holding a naked child on her
right and St. Roko kneeling beside them.

The Church of St. Mihovil
The Gothic-styled Church of St. Mihovil was built by the
Radasinic brothers in 1463, before it was extended in the latter
part of the 18th Century with the addition of a new altar and
Baroque facade,

Our Lady of Health Church
Perched on the top of Racic hill and accessed through the old
town, Our Lady of Health Church is an excellent vantage point to
observe the true beauty of Jelsa and its surroundings. Originally
built in 1535, the church has been extended twice, with the west
wing and steeple added in 1863. Inside there are 18th Century
wooden statues and a 17th century icon in a Renaissance frame.

As patron saint of Jelsa and its outlying villages, islanders gather every year on November 21 to celebrate mass in hour of Our Lady of Heath.

Augustinian Monastery and Jelsa Cemetery

Walking along the riva to towards the campsites and Hotel Hvar on the Gradina Peninsula, one comes to the town's cemetery. As with many cemeteries in the region, it is in a stunning location, some of the most prime real estate in the town. But not for sale... The site was an Augustinian Monastery from 1605 to 1787, and a church with bell-tower from 1605 still stands today.

A section of the ancient protective wall of the Civitas Vetus Ielsae (The Ancient City of Jelsa) can also be seen, dividing the peninsula from Mina beach to Bocic. There are two walls: a 172m long one surrounding Jelsa and a second, longer one (800m), which encircles the first. There are visible indents at the base of the wall showing where guards once stood.

Lapidary

The late Niko Dubokovic, head of Hvar's Cultural Heritage Centre, created a lapidary in Jelsa in 1970 in the area by the church-fortress, protective wall and bell-tower, a collection of approximately 20 stone monuments from ancient and Medieval times, including a tombstone of the Roman era, Venetian lion and a stone table which belonged to a knight named Ivan Obradic.

Perivoj – Jelsa's Public Garden

In 1870, the marshy ground was drained and a public park, Perivoj, created, a pleasant splash of greenery on the water next to the municipal building. Poplars, pine and palm trees have been added, and there are two statues in the park, a seated Captain Nikola Dubokovic (1835-1912) and composer Antun Dobronic (1878-1955).

The Tor – Greek Tower

About a one hour hike from Jelsa is what remains of the Greek Tower Tor, dating back to the fourth century BC. Situated 230m above sea level, the hike is worth it for the view alone, with the ancient watchtower offering spectacular views of not only Jelsa, but but also Vrboska and the Split and Makarska coastline. There are unfinished walls and man-made terraces around the tower, suggesting that it was also living quarters.

Galesnik – Medieval Town
Close by is what remains of the Medieval town of Galesnik. Some 210m above sea level, the fortress is twenty metres wide and is surrounded by a wall 80m long, 4m high and 50-60cm thick. The enclosed area is approximately 1,520m2, and the rectangular building, about 40m2, is partially preserved.

Most of the buildings are a leisurely walk from the pjaca and can be inspected at leisure. This is Dalmatia after all, where the main holiday activity tends to be lazing in the sun people watching over a cappuccino or two.

Vrboska

Top 5 Things to do in Vrboska

1. The Vrboska Wine Experience
Vrboska is a great place to explore the Hvar wine story, with two members of the Hvar Wine Association located in the village. In the heart of the old town, in a street behind the fortress church, lies one of the most authentic konobas on the island, Pinjata, which has vast experience of wine tourism,and will take you back in time, with cheese and a glass of the local varieties. In contrast, and opened on the canal last year is the Caric tasting experience, one of Croatia's most exciting wine producers (see wine section), a chance to sample some of Croatia's top-rated wines (which are exported to California).

2. Visit the Top of the Fortress Church

There is only one building which dominate Vrboska – the imperious and unique church fortress in the centre of the town (see below). After years of being closed to tourists, it is now possible to visit at certain times during the day (check with the Vrboska Tourist Board to be absolutely sure), and a climb up the narrow steps to the church's roof is rewarded by a spectacular view of the deep Vrboska bay, and an insight into what it must have been like as a guard watching the invading forces or pirates approaching...

3. The Fishermen's Museum

Founded in 1972 with the aim of preserving Vrboska's rich fishing tradition, the Fisherman's Museum has an interesting collection of traditional fishing nets, tools and equipment, as well as tools from the old fish processing factory. There is also a fascinating insight into the harsh conditions of life in a reconstructed fisherman's house. It is located on the waterfront of the old town. Check with the Vrboska Tourist Board for 2016 opening times.

4. A Walk along Little Venice

One of the most striking parts of Hvar is the canal in Vrboska. Known as 'Little Venice' because of it, the canal takes one away from the centre of town and into a haven of waterfront tranquillity. On the canal are two delightful stone bridges, a picture postcard moment. On the left of the last bridge, check out the stonework by the water – this is where the village women in years gone by came to wash their clothes.

5. Coffee in Jelsa, One of Hvar's Prettiest Walks

Vrboska is a safe and relaxed place, where the pace of life is decidedly on the slower side. It is why people some to do not very much, but if you are feeling somewhat energetic, the 35-minute walk to Jelsa, some 3km away, is one of the nicest walks on the island. There are plenty of enticing coves on this coastal walk,

120

which meanders round pretty little bays. Take your swimming things just in case you are tempted... And once in Jelsa, enjoy the feeling of 'the big city' with a coffee or ice cream on the main square before making the slow road home. A relaxing and affordable way to relax for a few hours.

An Overview of Vrboska Restaurants

Sailing into one of Hvar's prettiest towns and home to the main marina on the island can build up quite an appetite, an there are several bars and restaurants on the waterfront offering refreshment to tourists. Here is a quick overview.

Restaurant Lem
Located on the corner of the main bridge opposite the old town and next to the town's very helpful tourist office, Restaurant Lem has arguably the best location to enjoy a refreshing drink, as its south-facing orientation and stunning view of the old town make it an ideal place to while away an afternoon.

An additional bonus for families is the town's play area which is adjacent to the restaurant, while the wooden donkey (for guests only) is popular with children. Traditional Dalmatian fare with a large salad bar, there is ample space both outside and in the nicely restored interior. With the town's playground located nearby, it is an ideal place for families.

Luka
Away from the water and slightly elevated, Gardelin offers romantic views of the marina and beyond, a perfect setting to watch the to-ing and fro-ing of the active yachting community. Grab an outside table as close to the view as possible, and fish lovers will delight in the excellent fish platter. The restaurant can be reached via some steps on the way to the marina, or by car via a sharp right turn leaving Vrboska towards Jelsa.

Bonaca

121

Perdectly positioned for the incoming yachting community next to the marina, Bonaca is an excellent fish restaurant with extremely welcoming hosts. Excellent fish as one would expect so close to the sea, and the upstairs terrace area is both spacious and leafy, affording excellent views over the marina. A special location.

Skojic
Popular with the small expat population, Skojic is the only restaurant on the water in the old town. With a pleasant open courtyard and ample interior space, the pizzas are particularly good, and the restaurant is usually open at weekends throughout the year.

Soline
Tourists heading for the most popular beach just outside Vrboska, Soline, can eat at the restaurant of the same name. Pasta, pizza and local Dalmatian dishes provide sufficient sustenance to enable sun-worshippers to continue their main activity without returning to the town for lunch.

Paparazzi, Dalmatino
There are a number of cafes dotted along the old town's front, where the art of coffee drinking is taken seriously. Two of the best are Papparazzi, a favourite local hangout, which also serves Guinness, and Dalmatino, just above the Konsum supermarket. Lovers of German *Weissbier* will be pleased with the Erdinger on offer. Dalmatino has free wireless and the nicely restored stone interior and comfortable seating make it a popular destination in winter.

Things to See

Vrboska boasts a well-preserved old town, with a good selection of cafes and restaurants on the waterfront. While away from the water, the most impressive building is the church/fort of St. Mary, which dominates the central square of the old town. It dates from the 16th century and was constructed by the people of Vrboska as a fortification against the Turks. Recently renovated, its most curious feature is the giant stone triangular fortification which juts out from one corner of the church. There are other, smaller churches to be discovered in the narrow and atmospheric back streets, but the town's fishing museum, situated on the waterfront, is also worth investigating. The museum has exhibits of traditional fishing equipment, as well as tools for the fish processing plant, and even a reconstruction of an old fisherman's house, giving an idea of how tough life was for the Dalmatian fisherman.

Hvar's smallest town is also known as Little Venice, but tourists expecting a gondola ride will be disappointed as the only canal peters out soon after disappearing from view from the centre of the town. It is an extremely pleasant walk, however, with some picturesque foot bridges, as well as various original features such as the steps down to the stone plateau after the last bridge, where clothes used to be hand washed.

With the growing foreign interest in Croatian tourism, more boat owners are choosing to base their boats year round in Croatia, and the ACI Marina in Vrboska has been experiencing a boom and has expanded its capacity to cope with the increased demand.

Situated metres from Vrboska's historic old town and protected from the Maestral and Bura winds, the ACI Marina is an ever more popular place to for long-term mooring. The facilities are excellent and include a gas station, five ton crane, restaurant, repair shop, laundry service, toilets and showers. There are 85 berths and 25 boat places on land, with water and electric connections to all berths.

The Vrboska marina has been awarded the European Blue Flag, in recognition of the community's effort to maintain the cleanliness of the local beaches and marinas. It is open all year and demand is very high in peak season.

With sixteen marinas along the coast, ACI has by far the biggest network in Croatia, and sailors planning to spend more time on the Adriatic may want to consider ACI membership through the ACI Card, which is available to boat owners with an annual berthing or land storage contract.

Benefits of the card include: a 10% discount on daily berth rates throughout the year in any ACI marina; 50% off daily and monthly land storage rates; three days free mooring for holders of a land storage contract; and one high pressure wash of the boat's undercarriage per year.

While one can swim in the village opposite the marina, a much more popular option is Soline beach, a pleasant ten-minute walk through the pines. This wide beach of small pebbles is an extremely popular place for families, with its child-friendly approach and facilities. There are also various sporting facilities, including a volleyball court, and windsurfing can also be organised. Thirsty tourists can avail themselves of the bar, or grab a bite to eat at the restaurant. There is ample (paid) parking in the pine forests or why not hop on the daily train from Jelsa via Vrboska which terminates at Soline?

On the northern side of the Glavica peninsula is one of Croatia's most popular nudist beaches. Parking in the same place as Soline, the beach is a 5-10 minute walk through the pine trees to a more private beach comprised of rocks. Although there is no shade, many of the rocks are isolated, making it ideal for naturism. More adventurous naturists may want to check out the tiny island of Zecevo nearby.

Vrboska is also popular as a naturist holiday due to the nudist campsite, which is located 1km from the town close to the naturist beach. The camp has a capacity for 420 guests and facilities on site include restaurant, shop, gas service and various sporting activities.

Sucuraj

I am not an expert on Sucuraj. Although I am have been there
hundreds of times over the years, the main reason sadly is to catch
the ferry. I am therefore indebted to Ante Modric, who runs the
excellent independent website www.sucuraj.com for the following
overview:

Sućuraj is a small picturesque tourist and fishermen's town.
Located on the East cape of the island of Hvar (central Dalmatia,
Croatia), it is surrounded by the sea on three sides and is closest
to the mainland. There are 357 inhabitants in the town living
mostly from tourism, fishing and agriculture. The town evolved
around a deep and narrow bay in which the port lies. The main
parts of Sućuraj are named Gornja Banda (Upper Side) and Donja
Banda (Lower Side). Gornja Banda is located on a slight slope
north of the port and Donja Banda is located on the south side of
the peninsula. The architecture is typical Dalmatian with stone
houses and narrow streets. The place gets its charm from the
combination of blue seas of the Hvar and Children's playground
in the park in the center of SucurajNeretva cannel as well as the
view of the Biokovo Mountain, Peljesac peninsula and the islands
of Brac and Korcula.

Sućuraj is the center of the Municipality of Sućuraj, which also
includes the village of Bogomolje. The town has an elementary
school, a post office, infirmary with the heliport for emergencies,
local Port authority office, souvenirs shops, grocery shops,
restaurants, bars, a hairdresser salon, exchange office, ATM and
tourist info office. More information about Sućuraj:

Thanks to a climate with long sunny days, beautiful scenery,
crystal clear sea and temperatures suitable for swimming from
May to October, makes Sućuraj an attractive tourist destination.
All of those who want to spend the day swimming and or

sunbathing will find the place most enjoyable thanks to its more than 25 km of coastline with sandy, pebble or rocky beaches and bays.

The island of Hvar (and also Sućuraj) is well known for its mild Mediterranean climate and record number of sunny hours. The summers are dry, warm and long, and the winters are mild and short so the temperatures below 0°C are very rare. Thanks to such a mild climate, the flora and fauna surrounding Sućuraj is lush and diverse.

Tourism development started in Sućuraj at the beginning of the 1960s. Hospitable people offer their guests accommodation in numerous beautiful private apartments, boarding houses (pensions), holiday houses and rooms and in motor camp in the Mlaska bay, located 4 km from the town center. Gastronomically there is an excellent choice of restaurants, inns and taverns in Sućuraj which include traditionally local specialties such as fish, crabs, shellfish, wine and olive oil, as well as a range of meats and vegetarian dishes. There is also a pizzeria and an ice-cream parlour at your disposal.

Entertainment and culture
For those who wish to enjoy a relaxing pace and escape the noise, crowds and hustle and bustle of everyday life, Sućuraj is an ideal location. The pleasure is guaranteed, whether you enjoy a stroll through Sućuraj's narrow streets, a seaside walk, having your morning coffee or a refreshing drink. In the evening one can find entertainment in bars, occasional fishermen's night, and for those who prefer rock and electronic music, Sućuraj hosts the Tam Tam Music Festival. In the summer months there are some exhibitions and plays by traveling theater troupes.

Archaeological finds testify of life in this area from the antiquities. The most important historical sights in Sućuraj are: The Franciscan monastery (once Augustinian) from the 9th

126

century, the fort from 1613, St. Anthony's church from 1663, the lighthouse from 1889 and St. George's church from 1897, with the foundation of a much older church in its front yard. More details about history here, and about sights here.

Excursions
During the tourist season there are daily boat trips. You can visit the Makarska coastline, Peljesac peninsula and the island of Korcula. The rest of the island of Hvar is best visited by car, but there is a bus and or taxi services available. The vicinity to the mainland and good transport links make one-day trips to Split, Dubrovnik and numerous other destinations in Dalmatia and Herzegovina possible. You can also rent a small boat, bicycle, scooter or car in Sućuraj.

Those who love cycling, running and hiking can enjoy more than 40 km of paths and for those who love diving and fishing there is a lot of coastline available. Local football club Mladost has its own soccer field also available for all who wish to play.

Fishing and agriculture
The people of Sućuraj are known to be skilled fishermen, olive and wine growers and the tradition remains to this day. More details about fishing here, and about agriculture here.

The Drvenik – Sucuraj Ferry Route
For many, the main reason to visit Sucuraj is to enter or leave the island, and the regular half-hour crossing to the mainland at Drvenik is a very useful option for visitors heading up the coast. There are several crossings a day in winter and the schedule is increased in the tourist season.

Although a car ferry, vehicle capacity is only 32 cars, a number that can be reduced further with caravans in season, and there can be long queues in peak season. The good news is that two ferries will operate in tandem to cope with peak demand, but waiting times can be long. One tip which seems to work at the busiest time is to take the first ferry, leaving at 0630. It should be noted that the first petrol station on the island is 56km away in Jelsa.

Where to Eat

Life revolves around the pretty little harbour which has several good spots to laze away an afternoon watching the ferries go back and forth. Walking round the harbour towards the ferry are two pleasant restaurants with good fish and a typical Dalmatian menu – Gusarska Luka and Vlaka, while the walk to the lighthouse, where most of the beaches are, passes pizzerias Mizzarila and Guido and restaurant Fortica. The other place to try for a bite is Pansion Ivan, which has a small restaurant in addition to the apartments for rent.

Edge Capital and Nikki Beach Hotels

Although currently little more than a transit point for traffic heading to the bigger resorts on western Hvar, Sucuraj's profile may be about to change with the development of a luxury complex close to the town. Norwegian company Edge Capital and the Nikki Beach hotel group are in partnership to develop an exclusive resort on 80,000m2 of land, transforming the fortunes of the area.

In a recent interview, the Norwegian Ambassador Henrick Ofstad, said that "the decision was taken to build a large resort in Sucuraj, something similar to which only exists in Cannes. The project is mutually beneficial, as it will provide many jobs." The project, valued at 270 million euro and bringing 500 permanent jobs, has been stuck in bureaucracy for years now, but it is edging forward slowly. As they say in Dalmatia, pomalo...

CHAPTER 5: THE VILLAGES OF HVAR

The understandable tendency of most tourists on the island is to stick to the coastal towns, and with plenty to do and great beaches and nightlife readily accessible, it is not hard to understand why, but if you want to get a better feel for Dalmatian traditions and culture, as well as experience Hvar's spectacular nature close up, there is nothing like renting a scooter or car to explore the surprising diversity of village life on the island. The villages can be loosely grouped into those west of the Stari Grad Tunnel, the central belt towards Jelsa, and the largely undiscovered villages and bays of eastern Hvar.

Western Hvar to the Tunnel

Those looking to explore what is on offer to the north of Hvar Town past the fortress will find plenty of beauty, but little habitation. For here is pristine natural Hvar, where few people roam despite the close proximity of the island's largest town. Here, if you have access, you can see wildlife such as mouflon, enclosed in a large hunting area given to private concession, There are idyllic bays such as Pribinja, where Ringo's offers exquisite seafood, one of the best-rated restaurants on the island, a bay overlooked by the organic vineyards of Andro Tomic. Here too, you will find Camp Vira, the premier camping experience on Hvar, as well as perhaps the most spectactular setting for a restaurant on the island – Panorama – which, as its name suggests, offers fantastic 360 views of the area, including a bird's eye's view of the Pakleni Islands. A nice backdrop to some consistently good Dalmatian fare. But for villages, we must head east... Starting with the fast new road.

Milna and Malo Grablje
If you are looking for a snapshot of traditional Hvar, spend a little time in these two villages, for they are totally different, and yet so

inextricably linked. Now with helpful signposting, Malo Grablje is for me one of the most hauntingly beautiful places in Damatia, a totally abandoned village, whose church has celebrated just one wedding in 50 years, and that a German...

Let's start with the legend, and who knows, perhaps there is some truth to it. We are back to the 16th century, and an illegitimate son of Henry VIII is shipwrecked off southern Hvar, and he manages to swim ashore to the nearby bay of Milna, where a beautiful maiden is washing clothes. Despite the language barrier, love blossoms, and the two young lovers move inland, hidden from the pirates, and found the village of Malo Grablje. Their legacy is in the surname of each and every owner of property in the village, a most un-Croatian name – Tudor.

Myth or reality? Who knows, but enjoy a bottle of the excellent local wine at one of Milna's excellent seafront restaurants, and then check out the features of some of the local owners. Perhaps there is something to the story after all...

What makes Malo Grablje all the more fascinating for me is what happened in the second half of the last century. I have never quite got the full story, but the entire village decided to move the 3km to Milna on the coast. Tourism was starting, livelihoods from fishing were to be had, and off they went, digging up their dead and taking the corpses with them for reburial in Milna. The graves were still open when I last visited several years ago.

In the property boom of 2004, EVERYTHING was for sale on Hvar, and trade was brisk. Locals could not believe their luck when Brits were offering tens of thousands for goat sheds. Just one village, one of the most beautiful of all, refused to sell. You guessed it – Malo Grablje. And in case the Tudor surname is familiar to some of you football fans, yes, Igor Tudor, the Juventus legend, comes from Grablje, and today has a house in Milna.

True or not, I heard a story soon after I moved to Hvar that an Italian film producer had offered a large sum of money to have the village as a filmset for a period of time, an offer which included renovation – an offer which was refused.

What is certain is that Malo Grablje is hauntingly beautiful, and despite being totally abandoned, it does have one of the best – and most authentic – restaurants on Hvar, Stori Komin. Just try the lamb. But not before walking around the village and breathing in its unique atmosphere – a truly mysterious place.

Milna on the other hand could not be more different, a thriving modern seafront community, albeit with a small historic centre, where many swear the best seafood on Hvar is to be found. What is for certain is that there are a string of excellent seafood restaurants offering their version of waterfront heaven. Enjoy a hearty lunch then jump in the Adriatic for a swim, then come back for more. The Milna experience is understandably a favourite for many, and numerous fiercely loyal tourists return year on year. With plenty of accommodation on offer, it is a great base for a beach family holiday, for the two beaches there are spacious and child-friendly.

Restaurants to look out for on the water include Milina Kod Barbe Bozjeg and Moli Onte at the end, but the real gem in recent years has been set back from the water – Lambik. And if the main beach is crowded when you arrive, turn right and walk a little to sample the delights of Mala Milna beach, with accompanying restaurants. A Milna sunset is something not to be missed.

Zarace
For some, the most perfect place on the planet, and Zarace certainly has its charms. It comes in two parts – the upper village above the main road, whose stone houses have been partially restored over the years. Turn right and head down the winding path to the water, and discover two excellent waterfront

restaurants overlooking an idyllic bay. And Zarace is unique in that the quite bizarre stong formations on either side give it natural protection. So picturesque is it that the village has been used as a filmset. And it is also home to local musical celebrity, Gego.

Dubovica

Slightly further along and just before the tunnel and new 'road' to Sveta Nedjelja is one of the jewels of Hvar, considered to be one of its best locations by many visitors. Dubovica is a small settlement with a big reputation, for its beach, pretty stone houses almost in the water, and superb informal restaurant, Taverna Dubovica. With its imperious main house jutting out into the water, Dubovica is a picture postcard, and it regularly features in lists of the best beaches in Europe.

A word on Dubovica if you are thinking of visiting. There is no road access, and the walk down is a little off the beaten path. Parking is on the main road, but it can get busy in season, and take care with passing traffic when you park. Dubovica is the last village before the tunnel to Stari Grad, but a new road – passable but only with a strong stomach and good car – is now open to Sveta Nedjelja on the south side. Should the road ever get finished, it will be a great time saver for tourists wanting to visit the central villages on Hvar's southern side.

Brusje, Velo Grablje and Selca

The other way to reach Stari Grad from Hvar Town is on the old road, and for those experiencing vertigo on the journey, spare a thought for the fact that until the new road opened in 2001, this was THE road from Hvar Town to Stari Grad, complete with Italian caravans and impatient Germans in their Mercedes. We have come a long way.

The road is one of my favourite places on Hvar, a true escape from the pressures of life (as long as vertigo is not your thing),

and it is the route of the annual half-marathon, surely one of the
most outstanding runs in the world. The views of the Adriatic
from both north and south (and you can actually choose your sea
view by table at Konoba Vidikovac, the only restaurant on the
route) are amazing, as are the patchwork stone terracing that has
been painstakingly done over the generations – a true work of art,
and testament to how unforgiving the land can be. In June and
July of course, the area blooms with lavender, and don't be
surprised to see several cars parked by the side of the road, their
drivers making selfies in the lavender fields.

Velo Grablje is covered in a bit more detail in the introduction to
this guide under 'Village in Focus', and Brusje (the donkey capital
of Hvar) and Selca are both beautiful to wander around, but have
little else to offer tourists in terms of facilities, although both offer
holiday accommodation if you are looking to escape the masses.
Divine villages both.

Central Hvar

The villages of central Hvar fall into three categories – north,
central and south – and each has its own individual character.
Starting in the north...

Basina and Mudri Dolac
While the majority of tourists on the northern coast of Hvar head
for the historic towns of Stari Grad, Vrboska and Jelsa, the little
village of Basina has a loyal following of regular guests, attracted
by the quieter pace of life and excellent views.

Almost deserted in winter, the village comes alive in summer as
many owners open up their holiday homes either for rental or
personal use. It is also a popular stopping off point for sailors,
who are attracted by the village's three inlets, excellent swimming
and good restaurant.

The village consists mostly of holiday homes and, like Ivan

133

Dolac, there are plenty of accommodation offers on the web, but independent transport remains an issue, as there is no bus service to the village. Basina is situated about 4km from both Vrboska and Stari Grad, so it is possible to walk. A little shop is operational in season for essential supplies, with the supermarkets in the towns the best option for a more comprehensive shop.

To reach Basina, take the main Stari Grad to Jelsa road and turn left at the sign for the village, then continue for about 2km and a right turn takes a sharp descent into the village and down to the water.

Stonehouse Hvar: An Exclusive Stone Complex
Clearly visible through the pine forests above Basina from many points of the island is the ambitious Stonehouse Hvar project, an exclusive stone complex with accommodation for 22 in individual stone buildings of great character.

With luxury features such as a sauna and infinity pool and one of the most striking terrace views on Hvar, the complex is being restored with attention to authentic detail. Construction is currently on hold and the original investor is open to sale or co-investment. Once completed, Stonehouse Hvar will be one of the most exclusive destinations on the island.

The Village of Mudri Dolac
Driving past the turning for Basina, the road eventually comes to the tiny fishing village of Mudri Dolac, where a local family has built a small but modern camsite, with showers, toilets and 10 plots under pergolas of vines. There is also a restaurant, where fish caught by the owner appears regularly on the menu.

Both Mudri Dolac and Basina have the great advantage of being off the beaten track but very close to the main tourist centres, and only a ten-minute drive from the main Stari Grad ferry.

The Hilltop Villages

While most visitors to the island of Hvar base themselves close to the beach, a growing number of visitors looking to experience authentic Dalmatia are heading to the hills to the six inland villages that form the central spine of the island.

Much quieter than the coastal resorts, the inland villages offer a more peaceful alternative in a traditional stone environment, and an opportunity to view daily life in a typical Dalmatian community without the tourist hordes. While several of the villages feature on the infamous 22km Easter Procession, the main tourism focus is more understated, focusing on nature, walking and general relaxation. Here is a quick overview of the villages.

Pitve - 2000 Years of Tradition

One of the oldest settlements on Hvar and with an enviable view overlooking Jelsa and the neighbouring island of Brac, Pitve has long been a popular spot for tourists looking for authentic Dalmatia. The village comes in two parts, Lower and Upper Pitve, separated by the church and cemetery, and property was much sought after in the 2004 property boom, as foreigners flocked to buy traditional stone houses in the village.

According to the 2001 census, the full time population is 81, much reduced from the 756 people living there in 1921. One of the more curious features in recent history is the large sky blue building as the road bends on the way to Upper Pitve. It was a fully-functioning, very lively and infinitely popular nightclub, with youths from Jelsa and beyond heading up the hills at the weekend. The last time this correspondent was inside, five years ago, there were unopened cans of lager on the bar, best before 1999…

Lower Pitve has an excellent restaurant, Dvor Dubokovic, and many tourists pass through on the way to the Pitve – Zavala tunnel.

135

Vrisnik - Village of Heather

A winding road through vineyards and olive groves leads to the village of Vrisnik, named after the local heather, with the parish church of Sv. Ante towering above all. Built on the hillside, the views of Vrisnik from the road to Svirce are stunning.

Vrisnik is linked to the eco-village of Humac, a stunning abandoned shepherd's settlement, 10km east of Vrisnik, one of the undiscovered delights of Croatia, with villagers owning land and property in both places. The local restaurant, Konoba Vrisnik, has been attracting diners away from the more fashionable coastal restaurants with its excellent traditional fare.

Vrisnik is olive oil country, and just outside the village is the 'hacienda' of Borivoj Bojanic, who offers an alternative dining experience surrounded by olive trees and striking views of the surrounding villages and Adriatic beyond. And a little-known fact about Vrisnik and its olive oil is that it is officially the most expensive in the world! An enterprising American businessmen added gold flakes to 0.2l bottles of olive oil and packaged them superbly, before Harrod's of London offered them for sale at £750 each. Only 444 bottles were produced in this exclusive offer. All sold out...

Svirce - Wine and Oil Heaven

A short drive on from Vrisnik lies Svirce, nestled at the foot of Sv. Nikola, the highest point on Hvar (and a worthwhile trip for stunning panoramic views). It is the heart of wine production on the island with the biggest winery on the island – the Svirce Cooperative – whose organic Ivan Dolac Barrique has won organic gold two years running at Biofach Mundus Vini in Germany. There is a hive of activity in Svirce in autumn as local olive farmers bring their harvest to be processed at the village's large olive press. And here too, we find quality olive oil, but this time the gold is in medals – and as far away as New York – for the Bozic family. The winery and olive mill are the last buildings in the village, on either side of the road, as you head to Vrisnik.

One of the most curious churches in Dalmatia can be found at the entrance to Svirce: built in the 18th Century, the Mary Magdalene Church has an atypical dome and is surrounded by cypress trees and the local cemeteries, and is worthy of investigation. Stop for a spot of lunch at the excellent Kod None, before walking up the hill to discover the heart of the old village, set out around the pretty main square.

And in such a tranquil village, what would you expect to find but... a biker's club of course! It has been on my list for years, but I have never quite got there. From concerts to pole dancing, the mind boggles what goes on it there, and I WILL make it one day.

Vrbanj - Largest Village on Hvar
The largest village on Hvar, Vrbanj is undergoing something of a renaissance. It boasts some extra facilities to attract visitors, including a bus connection to the ferry, post office, bars and an excellent restaurant,Konoba Boga.

A curious recent addition by the garishly painted priest's house is a model village and miniature lake which is a source of entertainment for small children, while it is also possible to catch a game of balota, the local equivalent of boules, on the main road. The model village has recently been joined by a souvenir shop with flashing red lights. Vrbanj is known locally as Texas.

Dol – Yoga, Painting and Edible Dormice
For those not feeling relaxed enough, drive on 2km to Little Marrakesh, as Dol is known locally. It is really two villages in one and has proved a popular place for foreigners to claim a slice of Dalmatian tranquility. The views to the Stari Grad channel are spectacular, as is the organic food in Konoba Kokot.

A growing attraction in the village of Dol is the Suncokret Body and Soul Retreat, run by an American-Croatian couple, and specialising in yoga and meditation techniques, as well as offering a wide range of original activities to bring alive the Dalmatian experience. The tranquil ambience of Atelier Marinka is one of Hvar's true secrets (see Activities for Kids). There is also a very pleasant bar in Dol called Trocadero.

August is peak season on Hvar and while the perceived wisdom is that the main action is in Hvar Town and the Pakleni Islands, those in the know will be heading in their hundreds to the playground by St. Ana church in Dol for the annual Dolska Puhijada, cultural programme which concludes with a night of revelry and feasting on the 'puh', or edible dormouse.

The event, organised by local NGO Tartajun is now a week-long and celebrates many aspects of Dol culture and tradition, including the Dol Open balota tournament (the island equivalent of boules), wine tasting, art exhibitions, children's games and concerts for kids and adults, an exhibition of the puh in its natural environment, before the festival's conclusion, a night of revelry, with fire-eaters, jugglers and feasting on the puh.

And what, pray, is a puh? An edible dormouse which lives on the island. Voracious eaters, their early winter weight can be double the summer weight. Edible dormice can jump up to 7 metres when moving from tree to tree, and their hunting is a specialised skill. A raucous evening not to be missed and the 'I went to Hvar for a Full Moon Party and all I got was a Lousy Dormouse Festival' t-shirt concession is still available. This year's festival is in August – check the Tartajun website for more information closer to the time – www.tartajun.hr.

If dormice aren't your thing, there is plenty on offer at the excellent Konoba Kokot, where much of the food is produced by the family themselves.

The Kabal Peninsula

The peninsula is a tranquil place, almost devoid of human habitation, and an excellent place to enjoy a peaceful vacation, while being close to civilisation, with the port town of Stari Grad a two kilometre walk down the hill.

There are two villages on the peninsula, Velika Rudina and Mala Rudina (literally Big and Little Rudina), with Velika Rudina the central hub of activity, with a full time population of nineteen, of which seven are children of school age. Local parents are hoping for an increase in child numbers, as the State provides a free school bus service for villages with ten pupils or more.

Velika Rudina is known as 'Little Bosnia' and is a sociable and welcoming place, popular with Bosnians who have holiday homes in the area. Unusually for the island, the majority of the house is relatively newly built, although there is a small central square with traditional stone housing. The main employer in the village is the local fish processing factory, which employs people from the village, Stari Grad and beyond.

Driving from Stari Grad onto the peninsula, the road forks and a right turn will eventually arrive in the tiny hamlet of Mala Rudina, an exquisite stone hamlet with a full-time population of two. There are perhaps a dozen authentic stone houses assembled around a pretty courtyard. Real estate is sought after in this peaceful setting, with one stone ruin changing hands three times in 18 months in 2004-5, from an initial sales price of €43,000 to €150,000.

The main real estate story on the peninsula until recently are the Male Rudine villas, billed as the ultimate in luxury villa accommodation during the Croatian property boom. Billed as a unique luxury villa complex, complete with individual swimming pools, the almost-finished development is deteriorating slowly, a symbol of the collapse of the Croatian property market.

A much bigger real estate story could be about to start, however, as Four Seasons Hotels are planning to open a five-star hotel and build up to 100 villas in a bay where they have bought 16 hectares of land. After years of battling bureaucracy, it would appear that things are moving forward. Stay tuned...

An essential part of any Croatian island holiday is a trip to the beach, and the Rudine peninsula has much to offer in this regard. While beaches in the main resorts can get overcrowded in the season, this is rarely the case on the peninsula, as it is off the beaten track. The most popular beach is at Zukova, a few minutes' walk from Velika Rudina, while Kabal on the other side is also worth trying. For the more adventurous beach hunters, the rough track heading north out of Velika Rudina travels the 12km to the head of the peninsula, and there are many pretty beaches and coves to be discovered, although access is not always easy.

Tourists who do make the trek to the head of the peninsula are rewarded by a curious man-made attraction – tunnels created on orders by Tito to defend the island from attack. They are positioned at the top of the Stari Grad channel and can be seen from the ferry on the left as the ferry approaches the port. Apart from being a fun thing to investigate, the sunsets from the tunnel parapets are among the best on the island. To reach them, drive through Velika Rudina and continue 12km to the top of the peninsula, where you will see the word 'Tunel' painted on a rock.

Through the Pitve Tunnel

The tunneling through the rock to open the Pitve Tunnel in 2013 was not only a feat of engineering and one of the scariest tunnel rides in Europe, all 1.4km of it, but it opened up the south of the island for tourism. And how the South took advantage. For all the charms of the towns of the island, many tourists head straight for the southern side of the island.

Zavala

The southern coast of the island of Hvar has long been a favourite for many tourists, with its excellent swimming, numerous beaches and superb views of the islands of Korcula, Vis and Scedro. Far from the more crowded resorts of Hvar Town and Jelsa, it is a great place to relax, with the village of Zavala proving to be one of the more popular destinations.

Originally a small stone village in the hills, whose residents eked out a harsh existence from wine, olives and fishing, Zavala's fortunes were transformed with the construction of the Pitve-Zavala tunnel which began in 1962 as a means of transporting water to the south side. The resulting tunnel was then used for regular traffic, providing a lifeline link to the more developed parts of the island for local residents, as well as much easier access for tourists. The opening of a second road from Hvar to Sveta Nedelja recently has further improved access.

The old stone village has been expanded considerably with the addition of newer housing closer to the beaches and the village location was much sought after in the property boom of 2004. Sloping vineyards from the island's peak provide a stunning backdrop as the road winds to the small jetty and main beach at Zavala, a small pebbly affair, suitable for children and equipped with cafe and a pizzeria. Tourists wishing to visit neighbouring Scedro can take a boat transfer from the jetty. Ivo Jakas who has the restaurant Kod Ive has a taxi boat. Pre and post season there is one departure at 10 am, high season departures at 10 and 11. In both cases returns are by arrangement. There is a great little pizza place called Bistro Davor, which is just 7m from the beach, with ample parking. Other places worth checking out are Cafe bar/fast food Zaca, Restaurant hotel Skalinada & Beach bar Terra Nova and Villa Stella Mare.

As of this summer there will be speed boats for rent (daily and weekly, small and big), and SUP paddle boards (contact the owner for details- Slovenian guy, Damjan - 0994012095).

Gromin Dolac
One of the most picturesque and largely abandoned stone villages
on Hvar – Gromin Dolac – is only accessible by road from
Zavala. Coming through the village, the road swings round to the
right with a large church on the corner. Immediately after the turn,
there is a sharp turn to the left onto a rough road which leads to
Gromin Dolac. Lovers of old stone villages will enjoy the serene
setting and ruins. Although largely deserted, it is possible to find
accommodation there – a Belgian national has bought a house
there and welcomes guests through the Couchsurfing website
when he is there, usually in summer.

Zavala and Gromin Dolac are all about the beaches and the sun,
both of which it has in abundance.

The Island of Scedro
A hidden delight is the island of Scedro, which sits in splendid
isolation off the southern coast, opposite the popular resort of
Zavala.

There are two theories surrounding the origin of the island's
name, which the Romans renamed Tauris, both with Slavonic
origins. The old Slavonic word *stedri*, meaning "charitable" refers
to the two deep bays, Veli Porat and Mostir, which have offered
shelter to ships for almost 2,000 years, while *scedrota* means
"lovely" or "delightful," both words which can be used to describe
this pretty island 2.7km from Zavala.

Apart from enjoying the island's outstanding natural beauty, the
main tourist site is the remnants of a Dominican monastery in
Mostir, which dates back to 1465 and was finally abandoned in
the 18th Century, as the problems of piracy became too great.

Living on Scedro since the early 20th Century, the Kordic family are the only family who live almost all year round on Scedro, and they offer a unique accommodation package allowing tourists to experience the island through local eyes.

Visitors have the opportunity to see local life as a fisherman, wine and olive grower or bee keeper, as the family goes about its daily business. The majority of the excellent food on offer in the standard half-board package is grown or caught by the family, and includes a decent line in wine and *rakija*, the local firewater.

Accommodation is basic by necessity, as there is no electricity or mains water on Scerdo, but a limited electrical supply is available through the family's solar systems, while drinking water from a well is available. There are no problems charging phones and laptops. What may be sacrificed in creature comforts is more than compensated for in stunning sunsets and excellent hospitality on a large terrace.

Scedro is most easily reached from Zavala by water taxi (see Zavala, above)

Ivan Dolac
First mentioned in the 15th century, the old stone village of Ivan Dolac still exists above the main road, but most visitors turn left into the heart of the new village and keep going until they hit the beach, for that is Ivan Dolac's main attraction: quality family beaches on the island's southern shore.
Beaches such as Suplja Stina, Lucisce, Jagodna, Paklina and Petarcica have proved popular with tourists, many of whom return every year to the same places and host families.

Apart from the main towns of Jelsa, Stari Grad and Hvar Town, Ivan Dolac has the widest selection of rental accommodations on the Internet, with owners offering a combination of clean apartments, terrace views of the sea and easy access to the beach. Campers can pitch their tents at the family-run Camp Paklina on the beach.

For such a popular resort, facilities are somewhat lacking. While there is a shop for bare essentials, the nearest supermarket for shopping is in Jelsa, a 20 minute drive away.

The place to chill in Ivan Dolac is Vartal, a cocktail bar on the water, with friendly atmosphere, great cocktails and spectacular views, while recommended dining is Slavinka, where the homely atmosphere will be one of the first things you notice. A cafe, restaurant and apartments. There is a small supermarket, exchange office and tourist agency. Check out also the Big Blue lounge bar and Restaurant Spila.

Some of the wines in Ivan Dolac are among the best on the island, a combination of skilled wine-making and the sun-drenched south-facing southern vineyards, with the red wine from the *plavac mali* grape particularly worth trying.

The Deserted Stone Village of Jagodna
Shortly after Ivan Dolac and high above the sloping vineyard that are a feature of the southern coast is the deserted stone village of Jagodna, one of the prettiest and most unspoiled villages on the island. Largely a collection of stone buildings in various stages of disrepair, the small church has been recently renovated. It is possible to reach Jagodna by car, although the road is rough and a four-wheel drive is advisable. The journey is worth it for the spectacular elevated views on offer.

Sveta Nedjelja
Sveta Nedjelja is wine country. The small village on Hvar's south coast is dominated by the vineyards and winery of Zlatan Plenkovic, one of Croatia's most famous producers and a regular medal winner in international competitions.

From the sloping vineyards on the steep hills leading down from

144

Svetia Nikola, the island's highest peak at 621m, to the unique restaurant and jetty on the waterfront, the mark of the Zlatan Otok brand is visible throughout the village.

In addition to produce excellent wines, the Plenkovic winery also runs a guest house and restaurant on the small marina. The stone cone-shaped building is unique in its design and a good setting for the fish and meat dishes to accompany the Plenkovic range of wines. Boats up to 18m in length and 4m in draught are able to moor at the marina, according to the Zlatan Otok website, making it an attractive stopping off point for those sailing round the southern coast.

The Bilo Idro restaurant is open daily from 0900-0100 from May 15 and October 15 and its offer includes the choice of live crab and lobster from a sea pool, while wine tastings are easily arranged and include an underwater cellar with sub-marine view. As you descend the road to the water, there is a sign to the left for One other restaurant worth seeking out called Tamaris, a seafront restaurant with large terraces, traditional fare and easy access for swimming, a great place to laze away an afternoon. It is access by a sharp left turn along a dirt track as the main road winds to the jetty.

"I loved your guidebook, very useful, but there was nothing in your guidebook about the church in the cave," exclaimed one Sveta Nedjelja resident to me recently.

I had never heard of a church in a cave but went off to investigate, and sure enough, she was right. Below the mountain's peak of Sveti Nikola (621m), there is a cave in which the Augustinian monks built a church and monastery in the 15th century and stayed there until 1787. The remains of the church can still be seen today, and the hike is among the most spectacular on the island.

Access to Sveta Nedjelja, which literally means "Holy Sunday" in Croatian, has been vastly improved with the opening of a makeshift road from Hvar Town. Not yet ashphalted and perilous in places, it may not be for the fainthearted, but does offer access to some more isolated beaches, as well as an alternative to the main access road to the village, through the infamous Pitve Tunnel.

The road from the tunnel winds down to the water, the main destination for many visitors, but it is worth taking the right turn to the old village itself, a nicely preserved stone village with a pretty square, and affording great views of the sea and island of Vis in the distance. The backdrop of the cliffs gives a stunning contrast.

Cliffs mean rock climbing, and this activity sport is growing in popularity every year on Hvar, with Sveta Nedjelja one of the main centres on the island. There is also a rock climbing school where courses can be arranged by local activity specialists, &Adventure and Cliff Base.

Eastern Hvar

Humac and Grapceva Cave

Moving east, and situated 7km from Jelsa, the abandoned shepherd's village of Humac is one of the delights of Hvar. Totally abandoned for many years and dating back to the 15th Century, there is a magical atmosphere and some stunning sea views and picturesque ruins at every turn, arguably the most authentic village on the island.

There is currently no water or electricity in the village, although power has been promised, but Humac is not short of visitors – a mixture of tourists in the summer, as well as locals from the village of Vrisnik, whose inhabitants are the major landowners. Humac is at its most vibrant on June 26, St. John and St. Paul's Day, as islanders gather to celebrate in the village.

146

Restaurant and Accommodation

Despite its abandoned status, it is possible to eat and stay in Humac. The owners of the excellent Murvica restaurant in Jelsa have renovated an old stone house at the front of the village and overcome the utilities challenges to offer unique accommodation and an overnight stay in the small house, complete with an outdoor shower facing the Adriatic – a special experience.

While Murvica will organise an event on site with prior notice and sufficient numbers, a more permanent restaurant, Konoba Humac, offers superb local fare in a rustic environment, with memorable views of the sea and mainland beyond. The dining experience is probably best summarised in this TripAdvisor review:

"It was an amazing experience, getting there without expectations. Rustic place and food, but the view, the climate are great! Good house wine, delicious lambs, chicken and sausages, salads, the perfect olives and olive oil. No electricity, candles when the sun comes down, smell of lavender, rosemary, grapes... The waitress was so kind telling us about the place, wood tables with families, romantic couples, no noise... Perfect and I recommend! "

The restaurant also keeps the keys to the small museum in the church, offers the only horse-riding on the island, and is the starting point for tours to Grapceva Cave, which leave at 9am on Mondays, Wednesdays and Saturdays from June 15 – September 15. The tours can accommodate ten people and tickets can be booked at the Jelsa Tourist Office.

Walking past the church and continuing up the hill, there is a tiny path which, if you keep going for about 300 metres, brings you to a telescope from where you can zoom in on some of the island's most spectacular scenery. The telescope takes 5 kuna pieces only, so come prepared.

Grapceva Cave
Although access is not the easiest, the end result is worth the effort and Grapceva Cave dates back to Neolithic times (2,500 BC) and is one of the oldest discoveries in the region. There are two rooms in the cave, an entrance hall of approximately 13.5m x 5m and larger room (23m x 22) which is surrounded by chambers.

The stalactites and stalagmites which dominate the cave are a spectacular sight, especially when lit up by candlelight and the solitude and peacefulness provide a perfect spot for reflection. The excellent Museum of Archeology in Hvar Town has an array of weapons and tools from the period, including flint knives, hammers and arrows, bones of the human and animal variety, various shells and pottery of the era.

The cave can only be reached on foot – either from Humac itself or, more interestingly, by following the old path from Galesnik and over Vrh hill, where the views are spectacular.
Travel time from Hvar Town to Humac is about 45 minutes, leaving plenty of time for a change of pace to take in Grapceva, Humac and a traditonal feast, before heading back to the bright lights.

From Jelsa to Sucuraj

With most of the tourism focused on the west of the island, relatively few visitors venture east of Jelsa when visiting the island of Hvar, unless they are arriving on the notorious Sucuraj to Jelsa road from Dubrovnik. Although a lot less populated and developed than the more fashionable western neighbour, there is much to discover in the stone villages and exquisite bays. The road has been upgraded in recent years, and now there is a much faster inland stretch from Jelsa, which connects with the upgraded section to Poljica.

Poljica and Mala Stiniva

The first point of interest on the old winding winding road is the abandoned hotel complex, the Belgrade Health Resort. Once one of the most popular destinations on the island, the hotel was a victim of the war, and is an eerie place to wander around.

Passing Humac, the first village on the main road is Poljica, which has one of the best oil presses on the island and is an excellent place to buy some of the island's famous olive oil. While not as impressive as Grapceva, the Zemuinska Cave has striking stalagmites and is more accessible.

There are Roman walls and graves with ancient inscriptions, as well as the pretty parish church of St. John, but a diversion to the coast at the entrance to the village is also worthwhile. The road to Mala Stiniva is a curious one - by rights it should be worse than the main road, but it is more modern and better maintained, and comes with an intriguing fork: turn right and the road meanders along the coast before stopping abruptly (there is a stunning bay below, with difficult pedestrian access); turn right and the road also goes nowhere, although the delightful hamlet of Mala Stiniva, one of the most picturesque in Dalmatia, can be accessed on foot.

Zastrazisce and Velika Stiniva

Next up is Zastrazisce (which takes it name from 'guardhouse'), a village made up of the hamlets of Mola Bonda, Podstrana, Donje Polje and Grudac. The 19th Century parish church of St. Nikola dominates the hilltop, but there is an older church - St. Barbara - which was built in 1621 on the foundations of a 14th century church.

At 316m above sea level the peak of Vela Glava was an ideal observation point of marine traffic, commanding a view from the island of Solta to Makarsa, and there is a partially reserved Illyrian fort there.

One of the true gems of Hvar is close to Zastrazisce, and rarely visited by anybody, despite being protected since 1964 and dated at more than 2500 years. If true the imperious olive tree close to the village would be among the ten oldest in the world. It is extremely hard to find, and your best bet is to charm the owner of the olive press on the left halfway through the village, who has been known to take people there on request. If nothing else, check out Mr. Rubin's amazing oil and honey, some of the best on the island. On the way to the olive tree, you will pass what for me is Hvar's most unusual cemetery – the original Zastrazisce cemetery – surrounded by cypress trees. A serene spot.

As with Poljica, a left turn to the coast is essential, this time leading to Vela Stiniva, one of the hidden gems of Hvar. There is good climbing to be enjoyed on the steep cliffs, and tourism is surprisingly well developed given the remote location. Although the full-time population is only two people, there is a restaurant in summer, as well as wheelchair-friendly private accommodation.

There are few places to stop for a drink or bite to eat, but one that is worth checking out on the main road is Karmelino's on the left towards the end of Zastrazisce. And if, like many, you have problems pronouncing Zastrazisce, I call is simply the 'Z' village. Much easier.

The Bay of Pokrivenik
Another worthwhile detour before reaching Gdinj is the bay of Pokrivenik, a popular spot for sailors with its deep bay, hotel and restaurant. Of additional interest above the bay is Badan Cave, which is 61m long and inhabited in Neolithic times, and its entrance is clearly visible from the bay.
Pokrevenik's wonderful Hotel Timun is a popular stopping off point for sailors on the north-eastern coast, which has little in the way of hospitality between Jelsa and Sucuraj. A great place to stay for tourists looking for true peace and quiet. If you are

looking for a quality villa, check out the very remote and very fabulous Villa Amalia on the way to Pokrivenik, complete with pool, gym and the island's only floodlit tennis court.

Gdinj and the Gdinske Uvale
Continuing along the main road, the eight hamlets of Bonkovci, Stara Crkva, Banovi Dvori, Vrvolici, Visoka, Talkovici, Dugi Dolac and Nova Crkva compose the settlement known as Gdinj.

There are some fine buildings to enjoy, including the Church of St. Juraj with its 16th century cemetery, which lies outside the town, There is a protected building, once owned by Ivko Radovanovic, which houses a library and some of his paintings.

There are also prehistoric drystone walls from the Bronze Age and evidence of Illyrian burial sites, but most visitors who spend time in the Gdinj area turn right to some of the best, and least visited beaches on the island. South-facing and more than 60km from the glitz of Hvar Town, the bays of Rapak, Torac and Tvrdni Dolac are an ideal hideaway. There are few places to eat before Sucuraj unless you head to some of the bays, but Duga Grill, just before Gdinj, is a great little addition, fabulous food to match the view of the Adriatic, Brac and the mainland. It is on the road on the left all alone – impossible to miss.

Bogomolje to Sucuraj
The last village before the eastern port of Sucuraj is sprawling Bogomolje, a collection of hamlets which share a school, cemetery, parish church dating back to 1750, and a memorial for Second World War victims by Joka Knezevic. Nearby Bristova cove used to host steamships and there is a 13m long cave in the cove. Bogomolje used to be a thriving community and a major lavender producing area – indeed there was a ferry from the mainland to one of its northern bays until 1965, but the glory days are sadly long gone, leaving a pretty, but depopulated village, and some spectacular bays for tourists to enjoy.

151

From Bogomolje, the road straightens and the views of Biokovo Mountains on the mainland and the island of Korcula to the south are stunning. Apart from the occasional wild boar, the 21km to Sucuraj are a joy, from where one can catch the ferry to Drvenik and mainland discovery.

CHAPTER 6: BEACHES

For many visitors to the island, the beach IS Hvar, as a random sample of the travel forums of Poles, Czechs and Hungarians will tell you. Pictures of the prettiest beaches, the best swimming and great views are regularly posted throughout the winter, as people reminisce and look forward to their next holiday in Paradise.

There is an astonishing diversity of beach on the island, and you can pretty much find whatever you are looking for. Although sandy beaches are in short supply, they do exist, but it is the predominantly pebble and concrete beaches that contribute to the astonishing clarity of the water that many find so appealing.

Where to start? Perhaps with our top 5 beaches on Hvar...

Top 5 Beaches on Hvar

1. Dubovica
A regular in lists of best beaches in Croatia, Dubovica is one of the iconic photos of Hvar. Located on the south side just before one enters the tunnel to Stari Grad, for many Dubovica is the perfect beach, with its idyllic setting and unique stone house protuding into the sea. Parking is on the main road (come early) followed by a hike down.

2. Lucisca
Hvar's most heavenly beach for some, and the only beach on the island with reputed procreational powers, according to legend. Why not try it for yourself, along the new 'road' just before the Stari Grad tunnel from Hvar Town. Lucisca is not far from Sveta Nedjelja on the south side.

3. Kordovon
The Pakleni Islands have so many fabulous beaches and places to lose oneself in sun-seeking natural heaven, but Kordovon, on the

other side of naturist island Jerolim gets our vote. Great beach and probably the most chilled bar in Dalmatia - Mare's Place. Simply take a watertaxi from Hvar's waterfront to Jerolim, then walk through the trees to the other side for your own slice of paradise.

4. Grebisce
Looking for a sandy family beach on Hvar? They do exist, but they are relatively rare. The northern side of the Jelsa harbour is your best bet, and Grebisce is very popular with tourists and locals alike, especially for those looking for early evening sun.

5.Gdinj Bays
Eastern Hvar is not as popular as its western counterpart, which is good news if you are holidaying anywhere near Gdinj, where some of the island's best beaches are located on the south side. Known as the Gdinj Bays, take your pick from about seven, each with either a bar or restaurant (or both) to serve refreshments as you laze away the day.

Beach clubs on Hvar

Bonj les Bains
Looking to be totally pampered by the beach on your holiday to Hvar, preferably somewhere within walking distance of the centre of town? Look no further than the sexy Bonj les Bains resort, just below Hotel Amfora, a short stroll from the main square in Hvar Town, where you can enjoy the beach atmosphere that earned Bonj inclusion in The Times Online's 2010 list of the Top 20 Hottest Beaches in Europe.

The stunning 1930s stone colonnade has been completely restored and refurbished by owners Suncani Hvar after ORCO Group injected millions into the company from 2005, and there are luxurious touches at every turn, including divine waterfront sunbathing options. Or if you prefer to sit back a little in the shade and enjoy the view, there is plenty of space above to take in the comings and goings in one of the Adriatic's most popular nautical destinations.

There are various level of privacy and luxury, and one option is to rent one of the private stone cabanas for the day, where guests can enjoy individual massage, room service, sunbeds and private showers. Feeling hungry, but your budget does not stretch to private cabin rental? Choose from the Colonnade Beach Bar and Restaurant or Veranda Sea-court 'Steak and Fish' restaurant.

The water is pristine and Bonj has been a popular bathing spot for locals for decades, and there are few better places to laze away the day in style and luxury, with excellent service at your beck and call. For more information, and to book, check out the Suncani Hvar website.

Hula Hula Beach Club
Not that Hula Hula needed any more promotion, given its reputation as one of Dalmatia's coolest beach experiences, but Beyonce's decision to reveal her baby bump to the world over a non-alcoholic cocktail at the trendy Hvar beach club catapulted Hula Hula into the global headlines.
Further down the coast than Bonj les Bains, Hula Hula is a great combination of stunning location, great sunsets, fabulous service and a great atmosphere. Miss the Hula Hula After Beach party at your peril!

Carpe Diem Beach Club, Stipanska
A byword for Hvar's exclusive image, Carpe Diem has done much to promote the Hvar brand internationally. Its original location on the Hvar Town waterfront next to Restaurant Gariful is a magnet for celebrities and the jetset crowd.

The opening of the Carpe Diem Beach Club has taken the brand one step further, and a short water-taxi to Stipanska Bay brings you to a world of waterfront luxury and entertainment. Relax by day with some of the premier service on the Adriatic, then reconvene after dark for some of the best nightlight on the coast, the absolute highlights of which are the legendary Full Moon parties which take place from June to September.

Beaches on Pakleni Islands

While Hvar Town does have its own beaches, most people head to the emerald jewels of the Pakleni Islands to enjoy a day in the sun. There is so much to choose from, but the small island of Jerolim is one of the popular choices, a little more so this year after being named by CNN as the world's best naturist beach.

If you fancy something a little more tranquil than Carpe Diem at Stipanska, go to the other side of Marinkovac to Zdrilca, where you can enjoy some excellent waterside cuisine.
The most popular island is the biggest, St. Klement, and the two most popular points are near its marina and the oldest established tourism on the Pakleni, at Palmizana, where the beaches, atmosphere and fine cuisine match anything on offer in Croatia. Looking for a little sandy beach? Head to the bay of Perna just after Palmizana – small but absolutely idyllic.

Beaches in and around Hvar Town

While most people staying in Hvar Town head to the Pakleni Islands or Hula Hula and Bonj les Bains, there are other spots to the north and south of the town. One place making the effort to reach is Pokojni Dol on the island's southern coast, a wonderful beach overlooking the lighthouse island of the same name, with the excellent Konoba Mustaco on hand for refreshment.

The Brusje Bays and from Milna to Dubovica.
The beaches become much less crowded a little way out of town. Head north and take your pick of the inlets on the Pelegrin Peninsula. The view from Panorama restaurant in the middle of the peninsula has some of the best views of the Pakleni Islands, and an overview of the nearby bays. One of the best is Pribinja,

past the newly-planted Tomic vineyards, with waterside restaurant Ringo one of the best places to while away a long lunch.

Drive a little on the old road to Stari Grad and descend into the so-called Brusje bays, some of the prettiest coves on Hvar below the village of Brusje. Take your pick from Stivina, Sviracina, Lozna, Zastupac and Jagodna.

The choice is just as impressive on the southern coast slightly away from Hvar Town. Milna is one of the best beach and culinary combinations on Hvar, with some of the best fish restaurants and two great pebble family beaches.

Further down is Zarace, which last year was the film set of a Croatian movie starring ex-President Mesic, and also home to local pop star Gego. Some great restaurants and a lovely place to escape the crowds.

Just before the tunnel is arguably Hvar's most stunning beach, and certainly one of its most photographed. The rocky access down to Dubovica bay may not be the easiest (parking on the road above by the telephone booth), but the descent it surely worth it, with its flat beach, southern vista and stone house protruding into the Adriatic. Great food also available.

Stari Grad and the Kabal Peninsula

Hvar's former capital has some great beaches, including one with disabled access after local authorities installed facilities at the Bonj beach close to the old town. Popular beaches are Maslinica near the ferry, Lanterna in front of Borici district on the left of the town, while the beaches in front of the town's hotels are very child-friendly. Or rent a boat and explore the undiscovered Kabal Peninsula – Licisce, Gracisce, Zavala and especially Zukova, the peninsula's best-known bay. There is a small restaurant at Zavala (not to be confused with the village on the south side).

Vrboska and Jelsa

For many, the beaches of Vrboska and Jelsa are the embodiment of a perfect holiday. Soline, 1km through the pine trees from Vrboska is one of the island's most popular daytime destinations, as is the nearby (but very secluded) naturist beach next to the camp.

Or choose your own piece of heaven along the cute coves that line the coastal route to Jelsa, until you hit Vitarnja on the entrance to Jelsa, famous for its beaches and late evening sun. There are other great family beaches, with a bed of sand, which are popular locals and tourists alike – Mina beach below Hotel Hvar, Grebisce and Zencisce. If you are heading out that way, check out Corni Petar, a great beach bar.

The South side from Sveta Nedjelja to Gromin Dolac

The south side of the island is wine country, with the famous reds of Zlatan Otok and Ivan Dolac, but there are many great places for a swim too. Among the best are the two beaches in Zavala – by the harbour and at Skalinada – the family beaches of Ivan Dolac and some picturesque swimming

The Unspoilt Bays of Eastern Hvar

As soon as you travel east of Jelsa, the crowds disappear, with the eastern half of the island relatively undiscovered. There are some great beaches to enjoy, on both northern and southern shores. For many the beach at Velika Stiniva is one of the most enjoyable, surrounded by high cliffs which offer some of Hvar's best rock climbing.

Continue on down to Zastrazisce, with bays on either side, before reaching the village of Gdinj, and one of the beach gems of eastern Hvar – the Gdinj Bays. Turn right at the church and enjoy the sloping descent to the southern shores, and take your pick of several bays, many with restaurants.

Turn left in Bogomolje and make for Bristova, once an important port with regular trade traffic between Split and Omis, today one of several bays where relaxation and clear water are the bywords. Until finally you reach the port of Sucuraj – a transit point for many – but with some very nice beaches at Camp Mlaska, as well as Perna and Cesminica.

Naturism

Naturism in Croatia is big business, and few places do it better than the island of Hvar. Voted as one of the top ten most beautiful islands in the world by Conde Nast readers, and averaging 2,724 hours of sunshine every year, Hvar attracts a wide variety of tourists in search of sun, party action, meditation and beaches. With its fine selection of nudist beaches and campsites, it has long been a popular destination for the naturist community, especially from German visitors, where the FKK (Free Body Culture) is well-established.

History of Naturism in Croatia

Although there are references to naturism in Austro-Hungarian times, the history of naturism in Croatia is generally accepted to have started in the 1930s on the island of Rab, in northern Croatia. Local authorities gave permission for British monarch Edward VIII to swim au naturel with his wife in 1936, which is the reason Kandarola Bay is also known as Engleska Plaza, or English Beach.

Naturism developed into an important component of Croatian tourism in the 1960s with the establishment of commercial naturist resorts in Istria and Dalmatia, and Yugoslavia hosted the Naturist World Congress in 1972. At its height, FKK tourism brought in more than 100,000 visitors annually. The war in Yugoslavia severely affected tourism but naturists are returning in ever greater numbers, with many heading for the island of Hvar.

FKK Camping on Hvar: Vrboska and Sucuraj

Camping on Hvar is a popular way of spending time on the island and there are facilities for FKK tourists. The main nudist campsite is in Vrboska, with the auto camp at Glavica a short ten-minute walk through the pine forest. The campsite has a capacity for 420 guests and there is a nudist beach nearby.

The other naturist camping option is on the east of the island, 2km from the port of Sucuraj, at Camp Mlaska, a popular campsite which is divided into two parts, with one side allocated to FKK guests.

Nudist Beaches on the Pakleni Islands

The infamous Pakleni Islands opposite Hvar Town are a naturist's paradise, with its secluded beaches, hidden coves and stunning nature. Accessed by water taxis from Hvar Town, there are three main nudist beaches:

Jerolim is the closest of the islands, directly opposite Hvar Town and named after a fifteenth Century church of the same name. Water taxis ply the route every half hour from 0900, and there is an excellent nudist beach close to the jetty, complete with restaurant and shop, although there are also more private alternatives through the pine trees.

Palmizana on Veliki Otok (literally Big Island) is a very popular naturism spot, with its sandy beach in a pretty cove. Palmizana has long been a favourite haunt for locals, even more so after the addition of a marina and restaurants.

Stipanska is beach on the island of Marinkovac which is reserved for FKK tourists, and facilities include showers, a restaurant and a shop.

Naturist Beaches on Hvar: Vrboska, Milna, and Zecevo

On the northern coast, Little Venice, as Vrboska is known, is a popular destination. Apart from the highlights of its stunning old town, canal and the main marina on the island, naturists can stay in the nudist camp and take their pick of beaches. The easiest option is to make the short trip to the nudist beach at Glavica, while the more adventurous may want to take advantage of water taxis to the tiny island of Zecevo.

Another picturesque alternative for nude sunbathers is the fishing village of Milna, a few kilometres from Hvar Town on the new road to Stari Grad. Bathers will have to fight their way past some outstanding fish restaurants in an idyllic setting, but the rocky naturist beach is well worth the effort.

There is a much more relaxed attitude to naturism in Croatia and one of the joys of Hvar is discovering one's own deserted cove, the choice is as endless as the sea is pristine.

CHAPTER 7: ACTIVITIES

Sailing

Hvar is a sailing paradise, with the magical Pakleni Islands nearby for exploring. Before we look at options, here is an overview of sailing around western Hvar.

A Sailing Overview from Jelsa to Zavala

Sailing holidays on Hvar are an excellent way to discover the hidden gems and secluded coves of Croatia's premier island. Tourism is concentrated on the western part of Hvar, from Jelsa on the northern coast to Zavala in the south. Here are some tips for sailors to get the most out of the route.

From Jelsa to Vrboska, Basina and the Island of Zecevo

The pretty town of Jelsa, the third largest, is an ideal entry point to Hvar, with its compact central square the centre of its cafe culture, and several excellent waterfront restaurants tempting passing yachts with their traditional fare. Mooring for visitors is reserved on the western side of the harbour, opposite the harbour master's office, with the eastern side reserved for the daily catamaran to Split and the seasonal tourist boats.

A short sail round the Glavica peninsula brings the main ACI marina into view, a thriving business with the increasing popularity of sailing in Croatia. The marina is located at the entrance to Vrboska, also known as Little Venice, and well-known for its picturesque canal and church-fortress. On matters more practical, it also has a marine fuel station, showers and a range of boat repair and maintenance facilities.

A little out of the town is the naturist resort of Zecevo, a tiny island in deeper water, or continue on to the delightful village of Basina, ideal for a detour with its three inlets, excellent restaurant and inviting swimming.

The Kabal Peninsula to Stari Grad
Hvar is very long and thin, with the exception of the Rudine
Peninsula which must be circumnavigated to reach the oldest
town on Hvar, Stari Grad. Apart from two small settlements, the
peninsula is almost deserted, and there are numerous inviting
coves, but mooring is not allowed in many due to marine cables.
Head instead for the deep bay of Zukovo, which almost
resembled a lake and has excellent swimming.

Passing Kabal Point and into the Stari Grad channel, look up to
the left to see the tunnels that Tito ordered for the islanders to
defend themselves in case of attach, then choose between the
various coves in Tiha Bay, before sailing into ancient Stari Grad,
with its 2.400 years of history and UNESCO zone. Moor up at the
southern part of the harbour after the lighthouse.

Around Pelegrin Point to Hvar Town
The journey west offers a enviable selection of hidden coves, and
there are plenty to choose from, but among the best are Lucisce
and Stiniva, the latter having a small jetty and restaurant.
Rounding Pelegrin Point is the jewel in the island's crown, Hvar
Town and the stunning Pakleni Islands opposite, where the boats
and large and the clientele rich and famous. There are a few
moorings on the eastern side.

Pokojni Dol, Dubovica, Sveta Nedelja and Zavala
Onward sailing from Hvar Town means an introduction to the
south of Hvar, passing the lighthouse on the tiny island at Pokojni
Dol, past the fishing village of Milna, home to south of the best
restaurants on the islan, to leave three gems still to discover.

The hamlet of Dubovica is one of the most photographed in
Dalmatia, and with good reason, as its few stone buildings
encroach on an excellent beach. There are a couple of places to

163

eat, but if sampling the local wine is of interest, sail on to Sveta Nedelja and admire the imposing cliffs before dropping into the curious restaurant at the jetty, owned by the Plenkovic family, purveyors of the island's best known wine, Zlatan Otok.

Continuing the journey, the resort of Ivan Dolac comes into view, and the smaller and almost uninhabited island of Scedro comes into view, which can be accessed by water taxi from Zavala, the final destination, popular for its southern sun, family beach and superb cuisine.

From Jelsa to Zavala by boat can take as long as the holiday pace dictates, but the journey by road is about 20 minutes through one of the most interesting tunnel journeys in Europe.

Our friends from Hvar Adventure (www.hvar-adventure.com) have all sailing options covered, so contact them for your specific needs. Here is a selction of their sailing offer

One-day sailing (10am – 6pm, snack included)
A full day of pure sailing for those who love the sea, our popular one-day sailing tour is necessarily at the mercy of the weather, which guides us round some of the most spectacular sights on the Adriatic.

Starting at 10am from Hvar Town, we sail to the fabled Green Cave off the neighbouring island of Vis, the first stop (weather permitting), where there will be ample time for swimming and snorkelling. A stunning tour of the picturesque coves and bays of Vis will follow, regarded by many as Croatia's most beautiful island, before a lazy lunch on board, followed by a little more relaxing time in the water.

The homeward sail begins about 4pm, arriving back on Hvar two hours later, after a full day of sailing, swimming, beaches, coves, local food and great company. An outstanding experience to prepare you for your evening's entertainment.

Overnight sailing trips are open to your wishes. Our staring points are Hvar town or Split (airport, town center or Le Meridien Lav Hotel).

The itinerary varies depending on the type of experience you wish to have, the number of days you would like to book (two , three or four) and if you prefer a one way or round trip.

Example of our typical One way trip is:
• Day 1: Starting point Split, sailing to the islands Brac and Hvar (overnight in Hvar)
• Day 2: Sailing from Hvar to Vis island (overnight in Vis)
• Day 3 : Sailing from Vis to Korcula town (overnight in Korcula)
• Day 4. : Sailing from Korcula town to Mljet island National park
Day 4 afternoon (around 5pm) there is an official connection from Mljet to Dubrovnik or back toward Hvar and Split.

3-Day Island Tour
Day 1
Departing from town of Split at 14:30PM
Welcome drink on the boat and sailing towards Hvar town.
Overnight in Hvar
Day 2
Sailing to Island of Vis, visit to Green Cave and Stiniva beach. Wine tasting. Overnight in Vis.
Day 3
Sailing continues towards island of Korcula. Free time for visiting Marco Polo's birth town.
Overnight in town of Korcula.
Day 4
Check out at 09:00. Speed boat connection at 10:00 to Mljet island and tow of Dubrovnik. Estimated arrival in Dubrovnik

12:30 PM.

Sea Kayaking

Sea kayaking is growing in popularity, and it is a great way to discover the hidden bays and coves of Hvar close up. No previous experience is necessary, and there are some really great programmes offered by our friends at &Adventure (www.andadventure.com):
Daily Sea kayaking Tours

Join us every day at 10AM or at Sunset for a four hour scenic adventure around Pakleni islands.

The starting point of the kayaking tour is the town of Hvar. You set off to the group of small islands called the Pakleni. The origin of the name goes back to old days when the islands were the main source of resin for local shipbuilders. Today, just like then, the islands are covered with thick pine woods providing refreshing shade even during the hottest summer days. The route through narrow straits and along the islands reveals small hidden pebble beaches where you can enjoy the privilege of having, at least temporarily, a beach of your own, where you can swim, snorkel and relax. Returning back to Hvar around 2pm. Lunch in a restaurant on the beach.

Afternoon sea kayaking tour – a perfect ending to the day (2.30/3.30pm – 7:30pm* depending of the season)
Same program as the morning tour.

Tour price: 375 kuna (53 EUR per person) for either program. Price includes: sea kayak and paddle, life jacket, dry bag, spray skirt, snorkeling equipment, guide and introduction in paddling techniques and safety, light lunch
Min: 2 people.
Max: We can take groups of up to 15 kayaks.

Meeting point: Krizna luka beach, at our sea kayaking base. 7min walk from the city promanade, just after Franciscan monastery. Departure time: 10.00AM and for sunset program, 2.30/3.30PM (depending of the season)

This tour can also be arranged at a time that is convenient for you, so please ask us what your unique requirements are and we will be happy to get back to you with the particulars and our price.

What to bring: Sunscreen, hat, sunglasses, long sleeve (Lycra if you have it, cotton if you don't) shirt, quick drying sports shoes, swimming gear, bottled water, towel and snacks.
What's extra: gratuities to guide/skipper.

Wakeboard

There is a rather nice young man who you can find just past Hula Hula called Mario. A bodybuilder, fishermen and all round nice guy, Mario is slowly building a very popular business for himself, a business which started out with boat transfers, but now is growing nicely. He is offering things that nobody else is, such as Wakeboarding. In his words:

We provide quality wake board equipment. Wake boarding is Mario's everyday sport so he will gladly give you some tips and show you some tricks. If you want to experience the feeling of flying like Iron Man or swimming like a dolphin then fly boarding is the perfect thing for You. Fly boarding is for everyone! It's easy to learn and we guarantee everyone will fly in 10 minutes... You don't need any experience, we will help guide You one-on-one during your entire session! Great memories and photos guaranteed! **Learn more on** www.rentaboathvar.com

Flyboard

Mario is the man to speak to for flyboarding as well:

If you want to experience the feeling of flying like Iron Man or swimming like a dolphin then flyboarding is the perfect thing for You. Flyboarding is for everyone! It's easy to learn and we guarantee everyone will fly in 10 minutes... You don't need any experience, we will help guide You one-on-one during your entire session! Great memories and photos guaranteed!

Flyboard is a water jet pack that is attached to Your feet! Surf the sky! Swim like a dolphin! This awesome jetpack like device bolts onto the powerful motor of a jet ski, then directs the gushing water through a long hose that connects to a pair of jet boots. The arrangement lets You fly, Iron Man style! Flyboard is an amphibious water-powered jet pack that propels You into the sky or underwater!

If there is more than 4 people interested we can bring our equipment to your boat / yacht, or we can pick you up with our speedboat free of charge. Also we can give you mooring in our flyboard base, directly in front of popular Hula Hula Bar.

PRICE | LOW SEASON 500 kn (65€) 30 min | HIGH SEASON 600 kn (75€)
10 minutes of instruction and 15 minutes of flying. Website www.rentaboathvar.com

Stand Up Paddle

SUP has also come to Hvar, and there are no prizes for guessing – that man Mario again. No information is currently available, but contact him via www.rentaboathvar.com

Windsurfing

There have been limited opportunities for those wishing to windsurf on Hvar in recent times, with many going over to Bol to take advantage of the facilities there, but things are changing...

No longer! Vrboska now offers a full windsurfing service, from beginners to advanced, including individual and group courses, and equipment rental and storage.

In high season, the wind is perfect for beginners until noon, and in the afternoon the advanced surfers enjoy stronger winds Maestral or Bura 3 to 6 bufor. In pre and post-season the most common winds are Jugo 3 to 7 bufor and Bura up to 8 bufor. www.bota-vrboska.com

Cycling

Cycling has exploded in recent years as an activity on Hvar. Challenging terrain, spectacular views and authentic experiences combine to offer an exceptional experience. Hvar Adventure can take plenty of credit for this trend, and here is just a selection of what they offer:

Leisure Cycle Tour
Hvar is a natural paradise, whose fields are famous for their wine, grapes and olives, which produce world-class products. What better way to experience its magic close up than through a challenging bike ride through its fields and picturesque inland villages, where time has stood still, and whose secrets are there to be discovered.

Cycle with us through the inland villages of Dol, Svirce and Vrisnik, before hitting the coast through Jelsa and Vrboska, much of it the route of the 500 year-old UNESCO Easter Procession. Breathe in the nature and the heritage before finishing your ride at one more unknown treasure very much off the beaten path – the Stancic family farm in Dol. There is nothing fancy here, just great locally produced food expertly served in an ambiance which will give you an insight into the Mediterranean as It Once Was.

We reserve the fancy part of the day for the quality of our bikes, which are the best quality carbon fibre road bikes from Pinarello and they all come lovingly prepared and serviced to ensure the maximum pleasure of cycling.

Meeting point: Hvar-adventure office 8:00, Van transfer to Stari Grad, bike fitting and welcome drink by Apolon Stari Grad.

Cycling approx: 3h through some of the most beautiful small villages along the island. Lunch and wine tasting…
Duration: approx. 5/6h
Experience Level: Beginner / Easy
Mileage: 30 – 50 km / 18 – 30 miles
Elevation gain: 210 m

4-Day Cycle Tour of Hvar, Peljesac and Korcula
Hvar is becoming increasingly popular as a cycling destination, and it is not hard to realise why. With its pristine nature, spectacular views and challenging hills, it is an ideal cycling destination, and combined with the mainland and other islands, there are numerous options to discover the beauty of the region by bike, none more so than our 4-Day Cycle Tour of Hvar, Peljesac and Korcula.

DAY 1
Arrival to Stari Grad on Central Hvar. After a welcome lunch, introductions and bike fitting, it is time for the steep climb on the old road to Hvar via the village of Brusje through lavender fields, olive groves and vineyards, before a retun to Jelsa at 7pm and an overnight stay in Stari Grad.
Total: 60 km

DAY 2

A day of the mainland, two islands and two ferries, with plenty of cycling involved. Departing at 9am, the long cycle to the eastern port of Sucuraj takes the group through the lesser known but equally stunning eastern half of Hvar, a natural paradise of depopulated stone villages, pretty bays and greenery throughout. The 50 km ride to Sucuraj is followed by lunch and the short ferry to Drvenik on the mainland at 3pm, after which a 30km coastal ride to the port of Ploce leads to the second ferry of the day, to Trpanj on Peljesac, at 7.30pm. Dinner and overnight stay at Trpanj.
Total: 80 km

DAY 3

After a relaxing breakfast, the action on Day 3 starts at 10am with a ride to one of the most beautiful spots in all Dalmatia, the village of Loviste on the top of the Peljesac Peninsula. Go back in time and experience traditional Dalmatian fishing life over an excellent fish lunch in a local tavern, before continuing the journey to Orebic, some 25km away. The short ferry from Orebic takes us to the birthplace of the greatest traveller of them all, Marko Polo. Dinner and overnight stay in Korcula Town.
Total: 65 km.

DAY 4

Korcula is one of Croatia's greenest islands and famous for its white wines of Grk and Posip. Leaving the main town at 9am, there are plenty of its vineyards on display on the 25 km ride to the famous wine village of Cara, where lunch is served, before continuing along to the other side of the island, with a 30 km post-luncheon cycle to the western port town of Vela Luka, where dinner and accommodation is provided.
Total: 55 km

DAY 5

And after all those strenuous kilomtres, what better way to finish the tour than with some relaxed sailing and a visit to one of the timeless islands of Dalmatia, tiny Scedro off the southern coast of Hvar, whose full-time population consists of just one family? Swim, snorkel, sunbathe, relax, and enjoy a traditional lunch of freshly caught fish and freshly baked bread. You have earned it! Departure from Vela Luka at 9am, departure from Scedro back to Hvar at 5pm.

For more cycling options and details of Pinarello carbon bike hire, www.hvar-adventure.com

Triathlon Training Camp with Dejan Patrcević

Another initiative from the team at Hvar Adventure to maximise the adrenaline potential of Hvar.
Join us for an unforgettable week on the beautiful island Hvar and train with one of the top Ironman triathletes, Dejan Patrcević. With accomodation in luxury villa „Apolon" and a private chef, it will be a week to remember.patrcevic_logo

Swim in the waters of Stari Grad Bay, home to the legendary annual Faros Marathon, a 16km race which attracts Olympic gold medallists and is regarded as one of the world's toughest swims. Bike through vineyards, olive groves and fields of lavender through Croatia's premier island, known for its fabulous climate, as well as being officially the sunniest island in all europe. Then run through 2,400 years history through the UNESCO-protected Stari Grad Plain, a fully functioning agricultural colony still functioning today much as it did with the Greeks and the Romans some 2,000 years ago.

Analyse your swimming technique, work on and improve your weakest points an all three sports. Drawing on his many years of experience as a top athlete and coach, Dejan will share his knowledge with you and give a peek into some of the secrets of professional sport.

The camp is limited to a small number of participants in order to give everyone a chance for unlimited access Dejan and his team. More info on www.hvar-adventure.com

Skydiving

The small airport in the UNESCO Stari Grad Plain received a new dimension a couple of years ago, when a company offering skydiving in the peak season (from July 1 to August 31) took up temporary residence. In their own words:

A jump out of a perfectly good airplane :)

By now, you have probably decided to experience some adventure, so the skydive is a perfect one and you picked just the right location to do so :)

Whole process of jumping and free falling is called skydiving, and its by far one of the most satisfying feelings a human can experience. While skydiving You feel an amazing adrenaline rush combined with a great feeling of pleasure. Skydiving in Croatia is unique because of the beautiful terrain you free fall and glide over.

Adventure begins with a short ground preparation where your instructor will provide you with crucial information about the jump. You will go over the proper technique for exiting the aircraft, flying your body in freefall and controlling the parachute descent. Then you will put on a special skydiving jumpsuit, a para helmet and you are ready to go for The Skydive.

Board the plane with your instructor and enjoy the panoramic flight while climbing to 11,000 feet.
HERE WE GOOOO !!!! Free fall and enjoy the rush, sound of freedom and the feeling of limitless... After about 40 seconds of free falling the instructor will pull the ripcord and your main

173

canopy will deploy.. From this moment you will have about 5 – 7 minutes of a beautiful panoramic canopy ride to the landing point and you can take control of steering until your instructor brings you in to land. The skydive is over but the beautiful memory will remain :)

After landing you will receive a jump certificate and if you purchased a DVD video you can pick it up 1 hour after the landing or it can be uploaded to our servers and shared afterwards.

More info on www.skydivingcroatia.com

Hiking

Hvar is a hikers paradise. Nature, stunning views, varying terrain. Our experts are &Adventure, and here are a couple of sample hikes. For more info on the full offer, visit
www.andadventure.com
1 day hiking (5-6h walk)

The tour starts in Hvar Town where the group meets with the guide. A 20 minutes transfer from the bus station to our starting point takes us to the village of V.Grablje, which is approx. 14km from Hvar town. The road to the starting point will offer the group amazing views on the surrounding islands.We will hike through villages where you would see the beauties of traditional architecture and way of living, learn about medical herbs and much more. There is a possibility to try the homemade vine, prosek or grappa, prepared in a traditional way…

We start our walk from Velo Grablje towards Malo Grablje following the old trail which in medieval time used to be the main road connecting Hvar with Stari Grad on the north side of the island. The entire trail is downhill, starting with approx. 20 long steps and continuing as a small trail for approx. 1.5km. After that part we continue our walk to Malo Grablje on a wide, gravelly trail...

It usually takes us around 1h from Velo Grablje to Malo Grablje, including short stops for some explanations and pictures taking.

After arrival to this picturesque, hidden village of Malo Grablje we continue walking for about 45minutes on a wide, gravelly road to Milna. A walk from Milna back to Hvar follows a small, rocky trail and it lasts approximately 1.30h (depending on the speed).

When: 8:00AM every day (we can be flexible, so ask!)
Price: 350 kuna (50EUR) per person
Duration: 5 hours

1/2 day hiking (3h walk)
The tour starts with a 20-minute transfer from Hvar town to our hiking path. We will hike through villages where you would see the beauties of traditional architecture and way of living, learn about medical herbs and much more. There is a possibility to try the homemade vine, prosek or grappa, prepared in a traditional way...

Hiking from V.Grablje to Milna is quite easy trail to follow. It is the best choice for short walks during hot summer days and for perhaps less active groups who would like to experience the challenges of walking in the nature.

We start our walk from Velo Grablje towards Malo Grablje following the old trail which in medieval time used to be the main road connecting Hvar with Stari Grad on the north side of the island. The entire trail is downhill, starting with approx. 20 long steps and continuing as a small trail for approx. 1.5km. After that part we continue our walk to Malo Grablje on a wide, gravelly trail...

It usually takes us around 1h from Velo Grablje to Malo Grablje, including short stops for some explanations and pictures taking.

After arrival to a picturesque, hidden village of Malo Grablje we continue walking for about 45minutes on a wide, gravelly road to Milna, where our walking ends and we can spend some time on the beach before we take the return transfer to Hvar town. Duration of time on the beach is usually around 30min.

Return transfer from Milna to Hvar is approx. 20min.

When: 8:00AM every day (we can be flexible, so ask!)
Price: 350 kuna (50EUR) per person
Duration: 3 hours

Rock Climbing

Hvar has great rock climbing all over the island, with the two primary sites being at Sveta Nedjelja on the south side and Vela Stiniva on the north side, east of Jelsa. &Adventure are our friends again:
Discovery rock climbing – suitable for beginners.

You will meet instructor and choose right equipment for your climbing activity. When you are ready end equipped there is a short 15-20 minutes walk from the office to the rock climbing area overlooking Hvar town. A new developed location with some great easy routes for your initial climbing steps. We start with basic instructions about equipment and rock climbing before you get opportunity to climb your first route. How many routes you would climb during the session depends upon your progress, but you can count 2-4 routes for shore.

NOTE: we need your shoe size and whether you ware S, M, L, XL label.
When: 3:30PM every day* (we can be flexible, so ask!)*depends on the season

Price: 400 kuna (57EUR) per person
Duration: 4 hours
Price includes: guide, necessary equipment

For more information on all rock climbing options on offer,
www.andadventure.com

Adventure Park Jelsa

Jelsa recently got a really nice addition to their tourist over, an
adventure park. There is quite a lot on offer. In the words of the
owner:

We are a small adventure park in Jelsa on Hvar island directed
mostly at tourists visiting the island… Besides the fun activities
you may have never tried like paintball, splatmaster, cageball and
living table football our offer includes some of the more common
recreational activities such as sand volleyball, badminton, boccie
etc

Our paintball and splatmaster course is completely different than
any course you may have tried before. It blends into the natural
ambience of Hvar, located in a forest which provide shelter from
the strong summer sun and the places for cover are not just trees
but also stone walls and bunkers located throughout the course.
After being shot you enter the shielded area in the middle of the
course giving you an overview of the entire game and the feeling
of being in the middle of an action movie.

Coming to our Park is not just about sports and recreation in the
competitive sense, you get that just by entering, but also fun and
adventure and some of the best memories to take home from your
vacation.

With our 10+ activities you will surely find something to enjoy.
Email www.hvar-adventure-park-jelsa.com

Scuba Diving

With its pristine sea, clean beaches, hidden coves and numerous small islands nearby, Hvar is the perfect base for a water-based holiday, but what is on offer for tourists who want to go a little deeper into the Adriatic and spend a day or two scuba-diving?

Although diving centres have been in existence for more than 50 years in Croatia, there has been an explosion of interest in the last 10 years, and there are several dive centres on the island. The best are Nautika in Stari Grad and Hvar Town, adn Viking Dive Centre, which operates out of Hvar Town, and whose experienced teams have years of diving experience, both internationally and around the island. The main diving attractions in the Adriatic are wrecks, caves, some coral reefs, and an unlimited selection of interesting fish. Here is a brief overview of the diving highlights near Hvar.

Vodnjak– one of the most popular diving points is Vodnjak, the last of the Pakleni Islands opposite Hvar Town. Vodnjak was in the news recently as the town's mayor offered to rename it Facebook Island, but divers will be more interested in the canyon with red gorgons at 15-40m and the 5m long tunnel at 35m underneath the Campanile, a tower rising from nowhere to about 10m below the surface.

Vela Garska – a good place for beginners, there is a 70m long wall at a depth of 30m, which masks a 20m cave just 5m from the surface. There is some very colourful sea-life to enjoy.

The Wreck – the English trading ship, Paulina was sunk 150 years ago in a lagoon a half-hour boat ride from Hvar. Small sea creatures and a sandy sea bed give way to the wooden boat at a depth of 30m.

Poseidon Pile – a good dive to see scorpion fish, moray eels and sometimes a lobster is the Poseidon Pile, a chimney dive starting at 30m and exiting at 11m. Cracks in the ceiling allow sunlight to create some spectacular effects.

Anchor Wall – a drop of at 35-40m ending with an Admiral anchor hanging on the edge of the cliff, this dive is a great place to spot lobster, seabream and sleeping spotted dogfish.

Scuba Diving Courses and Safety Regulations
In addition to organising excursions for experienced divers, beginner's courses are available to enthusiasts as young as ten. While all courses are taken with professional instructors, there are certain diving rules which need to be adhered to when scuba diving in Croatia.

A permit must be purchased to dive from a registered centre and all instructors must have a Government licence. Experienced divers are required to present proof of their qualifications and to sign a liability release. Written permission is required from parents for divers under 18, while anyone over 45 requires a doctor's certificate. For more information visit www.facebook.com/nauticahvardive and www.viking-diving.com

Deep Sea Fishing

For an island surrounded with the rich and abundant Adriatic, I have always been surprised at the lack of fishing options for tourists. Several people have contacted me asking about big game fishing? Perhaps some organised octopus or squid fishing?

Although I had heard of the occasional fishing opportunity, there was nothing readily available for tourists as a concrete offer. Or nothing that I could find while researching for my guidebook until I met Mate.

An 'incomer' like myself - although he has not travelled quite as far, just from the next island of Vis - Mate is the answer to many people's fishing desires, and his comprehensive offer includes deep sea fishing, squid and octopus fishing, day and night snorkelling, boat transfers and excursions to places such as the Blue Cave.

Delmar offers fishing trips aboard our boat, the "Palagruža". As the name suggests, the boat is strong, robust, elegant and invincible, just like the most remote Croatian island, Palagruža.

The fishing trips are lead by a professional fisherman with years of experience.In our diverse fishing activities we use a number of tools and techniques, such as longlines, nets, traps, hooks, big game fishing, middle game fishing.

The fish caught during the trip remains on board. It is possible to arrange the preparation of fish delicacies on board (requires approval of the skipper), to purchase the fish or to arrange to store it in one of the restaurants in Hvar.

The price includes: guidance by an experienced skipper, fuel, drinks, fishing permits, appropriate bait, and fishing equipment – rods and reels (class 50/class 80 and 30 lbs).
Squid, Octopus, Night Snorkelling, Transfers and Excursions
Have a look at his website to see what else is available - there is a lot! From the relatively simple squid and octopus fishing and boat transfers, to night snorkelling and all-inclusive excursions.
www.taxi-delmar.com

Hvar Half Marathon

Hvar now has its own established half-marathon each August, with more than 80 entrants taking part from all over the world. The date of this year's event has been announced - August 20. Many of last year's competitors described it as the most beautiful run they had ever done. Why not give it a try yourself?

IMPLEMENTATION: Hvar Half-marathon Race Commitee

- Josko Domancić
- Boris Reinić
- Dragan Janković
START: 20th of August 2016, 18:00, Petar HektorovicSquare (trg Petra Hektorovića), Stari Grad, Island of Hvar, Croatia
ROUTE: Start is in Stari Grad. First half of the race is an ascent from the sea level to 400 m.a.s.l. The other half is a descent to the sea level in Hvar. The whole route is on paved roads, with markings at each 1 kilometer. Refreshment points are at 5km, 10km and at 15km.   www.mapmyrun.com/routes/view/32298370

PRIZES:
Trophies for the first 5 male and female runners each.
Medals and sponsor awards per each age category.
Race finisher medals, t-shirts, dinner and after-party for all runners.

CATEGORIES:
F-S (born in 1977 or younger) M-S (born in 1977 or younger)
F-35 (1972-1976) M-35 (1972-1976)
F-40 (1967-1970) M-40 (1967-1971)
F-45 (1962-1966) M-45 (1962-1966)
F-50 (1957-1961) M-50 (1957-1961)
F-55 (1952-1956) M-55 (1952-1956)
F-60 (1947-1951) M-60 (1947-1951)
F-65 (1942-1946) M-65 (1942-1946)
F-70 (born in 1941 or older) M-70 (born in 1941 or older)

All the participants registered via the website www.hvarmarathon.com should pay the start fee on the race day (15 EUR or 100 HRK) at the place of picking up the start number.

Keeping Fit on Hvar

(with thanks to Vivian Grisogono)
Hvar is a great place for keeping fit. You can walk, cycle or run, with a choice of flat or hilly routes. There is mountaineering and

181

of course swimming and a variety of water sports, especially sailing and kayaking. For the competitive, there are plenty of sailing regattas on the Adriatic, some centred on Hvar. There are several grass football pitches on the island, notably in Hvar Town, Jelsa, Stari Grad, Vrbanj and Sućuraj - the island's football league is fiercely contested. Hvar's tennis courts are excellent, the main ones being at the Hotel Hvar and Fontana complex in Jelsa and the Gariful Tennis Centre on the edge of Hvar Town.

Rowing a speciality
Jelsa's rowing club has a proud record of producing international level rowers - rowing is one of many sports in which Croatia, despite its small size, produces world and Olympic medal-winners surprisingly regularly. The club's leading light Jurica Gamulin is himself a successful competitor who still takes part in international veterans' events. Chief coach to the club is Jerko Božiković, who tirelessly trains rowers on and off the water, from novice to international standard. Children are especially welcome in the club, and Jerko organizes very popular fitness classes for four-year-olds upwards. Children are allowed on to the water in special training boats as soon as they have learned to swim. Experienced rowers who visit the island are welcome to contact the club to see if an outing can be arranged. Rowing times are dictated by sea conditions and the movements of larger craft, and there are strict safety regulations which must be adhered to.

Sports hall and gyms in Jelsa
Jelsa boasts a well-appointed sports hall marked out for indoor football, handball, volleyball and basketball, which can be hired for private use when it is not being used by the school. During the winter months regular Pilates, yoga and fitness classes are held there in the evenings.

There are also two gyms in Jelsa for those dedicated to fitness training or bodybuilding. The Figura Gym is on the outskirts of Jelsa towards Pitve, and the other gym is attached to the rowing club on the waterfront. Both have free weights, stands and benches. Figura offers more fixed-weights machines covering all the body's major muscle groups, while the rowing club's machines are (logically) geared to rowing and include trunk rotation and a heavyweight leg press. Figura has basic aerobic machines including a static bicycle and stepper, while the rowing club gym has a battery of Concept rowing ergometers, an elliptical cross-trainer and a reclined static bicycle.

Contacts for fees, times, bookings:
Rowing club gym and boats: Jerko Božiković, mobile: 00 385 (0)91 5242776
Figura gym: Sinisa Simić, mobile: 00 385 (0)95 8308952
Sports hall: Andro Balić, mobile: 00 385 (0)91 5850748

Yoga – Suncokret Body and Soul Retreat

One of the attractions of the island of Hvar is its ability to cater to the varying needs of tourists, and while the beaches, historical stone towns and excellent night life grab most of the attention, there is much to discover away from the coast.

With its stunning views, healthy climate and limitless sun, many visitors come to Hvar to enjoy its special natural setting. The land is central to local life, with the majority of local residents somewhat involved in the fields of the island, producing olives, wine, lavender and healthy food.

Suncokret Body and Soul Retreat in Dol
An excellent way to get away from the stress of modern life with some wholesome meditation and communing with Hvar's nature is to book in to the Suncokret Body and Soul Retreat in the inland village of Dol,

Suncokret (pronounced soon-tso-kret) means 'sunflower' in Croatian, and the word embodies the main goal of the centre, to provide and organic and nourishing environment for personal

183

development, enabling individuals to "blossom like a sunflower in the sun," according to the centre's co-owner and holistic programme leader, Evening Marie.

Evening is a native New Yorker who came to the island in 2004 and met her partner Stipe one fateful evening in Hvar Town. Together, the couple decided to open a boutique holistic healing centre in Stipe's home village of Dol.

As Suncokret enters its twelfth season, the results have been spectacular. Combining Stipe's local knowledge and Evening's spiritual energy, the couple have created a unique experience on Hvar, a holistic retreat with the chance to enjoy and engage in the island's nature. Suncokret was named one of the 23 Best Coastal Yoga Retreats by Coastal Living.

Organic Produce and Sunset Safaris

Stipe acts as local guide and chef, offering a delicious vegetarian menu of local produce, often produced by himself. Two of the most popular guiding tours he leads for guests are a trip to the family field in the Stari Grad Plain, where guests can pick their own food and learn about traditional farming techniques, while the end of retreat hike to the peak of the island is a spectacular sunset safari, with panoramic views of the sea. Stipe expertly guides his visitors around the historically significant sites along the way.

Holistic Yoga and Well-Being Retreat

Evening became a certified Reiki Master in 2001, a Vinyasa Yoga Instructor in 2004, a certified Bioenergy Therapist in 2008 and a Holistic Yoga Therapist in 2010. She describes Suncrokret as "holistic yoga & well being retreat that specializes in offering tailored retreat programs for individuals on a journey of personal transformation." Her bespoke holistic progammes run from March to December, in which she offers, among other things, individual yoga therapy and tuition, bioenergy and reiki therapy

184

treatments, and a Life Path Awakening workshop.

Accommodation is on-site, a delightfully rustic complex in the heart of the village, one of the six inland villages that comprise the less-visited hilltop villages. www.suncokretdream.net

Olive, Lavender and Grape Harvests

While tourism now constitutes a large part of the island's economy, this was not always the case, and the traditional harvests of olives, grapes and lavender are a great opportunity to mix with local farmers and reap the benefits of a day's work in the field.

The Grape Harvest
There is a marked change in the traffic from August to mid-September, as local residents reclaim the roads towards the end of another busy tourist season. Italian caravans, German Mercedes and expensive SUVs from Central Europe are much less visible than the Renault 4s, Golf 1s and Zastavas which meander slowly to the fields and park up at the roadside. For September is the wine harvest time on Hvar, as important to the island's culture and identity as tourism is to its economy.

The Wine Harvest on Hvar
Wine has been a mainstay of island life since vines were introduced by the Ancient Greeks more than 2000 years ago, and the island's wines are undergoing a resurgence after the devastating attack of phylloxera in the early 20th Century. Farming practices are similar to those first introduced and nowhere is this more apparent than on the Stari Grad Plain, an 80-hectare agricultural colony introduced by the Greeks and still thriving today.

While there are cooperatives and a handful of local producers with international reputations, such as Zlatan Penkovic and Andro Tomic, the majority of wine produced is by individual families on

185

private plots. The picked grapes are noisily transported in ageing motorised trailers through the small streets of the island's towns and villages, where they are crushed in the ground floor 'wineries' in private houses, the smell of the freshly crushed grapes pervading through the streets.

A day's grape picking is a lot of fun, a chance to mix with the local population and, particularly if the vines are on the south of the island, a chance to enjoy the spectacular views of vineyards sloping down to the Adriatic.

How to Find a Grape-Picking Opportunity
It is easy to find a grape-picking party to join for a fun day. There is no payment, but help is usually rewarded by a slap-up meal with wine prepared in the fields. With the main season over, the island relaxes and waiters in cafes have more time. Simply ask where you might find a grape-picking contact, and one will appear!

Grape-Picking at a Dalmatian Pace
This being Dalmatia, things happen at their own pace, as this correspondent learned in his first season. The early reporting time of 7am at the local cafe was taken as a sign of a long day ahead, but as the fourth round of *bevanda* (wine and still water, a popular beverage) was brought to the table at 9am, the realisation that rural Hvar is indeed far from the Western rat-race was beginning to take root. Finally underway at 10am, four hours of leisurely picking high above the Adriatic, was followed by a hearty and extended lunch of grilled fish, vegetables and more than a glass or two of the local red.

As a break from days at the beach, a day's grape picking is a rewarding experience, a chance to experience a little of local life, foster local friendships and sample some of the decent home-made wines in a picturesque setting.

The Olive Harvest
The summer tourists gone, the outdoor cafe chairs locked up for
the winter, the endless August sunshine a distant memory and
replaced by the biting *bura* wind, it would be easy to conclude
that Hvar was a less than attractive place out of season. While is it
certainly true that life is quieter, colder and (dare one mention it,
this being the sunniest island on the Adriatic?) infinitely wetter,
local interest turns from tourism to something altogether more
passionate: olives.

Olive Growing on Hvar
Olive growing has a long tradition on Hvar, dating back more
than 2000 years to its introduction by the Ancient Greeks, who
founded the settlement of Faros (present-day Stari Grad) in 384
BC. The supremely well-preserved agricultural colony, the 80
hectare Stari Grad Plain (now under UNESCO protection) is still
farmed in almost exactly the same way by modern farmers.

Given the long olive tradition, it is not surprising that growing
and picking techniques have been handed down from generation
to generation, and one of the perennial topics of debate inside the
cafes in winter is olive growing techniques, harvesting times and
picking methods. The debates can be lively!

The Olive Harvest in October/November
Visiting tourists looking for an alternative experience on their
holiday are more than welcome to help. Apart from giving an
insight to local life and helping out, a day's picking is a great way
to forge local friendships. There is no payment, but help is usually
rewarded with a hearty meal in the field or a bottle of oil as a
souvenir.

Given that most olive groves are family-owned, picking can take
several weeks, having to fit in with existing schedules such as
school and jobs. It is a team effort and a time for family to come
together, with successful businessman in Zagreb taking time off to

187

return to the family fields. Finding an olive-picking opportunity is easy - simply asking in any cafe should result in success.

Olive Picking Methods: To Shake or To Pick?
Picking methods vary from shaking the trees with the olives falling on sheets on the ground to the individual pick. Both have their fans, but both are time-consuming. Individual pickers often wear pouches to store the picked grapes, useful when stretching or climbing ladders to reach the less accessible olives. The pouches are frequently empties into buckets.

The work is quick physical, with lots of stretching, but the heaviest work is transporting the sacks or containers of olives over sometimes rocky paths to the trailer for onward transportation to the press.
Olive picking usually starts later in the day to avoid the early morning dew, and the picking is a very social affair, with neighbours and friends helping each other out and catching up on the latest gossip. Lunch in the field, usually a barbecue, is an essential part of the experience.

Processing the Olives
Once picked the olives are transported to one of the various presses on the island. The presses vary considerably in terms of technology, methodology and age (another cafe discussion point), with one of the more modern presses in the cooperative in Svirce.

Olives are pressed by appointment, while very small producers, of which there are many, add their haul is added to a larger consignment. The olives are weighed, and the generally accepted yield is 9-10kg for a litre. Processing is about an hour, after which the freshly pressed oil is ready for collection. While the oil can be used immediately, it is advisable to wait a few days for the oil to settle.

Olive oil from Hvar is of exceptional quality and makes for an ideal souvenir from Croatia.

A History of Lavender on Hvar

Tourists who can drag themselves away from the beaches or the party atmosphere in Hvar Town are often astounded at the colourful sights and aromatic smells of the flora and fauna of Croatia's premier island, and perhaps the best time to visit is June and July, when the fields are alive with lavender.

Known as the Lavender Island, Hvar has a long tradition of cultivating the crop, although the origins of lavender on the island are not clear. One local folklore version is that a poor villager went to his local priest in search of advice to find money for a dowry for his daughter. The priest suggested he plant lavender and, while the locals initially labelled him crazy, they eventually changed their mind, as the harvested lavender oil was sent to France as perfume and he became the richest man in the village.

What is known is that the Rosemary Cooperative of Velo Grablje, on the old road from Hvar Town to Stari Grad, was formed in 1892, and produced oils from both rosemary and lavender.

The Lavender Festival in Velo Grablje
Velo Grablje, an almost deserted village today, experienced a lavender boom in the late Twenties, and there was significant planting between 1928 and 1930, as the village became one of the biggest producers of lavender oil in Dalmatia.

The lavender tradition continues in Velo Grablje to this day, with the annual highlight being the Velo Grablje Lavender Festival every June, which is an opportunity to pay tribute to the hard work of lavender workers in the past, as well as motivate the youth of today to carry on the practice. The 2016 Lavender Festival in Velo Grablje will be in June.

Souvenirs from Croatia: Lavender Oil and Fragrant Bags

189

The lavender grown on Hvar is of exceptional quality and organically produced. It is widely available in the tourist boutique shops and makes for an excellent souvenir from the island. There are two main types of souvenir: lavender oil, which is packaged is attractive miniature bottles; and lavender fragrant bags, which are filled with dried lavender flowers.

Herbal Tours
Far from the glorious beaches and vibrant nightlife, there is another side of Hvar which attracts numeous tourists: its nature. Known as the Lavender Island, and with an annual festival in Velo Grablje to celebrate Hvar's famous crop, the stories of the plants of the island are no less fascinating that its history and traditions.

Away from the limelight, there are plenty of delicious natural products made from natural island products which make excellent souvenirs, and the rosemary honey made by Boris Buratovic won fourth prize in the international Apimondia in Argentina in 2011, for example. But how to learn more about Hvar's natural treasures, and where to taste them?

Meet Karmen Barcot, a qualified guide and aromatherapist, who offers an extensive and varied introduction to herbal Hvar, from guided tours of its fields, to herbal tea and talks in the relaxed atmosphere of one of Hvar Town's most exclusive restaurants, as well as introduction to a first-class range of natural soaps, oils and other products made from Hvar's natural gifts.

Together with husband Antun, whom she met at university in Zagreb, Karmen decided to return to Hvar ten years ago, swapping the fog of the capital for and island natural paradise for them and their children. Karmen and Antun's dream was to work in organic agriculture, and they decided that there was no better place for this than Hvar.

Their first venture was to create a rock garden from medicinal herbs, out of pine wood, but this did not last long, as it fell victim to the devastating forest fire which ravaged the island in 2003. Undeterred, they started again, and their herbal collection is now flourishing, with their native herbal collection now including St. Johns' wort, oregano, mint, marjoram, sage, lavender, thyme and curry plant.

Growing plants is one thing, but Karmen and Antun went on to produce a range of products from their herbal range, including herbal teas, essential oils of lavender and rosemary, St. John's wort oil (known as kantarion), natural soaps of lavender made of unrefined and cold pressed oils of castor, palm and coconut and essential oils.

The good news for visitors is that Karmen and Antun's products are very accessible to try and to purchase. Their stall can be found on the Hvar Town waterfront, the second stall from Pizzeria Mam Leone where their range of products are on sale.

Alternatively, head to the divine garden in Divino restaurant further down the riva, where Karmen provides a highly entertaining and informative talk about the agriculture and herbs on a rocky island, a talk which includes a light snack and herbal tea served on a 19th century terrace in a magnificent garden with an elevated view of the Adriatic and Pakleni Islands. Who said the best thing about Hvar was its nightlife... The Herbal talk is available from May to September.

For those wanting to get in amongst the aromatic fields of Hvar, Karmen also conducts a fascinating herbal walk from Hvar Town to Milna via the old road, giving visitors a chance to learn more about Hvar's flora and fauna in situ. The tour takes about three hours and includes return transport to Hvar from Milna, and it is available in Spring and Autumn. Contact Karmen by email karmen.barcot@gmail.com

Kids Activities

The beach of course if the main kids attractions on Hvar, but there is also a lively programme of activities for the little ones, particularly in Stari Grad. Stari Grad is a little hive of activity for the young ones during the summer. An overview of what your kids can get up to while on holiday this summer.

Little Swimming School

At the Bonj bathing area, the swimming club each year organizes a little swimming school in Stari Grad. The school lasts from July to the end of August every year, under the guidance of expert swimming teachers. Teachers will enable your children to learn all swimming styles, but once finished this school perhaps some of them will decide to train professionally in this sport. Swimming school takes place for three age group – Girice, children from 7 to 9 years old, Glamci, children from 10 to 13 years and Dupini, children from 14+ years. Email pk_for@net.hr for more details.

Sailing School

Sailing is a sport that has been practiced for years in Stari Grad, as is recognized by the numerous sailors who carry out their preparations in the Stari Grad Bay every year. The position of the bay is particularly favourable for sailing beginners because it has a deep channel and favourable winds. The Helios sailing club organizes a sailing school for beginners, under the guidance of experienced sailors. The school takes place during August every year, near to the church of St. Jerome where the club facilities are. +385 (0)91 564 1717.

Art Studio Atelier Marinka

The Marin+Marinka open atelier in the village of Dol, close to Stari Grad, is an ideal place for all art and nature lovers. During the afternoon children and their parents can visit the art atelier and have fun whilst learning something new, and they can visit the exhibition.

From 10 am until 6 pm children in groups can paint their T-shirts helped by artist auntie Marinka. Parents can also try their hand helped by their children.

The Small Town of Faros
The Children's festival 'Small Town of Pharos' has been organized for three years in Stari Grad, introducing children to creating a theatre performance. Every day there are workshops with Kristijan Ugrina, mainly of visual arts, scenography, literary skills, music and puppets.
The end result of working in the workshops is a performance that is conceived, designed scenographically, arranged and performed by the children themselves. There are also exhibitions and presentations of the children's works. The workshops take place in July and August. www.festival-mgf.com

The Gitarasta Guitar School
Every year in Stari Grad the International Summer School of Guitar GITARASTRA takes place under the expert guidance of professor Ante cagalj. The Summer school is particularly dynamic, with a full-day timetable whilst concerts by participants take place every evening in St.John's church. Besides that, every second evening we offer a particularly attractive programme by the guitar orchestra in prominent locations such as skor and Riva. www.antecagalj.com

Gariful Farm
Luxury fish restaurant Gariful opened a small farm a couple of years ago, with the aim of growing organic vegetables and keeping some animals. The project gathered pace quickly, and now there is an interesting variety of animals from all over the world for the kids to enjoy, including a llama, crocodile, eagle and white owl. Entrance is free, and you can see the Gariful sign on the right about 1km up the hill coming out of Hvar Town on the way to Stari Grad. www.facebook.com/Farmahvar

Agroturizam Pharos
Another great addition in recent years for a family day out is
Agroturizam Pharos, which is the only hospitality building
(indeed one of the only buildings) in the heart of the UNESCO
World Heritage Site, the Stari Grad Plain. There is a shuttle bus
from Hvar Town directly to the farm, which allows adults to
sample the excellent local wine, olives and various delicacies
(donkey salami was a new one for me...), while the kids can run
around and play with an array of animals. Horseriding can be
arranged on request. There are also plans to open a lavender
museum, while it is possible to buy your own organic vegetables
here on the 10,000m2 vegetable plot, much of which is used for
the owner's other business, Marinero restaurant in Hvar Town. To
reach Agroturizam Pharos, take the main road from Stari Grad to
Jelsa, and you will soon see three bizarre white posts sticking out
of the ground. Turn left there and you will see the farm on your
right after about 50m. A new addition for 2016 is the first
lavender museum on Hvar. www.hora.com.hr

Vrboska Water Park – Aquapark Soline
But the beach is never far from the minds of the little ones on
Hvar, and a nice new option appeared in 2014 in the popular
Soline beach near Vrboska, with slides and bouncy options in the
sea. There is a Facebook page, Aquapark Soline with more
information.

Day Trips

There are many great day trips both on and off the island, and the
best of them are mentioned in the 5 Tours Not to Miss section in
the introdcution to this book, so no need to repeat here.

Communications have improved considerably in recent years with
the arrival of the seaplanes and Krilo service to Dubrovnik and
Split, and this offers plenty of other options for day trips should
you want to explore.

194

Visiting Korcula has never been easy, despite the proximity of the birthplace of Marko Polo, But with the Krilo service to Dubrovnik, it is now possible to do a day trip to Korcula Town, something not previously possible, other than by speedboat transfer.

So too with the seaplanes, and two wonderful UNESCO World Heritage Sites are now less than half an hour away. Take the Jelsa flight to downtown Split, from where it is a short stroll to Diocletian's Palace, or head instead to Resnik, the seaport by Split Airport, from where a 5-minute taxi will take you to the old town of Trogir.

The other very popular day trip of course is to the world-famous Zlatni Rat beach in Bol on the island of Brac. The iconic beach is one of THE symbols of tourism in Croatia, and there are daily tourist boats leaving from Jelsa harbour from May to October, at 09:00 and 10:00 each morning, returning back about 18:00. The journey takes under an hour, and it is not uncommon to see dolphins on the journey, so look out for them. It happens occasionally that they come to play, and will swim under the boat in a zig-zag fashion. Wine lovers going to Bol should not miss the Stina wine tasting experience inside the imposing stone building on the waterfront to the left as you dock. Don't be fooled by the shabby exterior – inside is a whole new world. Tickets for the boats cost 80 kuna return and can be bought the night before – simply walk to the boat and ask.

CHAPTER 8: THE WINES OF HVAR

Imagine an island whose vineyards enjoy the most sun in the Adriatic, an average of 2,724 hours a year. Imagine an island whose wine tradition has continued uninterrupted since the Ancient Greeks planted the first vines in 384 BC. Imagine an island whose quality wines include Croatia's only Grand Cru.

Imagine Hvar. The good news is there is no need to imagine. The wines are ready for tasting, the picturesque vineyards are available to visit, the wine experts are waiting to share their knowledge and produce. A wine tour of Hvar should be an integral part of any visit to Croatia's premier island.

History of Wine on Hvar

Since the arrival of Greek colonists in 385 B.C., the Dalmatian island of Hvar, Croatia has endured many changes. Rulers, empires and foreign armies have come and gone. Today the marks and scars of these events remain a part of the island's cultural-historical ientity and economic position in the region, and the ethnic composition of the island reflects the genetic patchwork left behind by the influx of settlers over time.

But one thing remains virtually unchanged. This is a tale about the continuity of winegrowing and winemaking on Hvar, which has survived the many rises and falls caused by wars, social unrest, vineyard scourges, and economic hardship.

In the beginning, From the Aegian island of Paros the Greeks brought grapevines and planted them in the fields of Stari Grad, thus establishing the island's first vineyards. The Greeks then divided the fields of Stari Grad, also known as Ager (originally named Chora) into 73 equal parcels and allocated them to the local settlers.

One year after their arrival, a conflict between the Greek settlers and the local Illyrian tribes broke out. With the help of Dionysius I of Syracuse's fleet (winner in the war against Carthage and ruler of Sicily), the Greeks were able to defeat the Illyrians and strengthen their hold on the island.

According to Roman historian, Appian, the Illyrian mainland tribes considered wine from Hvar a valuable commodity. Clay amphora bearing the seal of Pharos, which were recently excavated near the Neretva River in southern Dalmatia, affirms the importance of wine in the cultural-historic lifestyle of the region.

During the time of Demetrius of Hvar, a great soldier and confidant to Queen Teuta of Illyria, Hvar returned to Illyrian rule.

In the 2nd century B.C. the Romans conquered Hvar and brought with them the methods to improve the local production of wine. The Romans built many villae rusticae in the fields of Stari Grad and elsewhere on the island, where the owners would reside for the greater part of the year.

During this time, in the city of Salona, the capital of the Roman region of Dalmatia, a Christian group was founded and guided by Domnius of Antioch (better known locally as Saint Duje). Since Hvar was a major port between Salona and major cities of the Mediterranean, the teachings of the Christian Gospel quickly spread among the islanders, an influence that remains today.

After the fall of Salona (7th century A.D.), some of the city resident fled to the islands, subsequently followed by the Slavic tribe, the Croats. The Croats soon adopted the traditions and winemaking skills that would sustain the continuity of grape cultivation and wine production until the present day.

During the Middle Ages, Hvar was subjected to a revolving door of rulers: the Neretvans, Croatian kings, Byzantine, Hungarian, Croatian-Hungarian kings, and finally the Venetian Republic all took their turns.

Despite all the turmoil, vine cultivation and winemaking endured and continued to be the backbone of the local economy. In the Middle Ages, two-thirds of arable land was owned by the Hvar Commune, and the remaining third belonged to royalty and the Church.

Public lands were offered for rent to the workers, royalty and the Church. Strict rules governed the division of property and the payment of land rent. Grape growers were required to pay 1/6 of the yield to the royalty and the Church. Discontent led to unrest, and under the leadership of Matija Ivanić, a civil uprising (1510-1514) broke out. The mission: to secure equality between the common folk and the royalty.

The uprising was followed by a period of Turkish incursions. The Turks raze the towns of Hvar, Stari Grad and Vrboska. Turkish invasions all along the coast led to demographic changes, as a large number of Croats from the Neretva region and the Makarska coast fled to Hvar in search of safety.

Hvar eventually came under control of the Venetians and continued to develop – despite ups and downs – as an economic center of Dalmatia. Wine exports were the leading source of revenue, although Hvar was also well known for its production and export of dried figs, olive oil, almonds, carob and other Mediterranean produce.

In the time leading up to the mid-19th century, Hvar was again subject to periodic regime change, coming under control of the Austrians and subsequently the French (beginning of the 19th century). It also came under attack by the British and Russians, during which time commerce was interrupted and the local economy stagnated.

Austria again gained control of Hvar in the middle of the 19th
century. As a result, Hvar gained access to new markets in the
Austro-Hungarian Empire, which boosted the importance and
production of wine.

Toward the end of the 19th century, the scourges of phylloxera,
peronospera (downy mildew) and oidium (powdery mildew),
devastated and ruined the vineyards of France and Western
Europe.

Wine from Dalmatia suddenly came under higher demand,
prompting the residents of Hvar to expand their vineyard holdings
to 5,750 hectares. With the increased production and revenues,
many wine-growers enlarged their homes and converted the
ground floors into wine cellars. The future suddenly seemed
bright, and Hvar enjoyed newfound prosperity.

To minimize the power of and offset any threat from the buyers
and traders, many of the smaller local wine growers decided to
organize themselves into the first island cooperatives. One such
cooperative, Svirce, remains today.

But the unfortunate cycles of history soon took a turn, and the
economic boon turned into catastrophe. The Wine Clause, a
mandate that allowed Austria to import cheaper wines from Italy,
forced a drastic and devastating 350-500% decrease in the price
of Hvar's wines.

If that were not enough, the vineyards of Dalmatia – including
Hvar – were also attacked by peronospera and oidium, followed
in 1909 by the ravaging effects of phylloxera. The glory days of
viticulture on Hvar seemed to die a slow death, leaving the
population without the means to earn a living, and the local
economy teetered on the verge of collapse.

A record of these dark days is still visible, engraved in 1901 in a stone panel on the chapel in the village of Ivan Dolac, which says:

In honor of the Mother of God, this Church was built by Ivan Caricof the late Juraj. Since 1852 oidium and peronospera have ruined the grapes. These were hard times. Root pests came from Zadar, and the vines whithered. In fear we await our doom. My People! Devastated by this affront from God, heed the Virgin Mother Mary. And may God protect us from these three evils.

While the diseases and pests that attacked Hvar's vineyards and wrecked the island's economy were eventually conquered, viticulture as a way of life never fully recovered to its previous level of importance. Total vineyard acreage fell by over 2,000 hectares to 3,500 hectares under vine. The economic and social impact would be felt for decades to come, resulting in a further decline in production as many residents of the islands (including Hvar) abandoned their vineyards and homes to go abroad to seek work and a means of steady income.

However, a local family, led by Niko DubokovicNadalini – a powerful ship and land owner, winemaker and the mayor of Jelsa – spearheaded an effort to restore the vineyards of Hvar. They introduced modern method of grafting grapes onto phylloxera-resistant American rootstocks and shared the technology with local wine growers. Their winery in Zavala earned numerous world-class wine awards in those times.

Yet after the nationalization initiatives of the early 20th century, their winery was abandoned. Today most of their vineyards are overgrown with pine trees and macchia, although certain sections have recently been replanted with young vines by local winemaking families, such as the Caricfamily in Zavala and Zlatan Plenković.

World War I brought the Italian occupation of Hvar, during which time the Croatian language and culture were suppressed. Soon thereafter Hvar was absorbed into the newly-founded Kingdom of Serbs, Croats and Slovenians, which later became the Kingdom of Yugoslavia.

The Great Depression (1929-1932) had an obviously negative impact on wine production, and many winemakers and co-operatives, because of large debts, imploded and ceased to exist. As a result, the local population set off on another large exodus to distant countries such as the USA, Chile, Argentina, New Zealand and Australia, where they hoped to find new lives and jobs.

Today you can still find living witnesses of this hard time. My grandmother, Danica, still recalls her mother's sad sighs while she was baking bread. "A board of bread, one hectoliter of wine", she would say. This meant that to buy 20kg of flour, one had to sell 100 liters of wine.

Modern mechanization, vehicles and roads were unheard of in these times. In order to reach the vineyards on the south slopes of Hvarske Plaže and the wine cellars of Ivan Dolac, wine-growers were required to climb over steep heights of Vorh Mountain.

It is interesting to note that before the arrival of phylloxera, mostly white indigenous grapes were grown on the south slopes of Hvar: Bogdanusa, Mekuja, Parc, Kurtelaska, Vugava. Only later did Plavac Mali, the most widely-planted red grape in Dalmatia, come to dominate and prevail in the area.

Up until World War II, every town on the south side of the island had its own quay where boats would dock to buy wine. Traders would visit wine sellers, sample the wines and set their prices. The price of wines from Hvarske Plaže was always significantly higher than those from the north side of the island where the grapes were of lower quality and sugar levels.

Transporting the wine from the cellars to the boats was a challenge due to the steep slopes. Donkeys often bore the burden of carting the wine from villages situated far from the sea to the docks. Once at the sea, the traders would fill wooden barrels with the wine and then throw them into the sea, where they were picked up by the boats.

Sometime after World War II, Peroslav Caric(Slavko) noticed a new invention – rubber hoses – while visiting a marketplace, and he purchased some 2000 meters of hose. His idea to use the hose for pumping wine from the seaside stone reservoirs into the barrels was a success, and he soon offered his service to all the villages on the south side of Hvar, as well as a few on the island of Brac.

With the building of the Pitve–Zavala tunnel in the early 1960s, life became easier for the locals, who no longer had to each make wine in their own cellars and then transport it to the buys. Instead they transported the grapes through the tunnel to the big wineries on the north side of Vorh Mountain for processing.

But this progress was not necessarily good news. The large wineries, such as Hvarske Vinarije, Dalmacijavino, and VinoProdukt (today the cooperative Svirce), shifted into quantitative winemaking. Quality diminished but was offset by positive developments regarding modernization and better organization of production, brands and sales.

Thanks to the hard work of Ivo Politeo, Hvar achieved its first wine with Protected Geographical Origin status, "Faros", which was produced by Dalmacijavino from locally indigenous Plavac Mali grapes from the south slopes of Hvar. This is Croatia's second wine with protected status, the first being Dingac from Peljesac.

The era of Socialism brought further degradation of quality and the number of acres under vine, due to the disparaging attitude towards agriculture and farmers.

Today it is estimated that there are only 300-500 hectares of vineyards on Hvar, a huge decline from the 5,750 hectares of the mid 19th century. However, a reassessment of current vineyard acreage is underway, which will hopefully provide more precise data about present day viticulture.

When faced with the global economic problems of the present day, we can't help but wonder what kind of a future awaits us. One thing is clear: we should endeavor to preserve the things most dear to us – our heritage and our vineyards – because crises come and go. Vineyards do not grow overnight.

We must learn from the mistakes of our past. Ironically, the vineyards that my family cultivates today were purchased by Ljubo Carić, my husband's father, even though the same land was once owned by his father, Juraj Carić. In fact, when widowed with six children, my husband's grandfather sold all his lands on the prime southern slopes to buy land on the north side of Vorh Mountain, which he thought would be easier to work.

Unfortunately, he lost almost all the value of his investments and savings when the Austrian Crown (currency at the time) was converted to the Yugoslavian Dinar. He never accomplished his dream of growing quality grapes in his new vineyards.

(Written by, and with thanks to, Hvar Wine Association President, Ivana Krstulovic Caric)

Grape Varieties on Hvar

No pinot noir or sauvignon blanc here, but Ivana has prepared this excellent overview of the local grape varieties grown in her company's vineyards.

Bogdanjusa (Bogdanusa) An ancient variety indigenous to Hvar island, grown today in the Ager area. Bogdanjusa is a well-regarded white variety that can be relied on to produce quality wines. A prolific grower, it gives reliable and good yields. It ripens in the third period. Normally used to produce monovarietal wines, but also a great team player in white blends. The name means "a godsend" (Bogom dana), which is explained by its traditional use during church holidays and festivities. The sugar levels are in the 17-20% range, and the acids between 6.5 and 7.5 g/l.

Kuc (Trbljan) Considered an indigenous Dalmatian variety. A prolific, high-yielding variety. The wine is harmonious, characterized by a mild and pleasant varietal aroma. It ripens in the fourth period. Sugar levels 15-18%, acids 6-8 g/l

Posip This white variety, indigenous to Korcula island, has an increasing presence on Hvar. It probably owes its name to the somewhat tapering shape of its grapes, which brings to mind the oblong side (sip) of a Dalmatian soil-tilling implement. The yields are good and reliable. Posip gives a typically intense and aromatic Dalmatian wine. It ripens in the second period. Sugar levels 17-25%, acids 6.0-8.5 g/l.

Marastina (Rukatac) The most widespread white variety in Dalmatia. Also known as Rukatac in Korcula and elsewhere: the shape of the grape is reminiscent of a body with two arms (Croatian "ruka" = English "arm"). Its origin is unclear. It could be indigenous or perhaps one of Italy's various Malvasias under a local guise. Its moderate alcohol and floral nose have earned it a reputation as a "ladies' wine". It ripens in the third period. Sugars 18-24%, acids 4-7 g/l.

Darnekusa (Drnekusa) A red variety indigenous to Hvar, grown in the Ager, sporadically in the Plaze area, as well as around the

Vorh (the island's peak). It ripens in the third period. Sugars 17-19%, acids 6-7 l/g.

Plavac mali Croatia's best indigenous candidate for rivaling the world's famous grape varieties. Its exact origin remains unknown, but genetic analysis has identified Dobricic and Crljenak (Zinfandel) as its parents. One might call it a variety that thrives on adversity: while it is exceptionally successful in the Plaze area, it finds it very difficult to ripen properly in the deep soils of Stari Grad's Ager. It also gives good results in the terraced vineyards around Svirce. Wines made from Plavac normally have a high level of extract and high alcohol, and are capable of evolving for many years in barrel and bottle. It ripens in the fourth period.
An Ancestor of Zinfandel: Plavac Mali
Plavac Mali comes out of a cross between two grape varieties, namely Zinfandel and Dobricić. Actually Zinfandel isn't the local name. That's what it was called on its arrival in the New World. On Hvar it was better known as Tribidrag, around Omis it's Pribidrag, in the Kastel area west of Split it's called Crljenak kastelanski, and in southern Italy it's Primitivo.

They can now tell that these grapes are all the same variety, isn't DNA wonderful! Anyway, after being a staple of Dalmatian wine production from around the 15th century (and for all we know, earlier than that), Tribidrag all but disappeared from local vineyards, to be replaced by the new, improved youngster – Plavac Mali!

Plavac Mali first gets an official mention in the 1821 publication on Viticulture of the Austrian Empire. A little later, as "Plavaz Piccola", it was included as a varietal in an experimental vineyard near Vienna. I imagine it probably didn't do too well that far north, as it really flourishes on the sunny slopes of its native Dalmatia.

Apparently the oldest known vineyard of Plavac Mali is in Dol, on the island of Hvar. There are actually still 20 vines originally planted in 1860 by Mate Stančić. These are self-rooted, since the soil is sandy enough to stop the dreaded phylloxera bugs. So many vines died off in the early 1900s, that this small remnant of 150 year old plants is quite a rarity.

Plavac=blue and Mali=small, so the Croatians are really calling these grapes "Small Blue". The blue refers to the lovely deep skin colour of the grapes, while small refers to the size of the bunches. Funny how a small blue makes such a great red!

The best growing areas for Plavac Mali are south or SW facing slopes down to the sea. They need to be protected from the cold winter winds off the continent, and they benefit from the extra reflection of sunshine off the water. So, where are we talking about for the absolute best Plavac Mali wines? That would be the southern slopes of Hvar (Sveta Nedelja, Ivan Dolac), and the Peljesac peninsula (Dingac, Postup). And now I know why they call those vineyards the south beaches!

If you want to read more, the book is Plavac Mali: A Croatian Grape for Great Wines by the Plavac Mali Association – Zagreb. Edited by Edi Maletić, Ivan Pejicand Jasminka Karoglan Kontić. ISBN 978-95355938-0-5

Hvar Rose: An Undiscovered Gem

In addition to its better known reds and whites, Hvar produces some very good rose wines, particularly near the village of Svirce. Also by Ivana.

The picturesque village of Svirce used to be famous because of the wine Opol, and there is saying on the island: Red from Vrbanj, White from Vrboska and Opol from Svirce.

Old people say that the production of Opol started in the late 19th century, because of demand from the Austrian wine merchant

206

Schiller.

It is a wine similar to rosé but usually a bit darker in color and with less acidity, but still fruity and soft. Opol is sometimes called Dalmatian rosé and is produced on the Dalmatian coast and islands.
The terraced vineyards close to the village of Svirce, from where the grapes (plavac mali) for these wine are grown, are a masterpiece of the human efforts of Svirce inhabitants. Small parcels of land where cleaned of stone, and the stone was used to make the dry stone walls, looking from above like lace covering the sides of the hills.

The peak of the production of Opol was in the 1960s according to Antun Franetovic- Ticica ,who worked at that time in Cooperative Svirce. The cooperative had their wine shops in other towns and even in the Slovenian capital, Ljubljana, which was a significant market for this wine. After that the demand for this type of wine changed and red wine became more popular. Today smaller quantities are produced.

The technology of the Opolo making is as follows; the grapes are smashed and then left to macerate up to 12 hours, then the juice is poured off the grape skins, so the juice takes in a small amount of pigments. Usually producers are bottling it a few months after harvest. This wine is great refreshment for the hot summer days.

Hvar Wine Association

On May 31, 2010, the winemakers of Hvar joined together to establish their own representative association ("udruga"). The Association includes thirteen wineries, from the smallest, local-business type up to big wineries, some of the internationally recognized. The first President of the Association of Hvar Winemakers was Mr. Andro Tomic, the famous winemaker and oenologist, who was succeeded by Ivana Krstulovic Caric.

The association's mission is to revitalise abandoned vineyards, protect and promote native grape varieties, and to promote the island of Hvar as a wine destination. Hvar's winemakers have organised wine tastings on the beautiful Dalmatian squares of Stari Grad and Jelsa this summer.

Hvar is a remarkable wine region and includes three grape varieties which are only gron here: Bogdanusa (white grape) , Prc and Drnekusa, known in Hvar dialect as Bogdanjusa, Parc and Darnekusa. Hvar is famous for its Plavac mali, grown on the south slopes of the island, but Plavac gives excellent results grown on the terrace vineyards around Svirce, and Vrisnik. The area was once famous for the wine Opolo, that could be described as the Dalmatian Rose.

The diversity of microclimate and soils on the Hvar gives winemakers the chance to produce large palette of wines. Bogdanusa and Prc are grown in the UNESCO-protected Stari Grad Plain, better known as Ager, and Drnekusa is grown on terrace vineyards around Svirce and on the area Vorh, a large plateau on Hvar's crest.

The association's president is Ivana KrstulovicCaricfrom Vina Caric in Svirce, and she runs the Hvar Wine Association website www.hvar-otok-vina.org where you can find all contact details of its members.

Wine Festivals

The Hvar Wine Assocation has been very active in promoting the wines of islands in recent years, a trend which is set to continue. Regulary tastings in pictureque Dalmatian squares, accompanied by live music, have become a regular feature of the Hvar tourist calendar in recent years, and look out for the latest events via the local tourist boards to make sure you catch one of these magical events. The tastings started in the heart of wine, Svirce and Jelsa, but now also include Vrboska, Stari Grad, Dol, Vrbanj and Hvar

Town.

The most famous wine festival on Hvar is Festa Vina in Jelsa, which traditionally takes place in the last weekend of August. It is a fun event for all, with tug-of-war, donkey races, climbing the pole to claim the prsut, live music, and all sorts of stalls and entertainment. The focus on quality wine has been somewhat lacking, but that is also starting to change, and this year's event will also encompass a more quality wine presentation the weekend before. Details will be available from the Jelsa Tourist Board. Jelsa will also be hosting weekly wine tastings with live music every Thursday until October, a great chance to get to know the fabulous wines of Hvar.

Hvar Wine Producers: 7 Not to Miss

Indigenous grapes, various micro-climates, different approaches to winemaker, a range of professional egos – for such a small place the wine scene on Hvar is truly fascinating. Here are some winemakers (and wines) not to miss:

Andro Tomic (Jelsa) – One of Croatia's most well-known winemakers, and certainly one of the most flamboyant, Andro Tomic is the ultimate Dalmatian bon viveur and the only Croatian winemaker to appear naked in Playboy. His Romanesque cellars in Jelsa are magnificent, as are his wines. A passionate Hvarophile with a wine education from France, Tomic produces outstanding local variery wines (Beleca in the white, Plavac Mali Barrique in the red), as well as working with international varieties, such as Sveti Klement, which is akin to a traditional claret. The most popular wine tasting experience on Hvar. Don't miss his dessert wine, regarded as the best in the country. Visit www.bastijana.hr or email bastijana@st.htnet.hr for more.

Ivo Dubokovic (Jelsa) – Another winemaker passionate about the island, Ivo Dubokovic has been named as Croatia's top boutique winemaker, and with good reason. Not afraid to

209

experiment and faithful to the grapes of Hvar, Dubokovic has come up with a unique football team of 11 excellent wines from his annual production of 25,000 bottles a year. Coupled with his professional marketing experience, the Dubokovic range is highly sought after in the top restaurants of Zagreb, particularly the reds, and bottles to look out for include 2718 (sunshine in a bottle, after the number of hours of sun Hvar averages annually), Medvedica and Medvid. The Dubokovic tasting experience is the most intimate and seductive, conducted as it is by candelit is his wine cellar, and accompanied by a tasting of his outstanding flavoured olive oils. ivo.dubokovic@gmail.com

Teo Huljic (Jelsa) – One of Hvar's smaller but most talented producers, Teo Huljic produces about 6,000 bottles a year in his cellar in the back streets on Jelsa's old town, next to an excellent restaurant which bears his name, but the quality is excellent. Passionate about the island's indigenous grapes, his range of whites in particular celebrate the very best of Hvar's white grapes. This year, he has added another local variety which is close to dying out, Mekuja, with just 350 bottles produced. He is also keen to experiment as well, and recently became the first to plant Chardonnay on Hvar, where he intends to blend with Prc and Posip and age in oak. If you can persuade Teo to do a tasting with his slow food menu, it is a divine experience. Contact him on teohuljic@gmail.com

Ivo Caric (Svirce) – One of the rising stars of the Croatian wine scene, the rise of Ivo Caric is a success story to be celebrated. Passionate about the traditions of the islands and the native varieites available, Caric has built up an excellent national (and increasingly international) reputation for his small range of wines, which are now exported to many countries in Europe, and as far away as California. His Bogdanusa was the first to get international awards for this signature Hvar white, while his Plovac Ploski and Plovac Ploski Barrique are regarded by a growing number of experts as among the best Plavac Mali wines in the country. Caric last year opened a tasting facility on the canal in Vrboska. He also has a shop in Stari Grad where you can buy his wines, as well as other island-made products. Email caric@vinohvar.hr, website www.vinohvar.hr

Svirce Cooperative (PZ Svirce) - Don't let the word 'cooperative' put you off, PZ Svirce oozes quality, as well as offering the most expansive range of wines on Hvar. The first winery in Croatia to have a certified organic Plavac Mali back in 2003, and they have an impressive range of organic wines today. Pride of the winery is the Ivan Dolac Barrique which has won international organisc gold two years running at Biofach Mundus Vini in Germany. Their standard Plavac Hvar is one of the best quality Plavac Mali wines at the more affordable end of the market, and do try and get to try their Posip Deluxe (only 5,000 bottles). PZ Svirce has shops in Jelsa, Stari Grad and Hvar Town, or you can visit them in Svirce (last building on the right as you head to Vrisnik – impossible to miss). PZ Svirce also has an arrangement with national drinks wholesaler Badel 1862, so you can pick up prime label spirits such as Bombay Sapphire and Bacardi Rum at the winery. Email pzsvirce@hi.t-com.hr, website www.pz-svirce.hr. Open Monday -Friday 7-15 From 1. of May we are open also on Saturday 7-14. Tasting wine is advisable to annoounce the day before.

Vjeko Vujnovic (Sucuraj) – Sucuraj does not get as much attention as the rest of the island due to its distant eastern location, which is a shame, as it is a pretty place, as well as being home of one of Hvar's better winemakers, Vjeko Vujnovic. If you are in town, tastings can be arranged at his waterfront cellars on the opposite side to the ferry. Three to recommend, the indigenous white Prc (pronounced 'parch') and two meaty reds, Plame and Ivan Dolac Barrique.

Zlatan Otok (Sveta Nedjelja) – Hvar's best known and most decorated winemaker on the island, Zlatan Plenkovic is one of the biggest names in Croatia wine, his bottles exported as far away as Russia and China. With vineyards sloping down to his native Sveta Nedjelja, Zlatan has made the village an imporant wine destination in its own right. The first Grand Cru in Croatia, his Zlatan Plavac Grand Cru is a consistent international medal winner, while his Posip won the presitgious Decanter Best Regional White Wine. Add to that he has a cellar under the sea below the divine materfront restaurant on the marina he has built for the village, and no wonder more people are making the journey through the Pitve Tunnel. Email zlatanotok@zlatanotok.hr, website www.zlatanotok.hr

Hvar Wine Tasting Tours

There is nothing quite like a Hvar wine tour to experience the island up close in all its natural goodness, and there has been a steady increase in wine tourism in the island in recent years. The market leaders, and with some truly innovative tours, are Hvar Wine Tours, a local agency with a passion for wine and individual relationships with each winemaker. From the standard two-winery tour to a personal session with a celebrated winemaker celebrating his top vintages, Website www.hvarwinetours.com

Standard tours usally include visits to two wineries (including the option of a speedboat transfer from Hvar Town to Sveta Nedjelja), with the most popular wineries visited including Zlatan Otok, Andro Tomic and Ivo Dubokovic, although it is expected that Ivo Caric's new cellar on the canal in Vrboska will be very busy this summer. Standard tours are either half or full-day, where lunch in an olive grove is also include. Check also www.secrethvar.com for other wine tour options.

Croatia's Master of Wine Capital

A couple of years ago at a wine seminar at Dalmacija Wine Expo in Split, I met a very nice lady from London, who seemed to know an awful lot about wine. There was a reason for that, I quickly learned, for she was Jo Ahearne, one of just 300 Masters of Wine in the world. We talked and I persuaded her to try the wines of Hvar, which I was happy to introduce. Jo emailed me later to say that she had been looking for a country to make her own wine, and one thing led to another – including a very successful introduction and now strong friendship with Andro Tomic and family – and today Jo can be found in Sveta Nedjelja producing what is bound to be a rather fine rose.

Her presence, as the only Master of Wine making wine in Croatia, is a huge PR coup for the Hvar wine story, and it was boosted in February 2016, as Ivan Barbic, who is co-signature on the imperious Dubokovic Medvid, became Croatia's first ever Master of Wine. Hvar, the island of wine, much loved by the experts...

The Rise of the Hvar Wine Bar

It is about ten years since the first wine bar opened on Hvar, 3Prsuta. Tucked away in the street adjacent to Hvar Town's main square on the fortress side, it offered quality Croatian wine by the glass, a wonderful atmosphere and a nice alternative to the nightclub nightlife that did not appeal to the older guest. With such a strong wine tradition I was always surprised that more wine bars did not open. And then they did...

Hedonist, Red Red Wine, Vintage, San Marco by Hotel Palace and more are due to open this summer. For a party town, Hvar has twice as many wine bars as nightclubs... The staff are knowledgeable, the ambience in all places is excellent, and this new aspect of Hvar nightlife is meeting a need for older tourists, as well as being an excellent showcase for the wines of Hvar.

Jelsa, the historical town of wine on Hvar, received a major boost in 2015 with the opening of the first wine bar/restaurant on Hvar, where one can order Hvar wines by the glass. Artichoke, which is located on the waterfront of the old town has added a new dimension to fine dining and wine appreciation in central Hvar.

213

CHAPTER 9: FOOD AND DRINK

It would be hard to want for anything gastronomic on Hvar, given the wealth of fresh produce and excellent drinks. A brief overview of some things to try while on holiday.

Some Dalmatian Specialities to Try on Hvar

Hvar is a gastronomic delight, with an abundance of fish, fresh local vegetables and excellent meat. No McDonalds here, but there is plenty to taste and enjoy, with some interesting dishes for the more adventurous. Here are a few to look out for on a Dalmatian menu.

Prsut and Pag Cheese
Served at every wedding and the most common starter in many a restaurant, a plate of smoked Dalmatian ham and cheese from the island of Pag is almost a prerequisite. Served with olives and bread, it is a good dish to nibble on before the main course. Pag cheese is salty and comes from sheep; it's the most popular cheese in Croatia.

Octopus Salad
Octopus is not a common dish in the West, and the common tourist reaction to the notion is revulsion, but probably the biggest culinary surprise is the change in attitude after the first mouthful. Served cold and mixed with onions, garlic, olive oil and lemon juice.

Lamb, Veal and Octopus *Peka*: Under the Bell
No trip to Hvar is complete without a hearty *peka*, a slow-cooked feast of meat (or octopus), potatoes and vegetables. The ingredients are placed under a large pot and then inserted into the embers of a fire and cooked over a long period. Orders usually need to be placed 24 hours in advance by a minimum of four.

Black Risotto
Risotto is a popular dish in Dalmatia, and black risotto is a local
specialty, a delicious mix of fish, olive oil, onions, garlic and rice.

***Bakalar*: Dried Cod for Christmas and Easter**
For more traditional fare at festive periods, it would be hard to
avoid *bakalar*, a dried cod dish served in every household over the
Christmas and Easter celebrations. Usually imported from
Norway, the cod is boiled and then served with potatoes and the
ever-present olive oil.

Scampi Buzzara
One of the best recipes to enjoy the local shellfish is scampi
buzzara, a messy but rewarding adventure with prawns, tomatoes,
garlic, parsley and white wine.

Pasticada
One of Croatia's more popular dishes at home, it is a shame that
this excellent meat stew appears so rarely on tourist menus.
Pasticada is a slow-cooked beef stew served with gnocchi. It is
possible to find and is well worth seeking out.

***Sarma* and Stuffed Peppers**
There is plenty on offer in the shape of hearty winter food, with
sarma and *punjena paprika* topping the list. Both dishes comprise
of flavoured minced meat stuffed inside either cabbage or
peppers. The dish is more popular in winter, for obvious reasons.

Blitva and Other Vegetables
Unlike British supermarkets, tomatoes are not available all year
round, but also unlike British supermarkets the vegetables in
season are fresh, full of flavour and colour. There is wild
asparagus in April, unlimited tomatoes in the summer, but one of
the most popular vegetables is *blitva*, or Swiss chard, a wonderful
side dish when mixed with potatoes and olive oil.

Bread, Bread and More Bread

A Dalmatian without bread is more bereft than a desert without sand. Bread is the staple of most Dalmatian diets, and there are an impressive range of locally produced loaves every morning.

Some Typical Dalmatian Recipes

Octopus Salad - Serves 4

1 large octopus, cleaned and rinsed; 2 to 3 wine corks, if at all possible; 1 red onion, thinly sliced; olive oil; wine vinegar; juice of 1 lemon; salt and pepper to taste; 1 clove garlic, minced; 2 to 3 tablespoons chopped parsley; 2 tablespoons capers (optional)

Pound the octopus with a meat mallet. Place in a saucepan with water to just cover the octopus, add the wine corks. Simmer over medium heat for about 3 hours until completely tender. Let cool in its cooking water, then chop or slice the octopus and place in salad bowl. Add the sliced onion. Season with olive oil, wine vinegar, lemon juice, salt, pepper, garlic and parsley. Add capers if desired.

Buy cleaned octopus at quality supermarkets and fish markets. You may also find octopus that is cleaned and frozen, just thaw and cook. Use fat-free or low-fat Italian dressing instead of the olive oil and vinegar.

Black Risotto – Serves 6

Prep Time: 10 Minutes, Cook Time: 20 Minutes
500 g cuttlefish or whole squid; 3 tablespoons extra virgin olive oil; salt and pepper to taste; 410g Arborio rice; 810g fish soup; 500 g shrimps; 500g shells (different kind); 3 teaspoons chopped parsley; 3 teaspoons chopped garlic; 3 teaspoons tomato paste; 1 dl white wine
Clean the cuttlefish by removing eyes, beak and transparent quill. Remove and reserve ink sac. Cut the cuttlefish into strips. Sauté garlic in the oil until translucent. Add the cuttlefish and cook over moderate heat until golden, stirring from time to time. Add salt,

pepper, parsley, and tomato paste and reduce heat. Add the rice and stir briefly over high heat to blend flavors. Add the ink from the cuttlefish sac, and then little by little the fish soup. Reduce heat to low and cook for about 15 minutes, stirring constantly. Add white vine, stir briefly until the risotto boils. Stir once more and serve.

Stewed Savoury Scampi
1 dl olive oil; 60 g red onion; 4 garlic cloves; 400 g tomatoes; 1,2 kg scampi; 1,5 dl white wine; salt and pepper to taste; 1 bunch of parsley; 10 g bread crumbs
Chopped red onion, put in tin and fry. When yellow add garlic. Stir 2 minutes and add tomato cubes and scampi. Stir occasionally and add wine at times. Put salt and pepper. After 10 minutes of braising add chopped parsley and bread crumbs.

Roasted Fish with Salt
1,5 kg white fish (in piece); 1,5 kg sea salt; 2 eggs; 20 grams flour
Remark: you need as much salt as fish is heavy. Take out offal but leave scale. From the head down cover the cuts with aluminium foil. Mix salt with flour, add eggs and pour into a roasting tin. Cover the fish with salt on both sides and put into oven on 180°C for 1 hour. Then take it out, remove salt and serve. Remark: the bigger the fish the longer it takes to roast it.

Hvar Rozata – Serves 6
Prep Time: 15 Minutes, Cook Time: 50 Minutes, Cooling time: 120 Minutes, Ready in: 3 Hours 5 Minutes
1 cup white sugar; 1/4 cup water; 6 egg yolks; 1 litre of milk
1.Preheat oven to 350 degrees F (175 degrees C).
2.In a heavy saucepan over medium heat, cook sugar with water, stirring, until melted and light brown. Pour into a pan or cake mold, tilting to coat the bottom of the pan. Set aside.
3.In a bowl, gently whisk together evaporated milk, condensed milk, and egg yolks and mix
4.Line a roasting pan with a damp kitchen towel. Place baking

dish on towel, inside roasting pan, and place roasting pan on oven rack. Fill roasting pan with water to reach halfway up the sides of the baking dish.

5.Bake in preheated oven 45 to 50 minutes, until set. Let cool completely.

6.To unfold, run a knife around the edges of the pan and invert the rozata onto a rimmed serving platter. Refrigerate 2 hours and pour with Caramel Sauce before serving.

Caramel Sauce

1 cup granulated sugar; 1/4 cup water; 1 cup heavy cream

1.In a small, heavy-bottomed saucepan, combine the sugar and water and bring the mixture to a boil, stirring often. Cook, stirring occasionally, until the mixture is a deep caramel color and has the consistency of thin syrup, 10 to 15 minutes.

2.Remove from the heat. Stir in the cream, return the saucepan to the high heat, and boil the sauce until it regains the consistency of thick syrup, about 2 minutes, then cool.

Traditional Drinks on Hvar

Tourists interested in trying local specialities will have fun with the beverages on offer. Here is a quick overview.

The Dalmatian Coffee Break

Dalmatia is a cafe culture, and very little comes between a Dalmatian and his coffee break. Administrative offices have a built-in break (marenda) in the daily schedule, and officials head out to the local cafes for a relaxing coffee and gossip.

The most typical coffee ordered is an espresso, which can turn into a *duga kava* (long coffee) with the addition of more hot water. A coffee will usually be accompanied by a glass of tap water and sometimes a small biscuit, and it is not unusual for a coffee to be nursed for more than an hour. Cappuccinos are also very popular.

Tea is also a popular drink, but English tourists expecting a

219

British equivalent are in for a surprise. A simple order for tea will result in a fruity variety -- mint, pomegranate or fruits of the forest -- with honey rather than milk offered as an accompaniment. The closest to the British cuppa is *indiski cai s mlijekom* (Indian tea with milk).

Award-Winning Wine, Wine With Water and Ice in the Red
Hvar has a long tradition of wine production, and the island, along with the rest of Dalmatia, suffered terribly from the devastating effects of phylloxera in the early 20th century, which led to mass emigration. The wines of Hvar are once more making a resurgence, with award-winning
products from producers such as Andro Tomic winning awards in international competitions.

Although it is possible to find wines from outside the region in supermarkets, the selection is very limited. A sweeter wine, prosek, is also worth trying, served as an aperitif.

There is plenty of domestic wine available for tasting and purchase in the various hillside villages on Hvar, and while the quality may vary, the strong conviction from each producer that his wine is the best remains a constant. Two popular local drinks are bevanda, a mixture of water and table wine (red or white), and *gemischt*, white wine and sparkling water, both of which can be ordered at cafes. It is not uncommon to have red wine served cold, or even with ice.

Vunetovo, the First Micro-Brewery on a Dalmatian Island
One of the great things about living on an island like Hvar is that you hear rumours about other strange foreigners, but you never to get to meet those people. For years. When I first heard that there was a Polish lady in Hvar Town making amazing beer, I was more than a little surprised. The rumours persisted, and finally I tracked young Anna down, just two doors away from Hotel Podstine, on the town's northern edge.

And what I find! Wheat beer, stout, flavoured beers – all delicious, and all made with passion. I was not surprise that she had already won a medal at the Zagreb Craft Beer festival, and her rise has been meteoric in the last two years, and deservedly so. The tasting experience, with a view to match the beer, is something else. More on www.vunetovo.com

Meet the Rakija Family: Turning Berries Into Fire Water
Be careful! Some of this stuff is strong. A typical act at the end of a restaurant meal is a complimentary glass of the hard stuff on the house. While some of these schnapps-like liqueurs are delicious, quality does vary enormously, especially when one wanders off into the realms of homemade *rakijas*. They can be flavoursome, however, with typical ingredients including figs, walnuts and even olives.

Beers and Cocktails
Local beers are in plentiful supply and extremely good. The most popular Croatian brands are Karlovacko and Ozusko, while Lasko from Slovenia is also prevalent. There is a wider selection of bottled beer, including established brands, which tend to come in 0.33l bottles. Draught beers are served in 0.2, 0.3 and 0.5l glasses.

There are numerous cocktail bars on the island, the most famous of which is Carpe Diem in Hvar Town, with its stunning quayside location and celebrity pull.

Water and Other Non-alcoholic Drinks
Tap water is safe to drink, as is the water that comes from public fountains, but there is ample bottled water as well, with several locally produced brands, as well as Jamnica sparkling water. It is acceptable to request a glass of tap water with a coffee. Soft drinks are relatively expensive by comparison, with a 0.25l of Coke costing about 14 kuna in a cafe. Some cafes serve natural juices (prirodna), but this is not the norm.

CHAPTER 10: SHOPPING

Supermarkets on Hvar

There are various wonderful options when it comes to shopping for groceries on Hvar. There is the green market and fish market to be found in some extend in every city (even smaller villages) on the island during the summer. There are several butcher shops on the island and for the rest of the groceries, you can visit one of the supermarkets. Here is the full list with opening hours:
Note: Usually, the summer opening hours are different, but at the moment, they are not published yet.

Hvar Town

There is a large supermarket (Konzum) right behind the bus station at Dolac. It is close to the green market and fish market and there are 2 butcher shops there as well. There is another supermarket (Studenac) at the Main Square and there are several other options off the city centre:
Konzum - Trg Marka Milicića 8
Opening hours - winter months - Mon.-Sat.: 07:00-20:00, Sun.: 07:00-13:00
Konzum - Demetrija Hvarskog 4
Opening hours - winter months - Mon.-Sat.: 07:00-20:00, Sun.: 07:00-12:00
Studenac - Trg Sv. Stjepana 17
Opening hours - winter months - Mon.-Sat.: 07:00-20:30, Sun.: 07:00-19:00
Studenac - Križna Luka b.b.
Opening hours - winter months - Mon.-Sat.: 07:00-20:30, Sun.: 07:00-13:00
Studenac - Pavla Rossa 1
Opening hours - winter months - Mon.-Sat.: 06:30-20:00, Sun.: 07:00-13:00
Studenac - Mate Hrasta 3

Opening hours - winter months - Mon.-Sat.: 06:30-20:30, Sun.: 06:30-12:00

Stari Grad

The largest supermarket is located at the ferry port (Tommy). Other smaller ones are to be found opposite the bus station (Studenac) and in the city centre next to the former Volat shop (Tommy) and on the Riva (Studenac). There is one butcher shop on Riva and another one opposite the kids playground next to the new Volat shop.

Tommy - Trajektno Pristaniste 2
Opening hours - winter months - Mon.-Sat.: 07:30 - 21:00, Sun.: 08:00 - 20:00
Tommy - Alojza Stepinca 1
Opening hours - winter months - every day: 07:00 - 21:00
Studenac - Put Križa 4P
Opening hours - winter months - Mon.-Sat.: 07:00 - 20.00, Sun.: 07.00 - 13.00
Studenac - Riva b.b.
Opening hours - winter months - Mon.-Sat.: 07:00 - 21.00, Sun.: 07.00 - 20.00

Jelsa

The two biggest supermarkets are located next to the bus station (Konzum and Ribola) with the butcher shop just behind the corner and another smaller supermarket opposite the gass station (Studenac), it is as close as a shopping area can get in Jelsa. Another 2 shops can be found in the centre - a smaller one at the waterfront (Konzum) and another one in the library building behind the fish market.
Konzum - Strossmayerovo setaliste b.b.
Opening hours: - winter months - Mon.-Sat: 07:00 - 20:00, Sun.: 07:00 - 13:00
Ribola - Strossmayerovo setaliste 1
Opening hours: - winter months - every day: 07:00 - 21:00

Studenac - Strossmayerovo setaliste
Opening hours: - winter months - Mon.-Sat.: 07:00 - 20:00 Sun.:
07:00 - 19:00
Studenac - Trg Tome Gamulina b.b.
Opening hours: - winter months - Mon.-Sat.: 07:00 - 20:00 Sun.:
07:00 - 13:00
Konzum - Riva b.b.
Opening hours: - winter months - Mon.-Sat: 07:00 - 20:00, Sun.:
07:00 – 13:00

Vrboska
Konzum - Vrboska b.b.
Opening hours: - winter months - Mon.-Sat.: 07:00 - 20:00, Sun.:
08:00 - 13:00
Studenac - Vrboska 44
Opening hours: - winter months - Mon.-Sat.: 07:00 - 20:00 Sun.:
07:00 - 12:00

Sucuraj
Konzum - Sućuraj b.b.
Opening hours: - winter months - Mon.-Sat.: 07:00 - 14:00, Sun.:
07:00 - 12:00

Typical Island Souvenirs

Tourists looking for souvenirs and gifts from a holiday to the
island of Hvar have a range of excellent local products to choose
from and, while the current restrictions on liquids on aircraft may
limit the options for tourists flying in, there are souvenirs on offer
for the air traveller.

Known also as the island of lavender, the fields of Hvar are a
colourful and aromatic delight in June and July as the lavender is
in bloom. Lavender souvenirs are widely available in the boutique
shops and waterfront stalls and make an ideal gift. The two most
popular are lavender oil, sold in small, stylish bottles, and
fragrance bags of Lavandula Croatica, filled with dried lavender

flowers.

The island is also well-known for the quality of its olive oil, and olive farming is an important part of island life. Most families have an olive grove and produce their own oil, using the various presses available locally, and there are many signs in the back streets of the various coastal towns offering olive oil for sale direct to the public.

With its aromatic garden of herbs, Hvar is a fragrant island and there is an excellent selection of homemade honey to whet the appetite. Beekeeping has a long tradition on the island, and there are currently more than 3,000 hives and 100 beekeepers on Hvar, many of whom belong to the Lavender Beekeepers Society.

The bees turn the nectar of the island's rich variety of herbs into honey, with honey made from rosemary highly recommended, with its clear complexion and mild taste. Look out for the word Med meaning 'honey' while wandering through the alleys of the stone towns.

There is a wide choice of local drinks on Hvar, with strong liqueurs made from every conceivable herb. Quality varies considerably and one should be prepared for an insistent host professing his to be the best rakija on the island. There are some excellent liqueurs, which make for good souvenirs, the more interesting ones made from figs, walnuts and olives.

Hvar also has an excellent wine-growing tradition, which is undergoing a renaissance. Led by the Zlatan Otok range from the Plenkovic winery in Sveta Nedelja, the only Croatian Grand Cru and winner of several international awards, there are some excellent wines available locally. Prices, like the quality, vary considerably.

Benedictine nuns have been working on the island since 1664, and they made a significant contribution to education on the island, running a girl's school in Hvar Town from 1826 to 1886, before the first state school was founded that year. Another tradition that they uphold to this day is making lace from the agave plant, making intricate patterns of sun, flowers and other cheery motifs, each pattern individual and left to the nuns' imagination.

An interesting tradition in the lace-making tradition remains, namely that the nuns will not weave when the strong northern wind know as the bura is in full force, as the wind stretches the filaments, but the southern Jugo is preferred for artistic inspiration.

There are more generic souvenirs on offer, but for a fragrant and local memento, the natural resources of this stunning island generate a range of gifts that will linger fragrantly long after the holiday has finished.

There are also a few boutique shops selling arts and crafts from the island. A good place to have a look is the Made in Hvar shop in Hvar Town.

5 Shops Not to Miss

Hvar has a surprising diversity of shopping for those with cash to spend, especially Hvar Town. Here are five shops worth popping into.

Tanja Curin Jewellery
Hvar's best-known jewellery shop. A rare woman would not be caught breathless before the beauty of the magical jewellery world built by Tanja Ćurin in Hvar for thirty years. Her lavish necklaces are known worldwide. Year after year some yachts drop their anchors in the metropolis of the sunniest Mediterranean island for the shop owner to grace their collections with another

imaginative and original piece. New collections always bring new stories. Composed of semi-precious stones the artist searches for all over the world, as she says herself, "of the coral from the Adriatic depths, turquoises from the Himalayan heights, rubies from Africa, ebony from tropical jungles, aquamarines from the Brazilian mines, rosewood from desert oases and amber from the North Sea..." Located just off the main square going to the fortress.

Thesaurus, Hvar Town

I discovered a few years ago that Beyonce and my wife have two things in common.
The first I had known for a while - they are both gorgeous - but the second was new to me. They have the same taste in jewellery, and one store in particular.

My wife and my favourite street in Hvar is the one just north of the square, which I often refer to as Gastro Street. While I will head for a chat and a drink with the friendly teams at Lucullus and Giaxa, or perhaps a glass of wine at 3 Prsuta, my wife never gets further than the first shop on the western entrance of the street.

Thesaurus is the Latin word for 'treasure', and it is indeed an apt name for the store, which also has outlets in Vodice and Zagreb. They use precious and semi precious stones, silver, gold, crystals, minerals, corals, wood, ebony, sandal and lots of pearls in their pieces, all of which are unique and handmade.

Thesaurus has a strong Asian connection, and the two owner-designers spend two months a year in India, where they have small gold and silver factories, producing gold and silver according to their unique designs.

The designers work a lot with crystals, and the positive energy they emanate appears to be sometimes stronger on Hvar, and crystals are an important inspiration and component of their work.

What I had previously regarded as just another jewellery shop in my mind was becoming something altogether more...

And it is not just the likes of my wife who are very impressed. As reported in the national media a couple of years ago, Katja presented Beyonce herself with a necklace from the store on her infamous visit to Hvar, a piece of jewellery that melted the pop diva's heart, according to the report, which described how impressed she was with its beauty.

The Coral Shop, Hvar Town
Although I had heard of the Coral Shop in Hvar Town, it was only a fews years ago that I visited for the first time, when I spent half an hour in the height of the summer madness finally meeting the owner, Aron Scwarz.

What struck me on that first meeting was how chilled he was about life, how non-commercial and how passionate he was about the traditions, history and heritage of Hvar, this at the heart of the commercial intensity that is peak season Hvar.

I returned to the Coral Shop for a chat, and I was introduced to his delightful artist wife Lukrecija, as a succession of tourists entered the shop to look at their highly individual and top quality range of jewellery, with a couple coming to collect pieces already ordered. The Coral Shop story is as interesting as its very talented owners...

The tradition of coral crafts dates back thousands of years (with the oldest dated back to Babel times in 6000 BC, and it is thought that the people of Hvar were first introduced to corals with the arrival of the Ancient Greeks in 384 BC. Rather than follow the trend of refining the coral into perfect shapes, Aron and Lukrecija decided to refine the shapes of coral and silver manually, a craft which is disappearing but one they are keen to resurrect.

The shop is situated just off the main Hvar riva in the first street behind the main waterfont drag.

Green House, Hvar Town
'Green house' is a find, tucked neatly into the small street parallel to Hvar's main waterfront, where the luxury yachts moor, a short walk from the main square. Hvar's exquisite natural environment is its biggest attraction for visitors. It's a paradox that looking after the environment is not the main priority for the island authorities nor the majority of islanders. Logically, damaging chemicals should not be allowed to taint the earth and the sea. While local people are becoming more aware of the need to avoid chemical pesticides and artificial fertilizers, there is much less awareness of the potential damage caused by most commonly used household cleansers.

Green House products'Green house' is Hvar's first primarily organic shop, and it stocks cleaning products by Ecover and Urtekram for all household cleaning purposes, whether washing up, washing clothes, cleaning floors and surfaces, or descaling toilets. The residues from household detergents go into the earth and its underground waters, and a lot gets into the sea. Using products which biodegrade without environmental harm is a choice every householder and buildings manager should make. In a better world, there would be government subsidies to encourage the use of these products.

'Green house' is small, but has a surprisingly wide range of goods on offer, from organic pastas and sauces, to coconut milk, jams, spreads, wines, olive oils, teas, supplements, biscuits, soaps and shampoos, not forgetting etheric oils. There's much to explore and choose from. By rights the business should expand, just as organic products sprang from a minimal market share to become big sellers in the UK some years ago. The next good development would be to have certified organic fruit and vegetables available on the island.

In my early days on Hvar, I used to bring in environmentally friendly cleaning products for my household chores from the UK, Germany or Italy. More recently, they have been available in Split in various organic shops, including Bio & Bio in Prima 3. Now it is a blessing to be able to buy organic products on Hvar. 'Green House' is a small step which should create a big wave in helping to 'green' the island. (with thanks to Vivian Grisogono)

Za Pod Zub, Stari Grad
A French couple Yvan and Chloé decided to open a small shop offering delicatessen in Stari Grad called "Za pod zub" earlier this year.

Located in the old town, the shop is a place to taste and buy various products from the island and Croatia, including: various types of salt, herbal syrops, olives, dried tomatoes, pasta, olive oil, vinegar, various spices, biscuits and sweets and of course, a rich local and regional wine list.

CHAPTER 11: PRACTICALITIES

Visas

Visas are not required for the majority of European and North American countries, and tourists are permitted to enter for 90 days without restriction. For more information on visa requirements for individual countries, the latest information can be found on the Ministry of Foreign Affairs (www.mvpei.hr). Please note that Croatia is NOT in the Schengen zone, so any foreign visas for the Schengen zone will not be applicable in Croatia – most likely you will need another visa. Croatia is due to join Schengen soon, although the recent refugee crisis may have muddied the waters somewhat.

Health and Emergency

There is no hospital on Hvar, and all serious cases are referred to Split. A very efficient emergency helicopter service to Split hospital exists, transferring patients in minutes from several helipads on the island, both actual and makeshift (the football pitch in Jelsa, for example). The emergency phone number is 112.

The main health centres for the island are in Hvar Town above Hotel Amfora and in a newly constructed bock on the outskirts of Jelsa. Head there if in need of medical attention. To reach the medical centre, take the first Jelsa just past the petrol station on the main road from Stari Grad, past the sports hall on the right, and the health centre is immediately on the left. Tel. 021 583 538. Croatia has reciprocal health agreements with numerous countries, including Britain.

Pharmacies are widely available in the main towns, and English is spoken.

The standard of dental care in Croatia is excellent. It is also affordable and there is a growing business in dental tourism. Should a dental emergency occur during your stay, there are a number of dentists operating on Hvar.

The police station in Hvar Town is next to the Suncani Hvar offices opposite the bus station.

Money and Banks

The unit of currency in Croatia is the Croatian kuna, which was introduced to the newly independent country in 1994, replacing the Yugoslav dinar at a rate of 1 kuna for 1000 dinar. Kuna literally means 'marten', a throwback to earlier times when the currency of the region was animal skins and marten pelts were considered valuable. One kuna is sub-divided into 100 lipa (which means linden tree).

Kuna notes come in denominations of 10, 20, 50, 100, 200, 500 and 1000, while coin consist of 1, 2 and 5 kuna, and 5, 10, 20 and 50 lipa. The exchange rate fluctuates with world currencies, but remains relatively stable to the euro in recent years, with 1 euro buying between 7.1 and 7.5 kuna.

Foreign currency is accepted in tourist areas in lieu of kuna, although a lower exchange rate is then applied (usually 7 kuna). Credit cards are increasingly accepted at outlets on Hvar, but not all restaurants, for example, have a credit card facility. It is advisable to check before dining. It is probably fair to say that credit cards are the exception rather than the rule outside of Hvar Town.

There are numerous exchange offices in the main tourist centres, as well as ATMs and two local banks with branches on the island. The ATMs have daily cash limits, but more can be dispensed against a debit card within the bank.

Office hours vary considerably according to the time of year with banks tending to be open early (8am) to late (9pm) in peak season, while 0800 – 1400 is the more common opening times in winter and the shoulder months.

Phone and Internet

The international dialling code for Croatia is 385 and the regional code for Split and environs is 021. The two main local network providers have SIM cards widely available on the island, with the pay-as-you-go vouchers the most popular choice.

There are numerous payphones on Hvar, which are no longer coin operated. Phone cards can be purchased in most shops and at the post office. If dialling another local number from a local phone, omit the 021 or the call will not connect.

Broadband came to Hvar a few years ago, and the general speed of connection is good. Dongles can be purchased at the Offero shop in Hvar Town (www.offero.hr), although there is increasing coverage and Internet providers. Most cafes offer wireless connection, and many apartments will now include free Internet in a booking.

Public Holidays

1 Jan	Fri	New Year's Day
6 Jan	Wed	Epiphany
28 Mar	Mon	Easter Monday
1 May	Sun	Labour Day
26 May	Thu	Corpus Christi
22 Jun	Wed	Anti-Fascist Resistance Day
25 Jun	Sat	Statehood Day
5 Aug	Fri	Victory & Homeland Thanksgiving Day
15 Aug	Mon	Assumption of the Virgin Mary
8 Oct	Sat	Independence Day
1 Nov	Tue	All Saints' Day
25 Dec	Sun	Christmas Day

Apps for Hvar

This being the modern world, one should not be surprised to learn that there are apps available for the island of Hvar. There are three on offer, two very good, and one you should avoid at all costs – mine.

Hvar: An Insider's Guide was the first app for the island, and I was proud of it at the time, but I am now a little embarrassed as two quality (and free) competitors have appeared on the scene, which are much better than mine. Hvar Island Travel Guide and Hvar in a Nutshell are both excellent.

Weather on Hvar

Nowhere symbolises the great weather in Croatia more than the island of Hvar, with the oft-quoted statistic that its 2724 hours of sunshine every year make it the sunniest place in Europe. For an island with so much sunshine, it is incredibly green, so what is the real story with the weather on the Croatian island voted among the world's ten most beautiful by Conde Nast readers?

A Free Hotel Room if it Snows...
Among the other claims bandied about is that guests are entitled to a free hotel room if it snows, further proof of the island's fine weather. This is a nice piece of marketing as the Dalmatian winter has little tourism, but it is true that it rarely snows on Hvar, and it is regional news when it does. It has snowed briefly about five times in the last ten years, although February 2012 saw some unusual sights on the island, including a Slovakian who skied 5km from the the peak of Sveti Nikola to the bay of Dubovica.

Summers tend to be hot with temperatures in the 27-35C range, another excuse, if one were needed, for spending more time in the pristine Adriatic Sea. May, June and September are more temperate months, with the sea warm enough for swimming, and many walking and cycling holidays take place in these months.

It does rain. A lot. In winter. Locals joke that the influx of British buyers of the island's stone properties in 2004-6 resulted in them bringing their weather with them, but the weather is relatively consistent when it matters most, the tourist season.

The Winds of the Adriatic: Introducing the Bura

Just as the clear blue skies are an almost permanent feature in the summer, so the winter has its constant weather companion, a biting northern wind known as the *bura*. When the *bura* is blowing, the catamarans from Jelsa and Hvar Town are frequently cancelled, with the Stari Grad car ferry also an occasional victim. While bitterly cold, the morning after a *bura* usually results in clear blue skies.

How to Check Weather Forecasts on Hvar

There are lots of online resources for checking the weather in Croatia, but not all of them are localised. Several online forecasters predicting the weather use Split readings for the island, but there are differences between the two. One reliable local source in the central village of Pitve for forecasting weather in Croatia was set up by a Scottish business weather forecaster who bought property in the village.

Beaches in Croatia: Checking the Sea Temperature

Of much more importance to many tourists is the all-important sea temperature. While there are a hardy few who swim all year, including a sprightly octogenarian in Jelsa, the generally accepted swimming season is from May to October.

In order to help plan the timing of your visit (and indeed the type of beach to visit), the Ministry of Environmental Protection maintains a useful website with information on all beaches on Hvar, recording data every fortnight in the season on sea and air temperature, cleanliness and facilities. Powered by Google Earth, the site allows visitors to zoom in to a particular beach, to assess it for accessibility, privacy etc.

The weather in Croatia along the coast is generally excellent, and beach holidays are increasing in popularity, but it is not all sunshine in the winter, when a combination of Dalmatian *bura* and British-induced rain can change the experience entirely.

Language

The official language is Croatian, although visitors from Zagreb will question the Croatianness of the language spoken by the locals, who speak a range of dialects, which vary from village to village.
There is a richness of different vocabulary, and a word in Jelsa will have a completely different name by the time you have reached Stari Grad. A favourite example is the word for 'chisel' which has eight different dialect words on the island, the bigger joke being that it is impossible to buy a chisel on the island. Soon after I launched Total Hvar, I started a Hvar dialect service with Professor Frank John Dubokovich – if you have two minutes and want to see the size of the challenge, search for 'Dalmatian Grunt' on YouTube.

Added to the mix is the strong Italian influence on the island's history, due to extended Venetian rule, and the adaptation of various Italian words into the Dalmatian dialect complicates things further. The word for tomato, for example, has three mainstream translations – pomidor, rajcica and paradeis.

Having said all that, Croatian – part of the Slavic language family – is actually a very logical language, pronounced phonetically, and with several ground rules and very few exceptions from that. This does not mean that it is easy for Westerners to learn, it isn't, but for those willing to spend some time, a local teacher in Jelsa runs 'Croatian for Foreigners' classes.

English, German and Italian are widely spoken on the island, and tourists have little difficulty communicating their basic needs. While local residents would not expect visitors to be fluent in Croatian, making the effort to learn a few basic words is much appreciated.

Safety and Hvar with Children

Hvar is an incredibly safe environment, and reported crime is very low. While it always pays to be vigilant, one of the benefits of the island is its safety, particularly for children, a throwback for many to a time when the worries of the modern world did no apply.

The island's many squares are filled with cafes and children playing, the younger ones taking care of the old, a chance for parents to relax in a safe environment. Croatians love children and downtown friendships between local and visiting children are common. A common language is secondary. The trampolines (behind the park in Jelsa, opposite the old town in Stari Grad) are popular in season.

Religion

Croatia is an overwhelmingly Catholic country, and religion is taken very seriously. Mass attendance is high, and on of the nicest times of the week is late morning on Sundays as worshippers in their Sunday finest descend from their churches for a coffee and gossip in the nearby cafés.

There are numerous religious festivals and processions throughout the year, most notably the Za Krizem procession through the night on Maundy Thursday. During such processions, sitting outside the neaby cafes drinking alcohol is frowned upon, so either refrain or take your drinks inside. It is considered best practice to stand while the procession passes.

A constant reminder of in the influence of the Church in daily life is the hourly ringing of the church bells. The only time the bells fall silent is between Good Friday and Easter Sunday, a silence more than made up for with the exuberant ringing on the morning of Easter Sunday. A local death is announced by bells ringing 33 times, akin to the lifetime of Jesus.

Water and Electricity

Water is safe to drink on Hvar. While there are some local sources of spring water, the demand is greater than the supply, and water is now piped in from the mainland via Brac. There are several fresh water supplies in fountains in the main squares. Electricity is 220 V / 50 hz

Laundry

Many private owners will do laundry for a fee, so just ask. There is a laundrette in Hvar Town by the market at the back of the main square.

Buying Property on Hvar

The price of real estate in Croatia is a common discussion topic for holidaymakers as they saunter through the picturesque cobbled streets of the various stone towns of Dalmatia, daydreaming about buying a waterside ruin to turn into the perfect holiday home. As the country's premier island, looking at property on Hvar has been especially popular.

The Croatian Property Boom of 2004

Fortunes were made on Hvar in 2004, as foreign buyers stepped off the ferry and bought what they could. Croatia was seen as the next property hot spot and prices were cheap, as the country emerged from the damage of the war in Yugoslavia. Stone ruins in hilltop villages which had been seen almost as a burden were selling for tens of thousands of euros, while prime coastal building land turned some locals into millionaires.

In one example on the Rudine Peninsula, a stone ruin in the pretty hamlet of Mala Rudina sold three times in 18 months, with the sales price increasing from 43,000 to 85,000 and finally to 150,000 euro. Such price rises were not atypical, but just as prices rose quickly, the property crash caused several distress sales, leaving general price levels not too far from prices in 2004.

The Buying Process
The basic advice is the same when buying property anywhere - get a good lawyer. Croatian property titles are complicated, and it is not uncommon for there to be more than fifty owners, with the registered owner on the paperwork having died fifty years ago.

The essential documents that you need are the title deed (*vlasnicki list*) and the catastar map. The title deed gives information on the plot number and size, the list of registered owners and a list of any mortgages or charges on the property, while the catastar map pinpoints the plot. It is common to pay a deposit (usually 10%) against a notarised pre-contract, with the balance on completion.

Prior to February 2009, all foreign buyers were required to apply to the Ministry of Justice for permission to own the property they had just bought, a formality which caused anguish and frustration due to the length of time it took to process (up to seven years). This restriction has been lifted for many countries, including members of the EU and some states in America.

Potential Pitfalls
Title issues apart, there are several additional things to check before purchasing property on Hvar:
Any property built after 1968 should have a usage permit. This is in addition to the location and building permits required to legally build a house. All illegal buildings built prior to 1968 were

legalised in a general amnesty, and so the usage permit requirement only exists for later properties.

Check the registered use of the property on the building permit. A recent law change means that a rental licence is required for properties rented to tourists. Currently only properties which have commercial use listed in the building permit can apply for these licences. As most permits 20-30 years ago were issued for residential use, it may not be legally possible to rent the property.

Land purchase should be thoroughly researched. There are different grades of building land and it is a minefield for the uninitiated, with building permissions rarely granted. Buy land with permission already granted where possible.

Hvar is a beautiful island and, although by no means overrun with foreigners, a sizable number have bought and renovated property. With the appropriate due diligence, now is an extremely affordable time to buy real estate in Croatia.

Hvar and the Environment

Hvar is one of the most beautiful places on the planet, a natural paradise which attracts thousands of tourists each year who are looking to escape the pressures of the modern world. Just as you can lose yourself in the party atmosphere of Hvar Town, so too you can find endless hidden bays where you are totally alone.

Paradise needs to be protected, however, and the threats to Hvar's fragile environment are real. The biggest danger each year comes from forest fires. It is one thing being the sunniest island in Europe, it is quite another when a chance fire starts on the parched land and quickly spreads. Hvar, like other islands, has lost lots of its greenery over the years through forest fires which quickly spread from one careless action. PLEASE BE CAREFUL.

As elsewhere, there are many environmental issues which need attention on Hvar. An essential focal point is the excellent Eco Hvar website – www.eco-hvar.com

CHAPTER 12: THE TOTAL HVAR PROJECT

Thank you for buying and reading this book,and I hope it contributes a little to your enjoyment of this fabulous island. If you have any strength left, I would like to introduce myself and the Total Project, which has now gone both national and international, but started out on sunny Hvar.

From Somalia to Hvar - How I Came From Hell to Paradise

My name is Paul and I am from near Manchester (posh part) and I have been living in Croatia since 2003. Prior to Croatia, I wandered the globe doing an array of random, but satisfying things, which have included chambermaiding in Munich, being a laser crystals salesman in Moscow, a report writer in Tbilisi, an English, French, German and Russian teacher in Hiroshima, a wine merchant in Oxfordshire and an aid worker in Siberia, Rwanda and Somalia. Which makes me perfectly qualified to write a book about Hvar.

Why Croatia? Simple really. I was sitting on a rooftop in Hargeisa, Somaliland in January 2002, when I got news that my house in the UK had sold. I had already decided to quit Britain and was looking for a place to keep my books, that my friends could use, a refuge from my aid worker career. I went down to grab a (smuggled) beer from the fridge and my Kenyan colleagues were watching CNN, the only channel available to us. It was advert time and there is was, a stunning 30 second ad.

Croatia - the Mediterranean as it once was.

Croatia. Stunning. Warm (or so I thought - after seven bura-filled winters, not sure I would agree), cheap and accessible (or so I thought - flights are a nightmare out of season). I did some preliminary research and I could afford the 2002 asking prices. A cheeky little house in an old town close to the sea would be perfect. I never imagined then that I would be a permanent resident and writing a guide book about Hvar.

I didn't know anything about Croatia, never mind about Hvar, or anyone from there, but a Canadian friend had been living in Sarajevo and so I went to stay with her, and she agreed to help. It was August 2002, and beers were being consumed on a balmy August evening (love that city), and she asked me where I would like to buy.

On realising I didn't have a clue, she took pen and paper and started making a list, explaining a little about each place. Number 1, Dubrovnik, biggest tourist attraction, number 2, Split, gateway to the islands, that sort of thing. She wrote down other names, some on islands, some not - none of them familiar to me.

And after she wrote down the tenth place, she asked which one sounded best. I hadn't really been listening too hard, so I closed my eyes and pointed to the paper. My finger landed on number six.
Hvar.

And that was the decision made. We left at 0300 on the Friday with her Bosnian boyfriend, Amko, driving, interpreting and being a general hero. We had to return Monday afternoon, so time was against us. As we took the first ferry at 0700 to Sucuraj, we stopped for a coffee. Amko, a man of many Malboro inhalations, but few words, finally spoke once the espresso had hit its mark. "Jelsa is the nicest place on the island." More inhalation. And that was that, I decided that Jelsa was the place to be. My choice was made easier by the fact that there was only one house for sale in the town. We were told to be at the catamaran for 1800 on the Saturday to meet an older man in a straw hat, the owner. Antun spoke German so we had a channel of communication.

Random does not begin to describe the house. It came in two parts, separated by a public right of way; one half had toilet but no kitchen, the other kitchen but no toilet. It was habitable (not for a honeymoon...), 30m from the main square, we loved it. An offer was made and accepted the next morning, a lawyer persuaded to prepare a pre-contract on a Sunday evening (should have seen that coming...), 2000 euro withdrawal from the bank the next morning, and we drove back to Sarajevo in triumph on the Monday late morning. It is now back on the market for a very reasonable 79,995 euro, one careful recent owner.

A month later, I completed. My new home! On an idyllic, happening Adriatic island. I knew nobody and had only three words of Croatian to my name: punomoc (power of attorney), hobotnice (octopus) and the imperious potpis (signature) - I heard some Aussies on Brac were so impressed with the latter that they named their company Potpis doo!

And then the internet cafe started reducing its hours, ditto the bank. A restaurant closed and the realisation that Hvar in August is very different to Hvar in January began to dawn. What had I done? And then I walked into the library and so began another happier and more permanent chapter in my life. But that is another story...

A story that is told in my second book, *Lavender, Dormice and a Donkey Named Mercedes*, available in paperback and on Kindle on Amazon.

About This Book and a Request

I really hope you found the book useful and that it helped you enjoy this magical island a little more. I am the first to admit it is far from perfect, as it is self-written, researched and published.

There has never been a really good guide about the entire island (and am sure many of you would still hold that to be the case) and

245

watching tourists wandering round my home town of Jelsa with guide books that summed up the town in a paragraph convinced me to have a go.

The book has been written completely from scratch and some areas are stronger than others. My aim was not to fill it with advertising and make some quick money, but to make a start and produce a much more professional version for future editions. I am not sure I am achieving that in this, the third edition, but the information is well-researched and up to date.

In order to get the best information possible, I would like to ask your help. I have started a Facebook group, Total Hvar, where I intend to keep sharing the information about the island. Please contribute any findings you have, including restaurants that were poor, quirky things, so that we can make the next edition even better.

If you are a local business and have not been included, the book, in its various forms will be constantly updated, so get in touch and give me information about your offer and I will endeavour to include in the updated version.

Alternatively, leave a note at Café Splendid in Jelsa if you are in the neighbourhood. I can be spotted there most days around midday behind a green bottle and would welcome feedback and suggestions (including the constructive negative). It is a great island with so much hidden depth, that it would be a shame not to make all its attractions available to all.

Croatian language purists will have noticed the lack of squiggles over the letters c, s, z etc. This is a deliberate omission as the book will appear in various forms and experience has shown that there are compatibility. Practicality over perfection, and apologies in advance for any offence this may cause.

Apologies too for the lack of maps, something I am working on. All the tourist offices have excellent maps when you get here and there are numerous maps of the towns and islands online. This year's edition appears without photos inside, the result of a decision to opt only for the print on demand services. While it is something of a thrill to have the postman deliver hundreds of copies of your own book, the reality of trying to distribute, track and account for copies made the decision to work solely with Amazon on the print on demand option much easier. It is better of course for tourists planning to visit, as they will be able to buy the book in advance.

Total Hvar: Quality Information for a Quality Island

In March 2011, I watched a tourist walking through the square in Jelsa with a copy of Lonely Planet Croatia (and this is no criticism of that publication). He was trying to make sense of the town from the limited information in the book which, after all, covered the whole country.

It was not the first time that I had come across the scene, but I determined that day to do something about it, to write the first comprehensive guidebook for the island of Hvar in English.

It has been quite a journey, leading me initially into a world of iPhone apps, Kindles and PDF downloads; then to an idea of running the first interactive and all-inclusive website for the island, with video, interactive maps and 4-5 blogseach day. Things snowballed very quickly, and I found myself reporting on aspects of Hvar life in Belgrade, Zagreb and Germany, with the first Hvar festival in Norway in the planning. I was published in places as diverse as New York and the Qatar Airways inflight magazine.

The Total Hvar website (www.total-hvar.com) started in October 2011, and now has more than 8,000 articles just about the island.

247

Total Split (www.croatia-split.com) started in November 2012, and Total Inland Dalmatia (www.total-inland-dalmatia.com) in December 2013. All three websites are now under the umbrella of our latest project, the Google News-affiliated site Total Croatia News (www.total-croatia-news.com), which now has almost 50 writers and is the first comprehensive daily online portal about Croatia in English, which a minimum of 15 articles daily. Find Total Croatia News on Facebook if you wish to know more. Our most recent expansion has been into Bavaria, with Total Munich (www.total-munich.com), an ongoing project.

We have also recently expanded into various sectors of Croatian life, creating the first ever national websites (some are still in process). Total Croatia Cycling, Total Croatia Wine, Total Croatia Technology and Total Croatia Islands are all projects that are either live already or will be completed by the end of 2016. If you would like to get involved, contact us on news@total-croatia-news.com.

The mission remains the same – to promote the very best that my adopted island has to offer, and to work to improve the information flow and increase the opportunities for tourism. If my mother-in-laws apartments are full five months a year, I will have succeeded. I am happy to work with anyone with a positive interest in Hvar, so get in touch!

Acknowledgements

Lots of people have contributed to this book and the Total Hvar project in general, and I have been heartened by the number of local people who have embraced Total Hvar and contributed to its initial success.

It quite possibly would not have got off the ground without the timely advice and support of one agency in Stari Grad, and I am particularly grateful to Majda and Dalibor from Hvar Touristik for all their initial (and ongoing) support from the very start. Their advice and early enthusiasm helped shape the path of Total Hvar and I thank them for that. And they really do have a great agency as well...

An essential pillar of Total Hvar is the meticulous Vivian Grisogono from Pitve, who abhors my slack self-editing and frequent typos, and has contributed an enormous amount behind the scenes, tidying up the site, advising and contributing some fabulous pieces as well (and her Easter Procession coverage was one of the most popular things on the site). Thank you, Vivian. Check out her website at www.viviangrisogono.com

Thanks to to Ivana Zupan, who joined the Total Hvar team in 2014, and who has been responsible for not only tidying up the considerable mess I have created on the back end of the website, but also by her informative blogging which had given people a different (and much healthier) insight into life on Hvar.

My three girls have been more than patient since I plunged us all into this latest escapade, and I do hereby publicly acknowledge I am behind on my parenting and marital responsibilities. It has been fun watching the enquiring minds on the little ones watching Daddy beavering away on his computer, and two quotes from my five year-old sum it up:

"Daddy, are you on Twitter? Can you tell all the tourists that there is a nice old lady in Jelsa – my grandma – who does not have much money, but has nice apartments to rent. And that Jelsa is a nice place and they should come and stay." Which was beaten only by...

"You don't know anything Daddy. Dr. Oz in America knows everything about health. My rowing coach Jerko knows lots about vitamins. But I suppose you do know something about tourism on Hvar."

Three great ladies – thank you for everything.

If you are going to work with people, work with the best, and I am privileged to have met some great photographers on Hvar, which is just as well because my photos are worse than useless. Mario Romulic and Drazen Stojcic (www.romulic.com) are among Croatia's top photographers, and the artists behind many of the promotional pictures about Hvar which circulate the Internet, including the Suncani Hvar portfolio. Their Timelapse Croatia film was hailed by many as one of the best promotions of Croatian tourism, and if you haven't checked out their viral hit, Hvar Storm, on Vimeo, I encourage you to do so. Hvar as you rarely see it in the summer. Thank you, kind Sirs, for your continued support, and generosity in allowing me to not only have your fabulous photos on the book's cover, but also for our photo of the day feature on Total Croatia News.

USEFUL NUMBERS

Agencies:

Atlas Hvar, Obala bb, Hvar, Tel +385 21 741 911, www.atlas-hvar.hr, info@atlas-hvar.hr
Lavanda tours, Jelsa, Tel +385 21 761-611, www.lavandatours.hr, mihael@lavandatours.hr
Islands of Croatia, Trg Svetog Ivana bb, Jelsa, Tel +385 21 718 560, www.islands-croatia.net, info@islands-croatia.net
Hvar adventure - Bastun, Obala bb, Hvar, Tel +385 21 717 813, www.hvar-adventure.com, info@hvar-adventure.com
Hvar Touristik, Jurja skarpe 13, Stari Grad, Tel +385 21 717 580, www.hvar-touristik.com, info@hvar-touristik.com
Hvar Travel, Dolac bb, Hvar, Tel +385 21 717 426, www.hvar-travel.com, reservation@hvar-travel.com
Secret Hvar, Dolac bb, Hvar, Tel +385 21 717 615, www.secrethvar.com, info@secrethvar.com
MB rent, Hvar, Tel +385 91 518 3608, matko.domancic@hotmail.com
Luka rent, Riva 24, Hvar, Tel +385 91 591 7111, www.lukarent.com, info@lukarent.com
Mario-rent, Vlade Avelinija street, Hvar, Tel +385 91 894 72 29, www.rentaboathvar.com, info@mario-rent.hr
Globus Tours, Strossmayerovo setaliste bb, Jelsa, Tel +385 21 761 955, info@globus-tours.hr
Pelegrini Tours, Riva bb, Hvar, Tel +385 21 742 743, www.pelegrini-hvar.hr, pelegrini@inet.hr

Tourist Boards:

Tourist Board Jelsa, Riva bb, Jelsa, Tel +385 21 761 017, www.tzjelsa.hr, info@tzjelsa.hr
Tourist Board Hvar, Trg sv. Stjepana 42, Hvar, Tel +385 21 741 059, www.tzhvar.hr, info@tzhvar.hr
Tourist Board Stari Grad, Obala dr. Franje Tuđmana 1, Stari Grad,

Tel +385 21 765 763, www.stari-grad-faros.hr, tzg-stari-
grad@st.t-com.hr
Tourist Board Vrboska, Vrboska bb, Vrboska, Tel +385 21 774
137, www.vrboska.info, info@vrboska.info
Tourist Board Sućuraj, Tel +385 21 717 288,
tz.sucuraj@st.htnet.hr

Hotels:

Adriana, Obala Fabrika 28, Hvar, Tel +385 21 750 200,
www.suncanihvar.com/hr/adriana-hvar-spa-hotel.html
Amfora, Ulica biskupa Jurja Dubokovića 5, Hvar, Tel +385 21
750 300, www.suncanihvar.com/amfora-hvar-grand-beach-
resort.html
Riva, Obala Riva 27, Hvar, Tel +385 21 750 100,
www.suncanihvar.com/riva-hvar-yacht-harbour-hotel.html
Pharos, Ulica Dinka Kovacevića 10, Hvar, Tel +385 21 750 500,
www.suncanihvar.com/hotel-pharos.html
The Palace, Trg Sv. Stjepana 5, Hvar, Tel +385 21 741 966,
www.suncanihvar.com/the-palace-hvar.html
Hotel Villa Dalmacija, setaliste put Križa 13, Hvar, Tel +385 21
741 120, www.suncanihvar.com/hotel-villa-dalmacija.html
Hotel Delfin, Obala Fabrika 36, Hvar, Tel +385 21 741 168,
www.suncanihvar.com/hotel-delfin.html
Lavanda, Priko bb, Stari Grad, Tel +385 21 306 306,
www.heliosfaros.eu/en/hoteli-helios-info-en/lavanda-hotel-en
Arkada, Priko bb, Stari Grad, Tel +385 21 306 306,
www.heliosfaros.eu/en/hoteli-helios-info-en/arkada-en
Jurjevac bungalows, Stari Grad, Tel +385 21 306 306,
www.heliosfaros.eu/en/hoteli-helios-info-en/jurjevac-en
Helios Apartments, Priko bb, Stari Grad, Tel +385 21 306 306,
www.heliosfaros.eu/en/hoteli-helios-info-en/helios-apartmani-en
Trim apartments, Priko bb, Stari Grad, Tel +385 21 306 306,
www.heliosfaros.eu/en/hoteli-helios-info-en/apartments-trim-en
Adriatiq Resort Fontana/ Adriatiq Resort Fontana Deluxe, Jelsa
94, Jelsa, Tel +385 21 761 008, www.resortfontana-adriatiq.com,

resort-fontana@adriatiq.com
Hotel Park, Bankete, Hvar, Tel + 385 21 718 337,
www.hph.hotelparkhvar.com, park.hvar@st.t-com.hr
Hotel Croatia, Vlade Avelinija 7, Hvar, Tel + 385 21 742 400,
www.hotelcroatia.net, info@hotelcroatia.net
Aparthotel Pharia, Put Podstina 1, Hvar, Tel + 385 21 77 80 80,
www.orvas-hotels.com/hr/anu/orvas-hotels/aparthotel-pharia,
pharia@orvas.hr
Heritage villa Apolon, setaliste Don sime Ljubića , Hvar, Tel +
385 21 778 320, www.apolon.hr, info@apolon.hr
Hotel Timun, Pokrivenik, Tel +385 21 745 140, www.hotel-
timun.hr

Hostels:

Dink's Place, Ive Roića 5, Hvar, info@dinksplace.com
Marinero, Put sv. Marka 9, Hvar, Tel +385 98 554 411,
hostel.marinero@gmail.com
Villa Marija, Lucije Rudan 7, Hvar, Tel + 385 21 717 110,
info@villamarijahvar.com
Hvar Out, Kroz Burak 32, Hvar, Tel +385 21 717 375,
www.hvarouthostel.com, hvarouthostel@gmail.com
Helvetia, Ul. Grge Novaka 6, Hvar, rino.hajduk@gmail.com
Villa Zorana, Domovinskog rata 20, Hvar, Tel + 385 91 723 1737,
villazorana@gmail.com
Earthers, Martina Vucetića 11, Hvar, Tel +385 99 267 9889,
www.earthershostel.com, earthershostel@gmail.com
Dvoshko, Ive Roića 56, Hvar, Tel +385 91 572 6357,
guesthouse.dvoshko@gmail.com
The Shaka, Marina Blagaića 8, Hvar, Tel +385 92 233 6368,
nezicamir4@gmail.com
The White Rabbit, Stjepana Papafave 6, Hvar, Tel +385 91 666
1985, whiterabbithvar@gmail.com
Villa Skansi, Domovinskog rata 18, Hvar,
hostelvillaskansi1@gmail.com
Luka's Lodge, S. Buzolica Tome 75, Hvar, Tel +385 21 742 118,

www.lukalodgehvar.hostel.com
Green Lizard, Hvar, Tel +385 98 171 8729, www.greenlizard.hr,
hostel@greenlizard.hr

Restaurants

HVAR/PAKLENI ISLANDS
Zori, Palmizana 19, Hvar, Tel +385 21 744 904, www.zori.hr,
info@zori.hr
Toto's, Palmizana 11, Hvar, Tel +385 91 617 5510, www.totos.eu,
info@totos.eu
Meneghello, Palmizana 12, Hvar, Tel +385 91 478 3111,
www.palmizana.com, info@palmizana.com
Bacchus, Palmizana, Hvar, Tel +385 91 253 3796, www.bacchus-
palmizana.com, bacchuspalmizana@gmail.com
Laganini, Palmizana, Hvar, Tel +385 91 174 4976, www.laganini-
novak.com, info@laganini-novak.com
Patak, Palmizana Hvar, Tel +385 95 8649 544,
www.antoniopatak.com, dujmovic.k@gmail.com
Amo, Jerolim, Hvar, www.veneranda.hr, amo.beach@makart.hr
Dionis, Sv, Klement, Hvar, Tel +385 98 1671 016,
www.pakleniotoci.hr/dionis.htm, pjerino@pakleniotoci.hr
U Toncijevu dvoru, Sv. Klement, Hvar, Tel +385 98 589 613,
www.svetiklement.hr, perinam@yahoo.de
Gariful, Riva, Hvar, Tel +385 95 8540 387, www.hvar-gariful.hr,
ivangospodnetic@yahoo.com
Divino, Put Križa 1, Hvar, Tel +385 91 437 7777,
www.divino.com.hr, info@divino.com.hr
Đorđota Vartal, Uvala križa, Hvar, Tel +385 91 53 20 382,
www.restoran-vartal.com, djordje.tudor@st.t-com.hr
Kod kapetana, Fabrika 10, Hvar, Tel +385 98 312 161,
kodkapetana1998@gmail.com
C'est la vie, Križna luka, Hvar, Tel +385 95 902 000,
stipe@lucullus-hvar.com
Marinero, Banketi bb, Hvar, Tel +385 98 337 120,
fzuvela@gmail.com

Villa Dinka, Hvar, Tel +385 21 741 192, villa.dinka@hi.t-com.hr
Palaca Paladini, P. Hektorovića 4, Hvar, Tel +385 98 933 8915, paladinis@tihi-hvar.com
Paradies garden, Groda bb, Hvar, Tel +385 91 17 42 066, www.paradies-hvar.hr, karlo.trogrlic@st.t-com.hr
Dalmatino, Sv. Marak 1, Hvar, Tel +385 91 529 3121, www.dalmatino-hvar.com, dalmatino-hvar@post.t-com.hr
Passarola, Dr. Mate Milicića 10, Hvar, Tel +385 99 733 2438, www.restaurant-passarola.eu
Il Porto, Put Križa 17, Hvar, Tel +385 98 661 982, ilportohvar@gmail.com
Menego, Groda bb, Hvar, Tel +385 21 717 411, www.menego.hr, menego.hvar@gmail.com
Macondo, Groda, Hvar, Tel + 35 21 742 850
Alviž, Dolac, Hvar, Tel +385 21 742 797, vjekoslav.alviz.zaninovic@st.t-com.hr
Asian spice, Trg Svetog Stjepana 30, Hvar, Tel +385 98 938 6035
Junior, Kroz Burak 10, Hvar, Tel +385 99 195 3496
Fig, I.F. Biundovica 3, Hvar, tel +385 99 422 9721, www.figcafebar.com, info@figcafebar.com
50Hvar, Sverti Marak 10, Hvar, Tel +385 91 7399 972, www.50hvar.com, info@50hvar.rocks
Luviji, Jurja Novaka 6, Hvar, Tel +385 91 519 8444
Mizarola, Trg sv. Stjepana bb, Hvar, Tel +385 98 799 978
Kogo, Trg sv. Stjepana bb, Hvar, Tel +385 21 742 136, u.o.kogo@st.t-com.hr
Giaxa, Petra Hektorovica 3, Hvar, Tel +385 21 741 073, www.giaxa.com, giaxahvar@gmail.com
Luna, Petra Hektorovica 1, Hvar, Tel +385 21 741 400, www.lunahvar.com, lunahvarcro@gmail.com
Golden Shell, Petra Hektorovica 8, Hvar, Tel +385 98 9177 386
Paladini, Petra Hektorovića 4, Hvar, Tel +385 21 742 104, www.paladinihvar.com

STARI GRAD
Kod Damira, Trg Stjepana Radica 5, Hvar, Tel +385 91 573 6376,

www.kod-damira.hr
Antika, Duonjo kola, Stari Grad, Tel +385 21 765 479,
antika@yahoo.com
Marko's Pizzeria & Spaghetteria, Trg Ploca, Stari Grad, Tel +385
21 765 889
Ermitaž, Obala hrvatskih branitelja, Stari Grad,
jaksa_dulcic@yahoo.com
Zvijezda Mora, Trg Petra Zoranića, Stari Grad, Tel +385 21 766
133
Pineta, Ulica Ljudevita Gaja 3, Stari Grad, Tel +385 91 505 3672
Apolon, Setaliste Don Sime Ljubica 7, Stari Grad,Tel +385 21
778 320, www.apolon.hr

JELSA
Me&Mrs Jones, Mala Banda bb, Jelsa, Tel +385 21 761 882,
meandmrsjones.jelsa@gmail.com
Artichoke, Obala Cire Gamulina, Jelsa, Tel +385 98 908 8667
Murvica, Jelsa, Tel +385 21 761 405, www.murvica.net,
info@murvica.net
Faros, Jelsa 532, Jelsa, Tel +385 21 751 351
Nono, Jelsa, Tel +385 91 735 2335
Pelago, Jelsa, Tel +385 91 940 2445
Bistro Hit, Jelsa 503, Jelsa, Tel +385 91 581 0173

VILLAGES
Zbondini, Velo Grablje 21, Velo Grablje, Tel +385 91 532 0382
Stori Komin, Malo Grablje, Tel +385 91 527 6408
Konoba Ringo, Pribinja, Tel +385 91 510 3686
Kokot, Dol, Tel +385 91 511 4288
Konoba Bogo, Vrbanj 3, Vrbanj
Konoba Vrisnik, Vrisnik 5, Jelsa, Tel +385 91 522 9949,
www.konoba-vrisnik.com, info@konoba-vrisnik.com
Konoba Dvor Duboković, Pitve, Tel +385 98 172 1726,
www.dvordubokovic.hr, dvor.dubokovic@mail.inet.hr
Kod none, Svirce, Tel +385 91 528 5936,
veronikamatkovic@yahoo.com

Davor Zavala, Zavala bb, Jelsa, Tel +385 95 541 5830,
www.restaurantdavor.com
Bilo idro, Sveta Nedjelja, Tel +385 21 745 703,
www.zlatanotok.hr, booking@zlatanotok.hr
Tamaris, Sveta Nedjelja, Tel +385 91 5166 255, www.apartmani-
jurica-hvar.com/, tamaris@hi.t-com.hr
Konoba Humac, Humac, Tel +385 91 523 9463

Winebars

Tri prsuta, Petra Hektorovića, Hvar, Tel +385 98 969 6193
Vintage, Obala Fabrika 4a, Hvar, Tel +385 91 489 3377
Marco's Wine Bar, Trg Sv. Stjepana 5, Hvar, Tel +385 91 1741
500, www.suncanihvar.com/hr/palace-hvar/marcos-wine-bar.html,
concierge@suncanihvar.com
Hedonist, Ulica Marije Maricicbr.9 , Hvar, Tel +385 98 192 4150
Red Red Wine Bar, Kroz Burak 31, Tel +385 95 455 4554
rrwbar.hvar@gmail.com

Emergency numbers

HVAR
112 - general emergency number for all services
Dentist - dr. Maja Vajagić, Trg Sv. Stjepana, Hvar, Tel +385 21
742 122
Emergency medical aid,, Zastup, Hvar, Tel +385 21 717 099
Emergency medial aid, Majerovica bb, Hvar, Tel +385 21 778 040
Pediatrician - dr. Nađa Novak, Zastup, Hvar, Tel +385 21 742 716
Family medicine - dr.Divna Lazatović, dr. Natalija Granić, Trg Sv.
Stjepana, Hvar, Tel +385 21 743 103, +385 21 717 422
Family medicine - dr. Suncana Draganić, Zastup, Hvar, Tel +385
21 778 046
Pharmacy, Trg Sv. Stjepana, Hvar, Tel + 385 21 741 002
Police station, Ive Milicića 5, Hvar, Tel +385 21 307 565, +385
21 504 239

STARI GRAD
Veterinarian, Stari Grad, Tel +385 21 765 388
Medical clinic, Stari Grad, Tel +385 21 765 200, +385 21 765 373
Dentist, Stari Grad, Tel +385 21 765 917
Pharmacy, Stari Grad, Tel +385 21 765 061

JELSA
Pharmacy, Jelsa, Tel +385 21 761 108
Medical clinic, Jelsa, Tel +385 21 583 538, +385 21 583 537,
+385 21 583 533
Emergency medical aid, Jelsa, Tel +385 21 765 122, +385 99 471
148

SUĆURAJ
Medical clinic, Sućuraj, Tel +385 21 773 210

Post offices
Post office, Riva bb, Hvar, Tel +385 21 742 588
Post office, Stari Grad, Tel +385 21 765 164, +385 21 765 775
Post office, Jelsa, Tel +385 21 761 207
Post office, Sućuraj, Tel +385 21 773 202

Shops
Tanja Ćurin Jewellry, Mesnicka 22, Hvar, Tel +385 91 5067 140,
www.tanjacurin.com, tanja@tanjacurin.hr
Green House Hvar, Tel +385 92 1307 808,
www.greenhousehvar.com, greenhousehvar@gmail.com
Coral Shop, samovitov dolac bb, Hvar, Tel +385 91 897 2151
Thesaurus Jewellery, Kroz Grodu 10, Hvar, Tel +385 91 51 66
222, www.theasurus-jewellery.com, info@thesaurus-
jewellery.com
Za Pod Zub, Srinjo kola 11, Stari Grad, Tel +385 98 819 7792,
www.zapodzub.com, info@zapodzub.com

Travel
Krilo High Speed Ship Services, Pelegrini Tours, Riva bb, Hvar,

Tel +385 21 742 743, www.krilo.hr, www.pelegrini-hvar.hr
Jadrolinija Ship Services, Riva bb, Hvar, Tel +385 21 74 11 32,
www.jadrolinija.hr
Jadrolinija Ship Services, Stari Grad, Tel +385 21 76 50 48,
www.jadrolinija.hr
cazmatrans Bus Services, Ivana Mestrovića bb, Stari Grad, Tel
+385 21 765 904, http://www.cazmatrans.hr/cazmatrans-otok-
hvar/cazmatrans-otok-hvar.html, cazmatrans.otok.hvar@st.t-
com.hr
Suncity Taxi, Dolac bb, Hvar, Tel +385 91 602 7177,
www.hvartaxi.com, reservations@suncity.hr
Suncity Taxi, Riva 20, Stari Grad, Tel +385 98 178 9678,
www.hvartaxi.com, reservations@suncity.hr
Suncity Rent a car, Vlade Stosića 5, Hvar, Tel +385 98 178 9678,
www.suncity.hr, info@suncity.hr

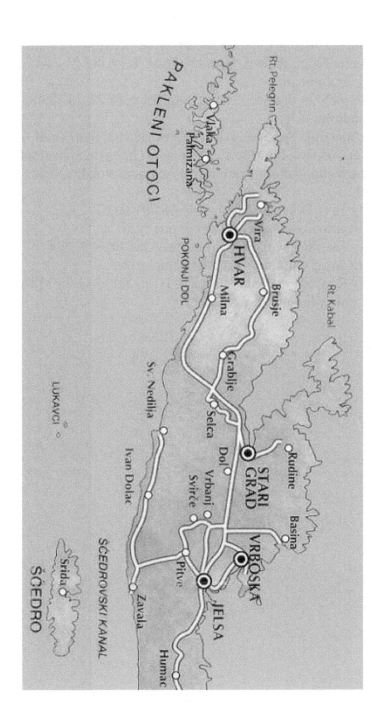

260

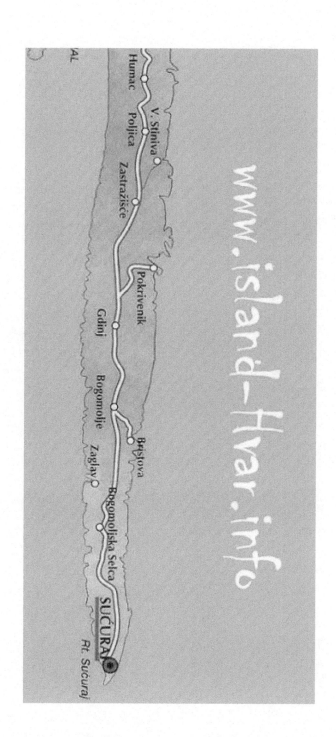

Made in the USA
Coppell, TX
26 July 2023

19635750R00144